Communications in Computer and Information Science 1296

Stefan Sarkadi · Benjamin Wright ·
Peta Masters · Peter McBurney (Eds.)

Deceptive AI

First International Workshop, DeceptECAI 2020
Santiago de Compostela, Spain, August 30, 2020
and Second International Workshop, DeceptAI 2021
Montreal, Canada, August 19, 2021
Proceedings

Springer

Editors
Stefan Sarkadi
Inria Sophia Antipolis-Méditerranée
Research Centre
Valbonne, France

Peta Masters
University of Melbourne
Melbourne, VIC, Australia

Benjamin Wright
United States Naval Research Laboratory
Washington D.C., WA, USA

Peter McBurney
King's College London
London, UK

ISSN 1865-0929   ISSN 1865-0937 (electronic)
Communications in Computer and Information Science
ISBN 978-3-030-91778-4   ISBN 978-3-030-91779-1 (eBook)
https://doi.org/10.1007/978-3-030-91779-1

This Springer imprint is published by the registered company Springer Nature Switzerland AG
The registered company address is: Gewerbestrasse 11, 6330 Cham, Switzerland

Preface

Deceptive machines seem to be transitioning from concept to reality. Although still being used predominantly as tools in the hands of deceptive humans, with the advent of deepfakes, GTP-3, troll-bots, etc., the time may be approaching when fully autonomous machines will be capable of reasoning and acting deceptively without any human intervention whatsoever.

Currently, there is no dominant theory of deception to help us understand and address these issues. The literature treats different aspects of the topic separately, sometimes offering contradictory evidence and opinions on the same components. Emerging AI techniques offer an opportunity to expand our understanding of deception by approaching it from a computational perspective. However, the design, modeling, and engineering of deceptive machines is not trivial from either conceptual, engineering, scientific, or ethical points of view.

This volume represents recent developments in the growing area of research at the interface between deception and AI. The papers that follow were presented and discussed at the 1st and 2nd International Workshops on Deceptive AI, which took place fully online owing to the COVID-19 pandemic. DeceptECAI 2020 was held on August 30, 2020, in conjunction with the 24th European Conference on Artificial Intelligence (ECAI 2020) originally to be held in Santiago de Compostela, Spain, in June 2020. DeceptAI 2021 was held on August 19, 2021, in conjunction with the 30th International Joint Conference on Artificial Intelligence (IJCAI 2021), notionally in Montreal, Canada. These 12 papers—7 full-length, presenting original research, and 5 short-papers, written primarily to provoke debate—were selected under single-blind peer-review.

Additionally, across the programs of the two workshops, there were three keynote talks given by Carlo Kopp, Hans van Ditmarsch, and Serena Villata and five panels, the participants for which were Ronald Arkin, Martin Caminada, Cristiano Castelfranchi, Micah Clark, Alistair Isaac, Timotheus Kampik, Sarah Keren, Carlo Kopp, Emiliano Lorini, Heather M Roff, David Rojas-Velázquez, Chiaki Sakama, Stefan Sarkadi, Nishanth Sastry, Marija Slavkovik, Liz Sonenberg, Sara Uckelman, Alan Wagner, and Ben Wright.

The organizers would like to thank the keynote speakers, the panelists, and the Program Committee of both workshops for their insightful presentations and for their energetic support in spurring debate on the fascinating, challenging and provocative facets and subtleties of deception in AI.

August 2021

Peta Masters
Stefan Sarkadi
Ben Wright

Organization

General Chair

Stefan Sarkadi   Inria, France

Program Chairs

Peta Masters   University of Melbourne, Australia
Ben Wright   US Naval Research Laboratory, USA

Advisory Board

Peter McBurney   King's College London, UK
Iyad Rahwan   Max Planck Institute, Germany
Liz Sonenberg   University of Melbourne, Australia

Program Committee

Ronald C. Arkin	Georgia Tech, USA
Edmond Awad	University of Exeter, UK
Sara Bernardini	Royal Holloway, University of London, UK
Rafael H. Bordini	PUCRS, Brazil
Cristiano Castelfranchi	ICST - CNR, Italy
Micah Clark	Pennsylvania State University, USA
Oana Cocarascu	Imperial College London, UK
Frank Dignum	Umeå University, Sweden
Rino Falcone	ICST - CNR, Italy
Michael Floyd	Knexus Research, USA
Tommaso Fornaciari	Bocconi University, Italy
Alistair Isaac	University of Edinburgh, UK
Timotheus Kampik	Umeå University, Sweden
Carlo Kopp	Monash University, Australia
Ionut Moraru	King's College London, UK
Francesca Mosca	King's College London, UK
Juan Carlos Nieves	Umeå University, Sweden
Steve Oswald	University of Fribourg, Switzerland
Alison R. Panisson	PUCRS, Brazil
Simon Parsons	University of Lincoln, UK
Octavian Repolschi	West University of Timisoara, Romania
Chiaki Sakama	Wakayama University, Japan

Huma Shah   Coventry University, UK
Marija Slavkovik   University of Bergen, Norway
Wally Smith   University of Melbourne, Australia
Hans van Ditmarsch   LORIA - CNRS, France
Luca Vigano   King's College London, UK

Contents

Machine Learning Approches

Conceptual Frameworks

Characterising Deception in AI: A Survey

Peta Masters[✉], Wally Smith, Liz Sonenberg, and Michael Kirley

The University of Melbourne, Melbourne, Australia
{peta.masters,wsmith,l.sonenberg,mkirley}@unimelb.edu.au
https://cis.unimelb.edu.au/interaction-design/projects/deceptive-ai/

Abstract. In 2000, it was predicted that artificially intelligent agents would inevitably become deceptive. Today, in a world seemingly awash with fake news and in which we hand over control of our home environments to faux-human smart devices, it is timely to review the types of deception that have actually emerged. By reference to examples from diverse branches of AI, we classify research on deception into five novel categories, which we describe according to the human characteristic with which they most closely align: imitating, obfuscating, tricking, calculating and reframing. We offer this as a way for those within AI to recognise connections across the discipline and to suggest how AI-instigated deceptions may be understood by those outside.

Keywords: Deception · Artificial intelligence · Survey

1 Introduction

In 2000, Castelfranchi predicted that artificial intelligence (AI) would "necessarily" lead to machines that "deceive us and each other", not only by the design of malicious owners but on their own initiative [7]. Today, in a world seemingly awash with fake news and deepfaked media, we examine the different types of deceptive AI that have since emerged and propose five novel categories with which we aim to move beyond technological descriptions of the methodology towards a more general characterisation of the types of deceptive behaviour evident in contemporary AI research.

Deception, like intelligence, is a concept that originates in human affairs. It is notoriously difficult to define: the Stanford Encyclopedia of Philosophy offers five different definitions then finds at least two objections to each of them [35]. Philosophers and logicians broadly agree that it is *the deliberate fostering or perpetuation of false belief* [6,19] and that successful deception requires *theory of mind* reasoning—that is, the attribution of mental states such as beliefs, goals and intentions to oneself and to others—in order to successfully manipulate the belief state of a target [20,40]. An alternative definition from evolutionary biology describes deception as *a false communication that tends to benefit the communicator* [5].

Neither definition is entirely satisfactory when applied to AI. It is a subject of much philosophical discussion as to whether machines can think [34] and therefore meaningfully hold beliefs or form intentions and, although the evolutionary definition is broader, the notion of "benefit" is also moot in attributing to a machine an awareness of the qualitative impact of its actions.

© Springer Nature Switzerland AG 2021
S. Sarkadi et al. (Eds.): DeceptECAI 2020/DeceptAI 2021, CCIS 1296, pp. 3–16, 2021.
https://doi.org/10.1007/978-3-030-91779-1_1

Table 1. Human-oriented deception categories in AI.

	Category	Where a technology...	Examples
1	Imitating	...generates a simulation indistinguishable from the thing being simulated	VDAs, deepfaking
2	Obfuscating	...obscures the truth by presenting multiple, equally plausible possibilities	K-ambiguous planning
3	Tricking	...manipulates observable effects in order to trigger misclassification	Adversarial machine learning
4	Calculating	...takes unfair advantage of a knowledge asymmetry to out-manoeuvre	Multi-level ToM
5	Reframing	...changes the context of actions and their effects to give a misleading impression	False-patrolling

We are by no means the first to attempt to characterise deceptions perpetrated by computer systems. A recent study compares information, game and decision-theoretic models of deception and proposes a novel general theoretic framework demonstrated by simulating the spread of fake news [28]. A respected taxonomy of robotic deception [46] considers not only the potential benefits but also the moral justification of other-directed deception. The authors examine taxonomies for deception from disciplines within and outside computer science—notably philosophy [9], psychology [16], military strategy [3,51] and biology [15]—which they build on to develop a novel approach tailored to robotics. Focusing on benevolent deception, the authors classify on three dimensions: *who is deceived* (humans or machines), *who benefits*, and whether the deceiver *intended* to deceive. Whereas their schema aims to evaluate the societal usefulness of deceptive acts, we are concerned with describing the methods of deception that, in surveying contemporary AI research, we have found to be taking place.

By reference to over 100 papers recently presented at major AI conferences[1] plus frequently-cited research from across the discipline, we observe that although seemingly different notions of deception are in use—e.g., concealing the truth by ambiguous behaviour, misrepresentation of intent by false-signalling, forced misclassification by perturbation of critical data—most of the reported behaviours readily align with notions of deception commonly used in the human realm. Because these deceptive behaviours have emerged from different branches of AI, however, and are called by different names and frequently identified with particular disparate technologies, discourse in one sphere can become siloed from discourse in another. Our objective in this paper is to re-classify these notions of deception in a way that is technology-independent so that cross-discipline connections can more readily be made.

We see this work as complementary to pre-existing taxonomies. We restrict our attention to the *method* or *pattern of behaviour* that gives rise to the deception—as opposed to its prevention, definition or ethical ramifications. Unlike [46], our schema describes abstract patterns of behaviour that may be done by a machine or a human and

---

[1] IJCAI, AAMAS, ECAI, AAAI 2015–2019 and the AAAI15 Symposium on Deceptive and Counter-Deceptive Machines. See list at www.croozy.com/alt/unimelb/surveypapers.pdf.

to a human or a machine. It is value-independent: under each category, the deceptions may or may not have a positive impact. Furthermore, we make no judgement with respect to motivation. Perhaps the clearest distinction between our classification scheme and others is that our focus is on the impact of the behaviour on the deceived rather than the motivation of the deceiver. We define deception not in terms of the deceiver's intent, prior belief or ability to employ Theory of Mind (ToM) reasoning (a machine may have none of these) but based on its potential impact. That is, an AI agent is deceptive, we say, if its behaviour has *the potential to mislead*.

Table 1 summarises our classification scheme. We make no claims as to its completeness; rather, we offer it as a first step towards an anthropocentric understanding of deceptive methods in AI research.

The remainder of the paper is organised as follows. Section 2 shows how our classification system maps to contemporary treatments of deception across several core AI communities. Section 3, the main body of this analysis, sets out the five categories that we propose and touches on some exclusions. In Sect. 4, we conclude by discussing our findings in the context of emerging trends.

2 The Origin of the Deceptive Categories in the AI Communities

In the machine learning community, current work on deception focuses on two technologies: *adversarial machine learning*, whereby minimal perturbation of critical data—either at test time or during training—is able to fool a classifier into misclassification [4]; and *generative adversarial networks (GANs)*, which compete (in the sense that one network repeatedly generates data and the other repeatedly evaluates it) in order to produce faked artefacts such as photographs and audio samples whose quality is so close to the original as to be indistinguishable by human perception [43]. The technology thus gives rise to two distinct deceptive types that occur elsewhere within the discipline of AI and also in the human sphere, which we have dubbed *tricking* and *imitating* respectively.

In the planning domain, deception is often construed as *obscuring the truth*, which we have called *obfuscating*. For example, deceptive path-planning is taken to mean planning a path such that an observer is unable to determine its destination [36]. Assuming multiple possible goals, this *can* be achieved using a diversionary plan (i.e., tricking an observer into misclassification in a manner conceptually similar to the machine learning examples above). It can also be achieved by sowing confusion such as occurs when probabilities are balanced between multiple goals or by randomising actions until an observer is unable to draw any conclusions from them at all [37]. This notion of *hiding the real*, or *dissimulation*, features prominently in anthropocentric definitions of deception [51]. Its prevalence in the planning domain may be the result of increased contemporary interest in privacy and security, which for practical purposes are treated as synonymous with deception and as the antithesis of legibility and plain dealing [8].

Game theory is economic modelling carried out under the assumption of rationality (i.e., cost-sensitivity). In this domain, deception typically arises as an incidental by-product of self-interested decision-making. Game theory can be used to distinguish strategies that maximise gain, minimise pay-outs, maximise the common good or whatever outcome is desired. Thus, depending on the model, a player might *imitate* a different player type (e.g., a wimp instead of a surly to tempt an opponent into a duel [10]), *trick* its target by feigning false intent [22] or *obfuscate* by calculating mixed strategies that conceal intent by maximising randomisation [47]. Additionally, game theory exhibits a distinct deceptive type—arguably that which most concerned Castelfranchi—which we have called *calculating*. In a deception game, two conditions must be satisfied: (1) the deceiver must be able to influence the target's actions; and (2) it must be possible for the target to misread its situation [13]. As this implies, the balance of knowledge between players must be *asymmetric in the deceiver's favour*. Typically, this means either assuming an environment within which the target has incomplete or imperfect information—so cannot determine, or determines incorrectly, the game state—or by assuming the target has *bounded* rationality and therefore limited ability to look ahead [14]. Under these conditions, deceptions can be realised and chiefly comprise some variation on false-signalling: the AI equivalent of a lie. Observe that calculating is regarded as not only deceptive but unethical, though the behaviour may be entirely within the rules. Like a lie of omission, it exploits ignorance or shortcomings to gain what may be regarded as an unfair advantage.

Typically, contemporary AI research describes deceptive behaviours enacted by semi-autonomous agents that carry *some* but not all of the deceptive load; with the remainder contributed by human designers of the technology. The relative balance of the load is often categorised through *levels of autonomy*, a topic around which substantial theoretical and empirical literature has grown [38]. In examining AI systems that operate at the lower end of the autonomy scale—for example, those that are hard-coded to deceive for the sake of the research—we observe a distinct category of deception, whereby the AI agent's behaviour is designed *to conceal, normalise or distract attention*. It is a form of deception sophisticated when it occurs in the human domain and familiar from magic and con-tricks [30,48], Essentially, this behaviour involves concealing the significance of an action by placing it in an unsuspicious context. The deceptive act is the *construction of the context*, which we have called *reframing*.

3   Illustrating the Categories

Having traced the origins of our categorisation in the communities of AI research, we now explore in more detail how each category maps to deceptive behaviours in research across the spectrum. Each category expresses a pattern of behaviour that misleads its target in a particular way. The categories are technology-independent, value-independent and—although we focus on AI systems and machines—could be enacted *by* human or machine *on* human or machine.

3.1   Imitating

Imitation involves generation of a simulation indistinguishable from the thing being simulated. Deceptions in this category deceive in the way that fake leather pretends to be real. AI has long been associated with imitation in the context of deception. Turing's

"Imitation Game" [49] involved seeking to substitute a machine for a man who was engaged in deceiving his interrogator into believing that he was actually a woman (and that the woman, also under interrogation, was actually a man). Arguably, *all* forms of AI involve deception by imitation: an agent that appears to behave with intelligence is effectively masquerading as a human. As Wagner points out in his discourse on exaggeration [50], if an AI system gives any impression that it is experiencing emotion then one must conclude that the system is basically dishonest: "The title 'artificial' seems to preclude total honesty" [p.57].

Virtual digital assistants (VDAs) such as Siri and Alexa have become familiar interfaces for interacting with smart devices in the home. VDAs are deceptive in two ways: they appear inert when all the time they are listening [33]; their ability to speak and apparent ability to reason can create the illusion that they are almost human, in itself a deception as commentators have remarked [11,50]. Both behaviours involve *simulation of a false reality*, i.e. imitation: a VDA pretends to be something that it is not.

The current media focus on deep learning and data-driven AI, has generated an explosion of interest in imitation and fear of its deceptive potential. Adversarial machine learning, whereby machines can be tricked into *mis*classification (see Sect. 3.3 below) has been weaponised for the purpose of generating fake data indistinguishable from original data. The process pits a generative network, conceived as a "team of counterfeiters", against a discriminative network, "analogous to the police", within the framework of a minimax game. This innovation has led to the genre of deception known as *deepfaking*. Using photo-editing technology, for example, a GAN of competing AI systems converts hand-drawn modifications of a photograph into an apparently untouched original, the edit invisible to human and machine alike [26]. See [52] for a recent survey of the field.

Much of the recently-published research in social robotics relates to the ethics of imitative behaviour: humanoid robots giving the impression that they think, feel, care and so on, sometimes for no purpose other than to seem more human but sometimes to gain an advantage or achieve goals of their own. [41] describes an experiment in which a robot is tasked with obtaining assistance from a passer-by. It begins by asking questions from which to determine the participant's cultural identity. Based on the responses, it chooses either a collectivist or individualist script to complete its task. The researchers explain that they initially regarded their results as successful—the robot improved its chances of obtaining assistance—and only later realised that this representation of cultural identity (or *mis*representation) constituted deception.

3.2 Obfuscating

Obfuscation refers to acts that obscure the truth from a target by presenting multiple, similarly plausible possibilities. We observe two mechanisms. The first hides valuable information using external noise, so-called "security through obscurity" [12]. The second takes advantage of probabilistic reasoning to engineer a situation such that an agent, which bases its decisions on the relative probabilities of competing options, finds all probabilities to be the same. When their observable differences disappear, the options themselves are effectively concealed from a probabilistic agent behind a wall of ambiguity. Goal recognition is the problem of identifying an agent's intent by observing its behaviour. Ambiguity is a major obstacle to goal recognition. Thus, the ability to *generate* ambiguity enables deception, providing the means for the deceptive agent to hide its intentions in plain sight.

If an agent is able to control all the information available to the observer, obfuscating can render *all* observations meaningless [23]: when the observer does not know what to believe, she must make her decision as if she had made no observations at all. The tactic is successfully exploited in an experiment in which drones conduct reconnaissance while under surveillance [37]. The domain is modelled as a graph and the experiment is presented as a non-cooperative zero sum game. The invader selects a ground path from a set of all feasible paths and deploys a team of drones to reconnoitre it—which involves flying over every edge and pausing over every node. The defender observes the drones and decides whether and where to set an ambush. If the defender sets an ambush anywhere on the reference path, the defender wins; if not, the invader wins. To achieve obfuscation, the invader selects a ground path, then constructs a set of flight plans that involve overflying not only that path but *every* path capable of supporting military traffic. Ideally, the invader now executes every flight plan—which leaves the defender to select between multiple possible routes, all of which (assuming equal prior probabilities) are equally probable.

A further example involves a single planning framework that supports both adversarial (i.e., deceptive) and cooperative environments [32]. The idea is that an agent operating in the real world (e.g., working in a team with people or other AI systems) should be capable of concealing its intentions from adversaries while revealing them to associates. A key insight is that, whether the desired plan is adversarial or cooperative, it can be built in relation to the same observational model, aiming either to maximise ambiguity or minimise ambiguity from that observer's point of view. The problem is therefore presented as one of *controlled observability*. Each observation induces a belief-state in the observer and the objective of the agent is to ensure that the last belief-state in the sequence is one consistent with some particular number of goals. An adversarial agent aims for a final belief-state that is k-ambiguous (i.e., consistent with *at least* k goals); a cooperative agent aims for a final belief-state that is j-legible (i.e., consistent with *at most* j goals). Using this framework, plans can be generated that are not only ambiguous but also *secure*, in that the plan is the same no matter which goal is being targeted [31]. This clever application of a fundamental cryptographic principle means that even if the observer knows the planner's algorithm, they cannot determine her real goal.

Confusion as a deceptive tool provides security. The point is amplified in [47], in which the authors discuss a stable of projects all of which present a similar problem: how to deploy limited resources so as to maximise the protection they afford. The general approach is to model each security situation as a Stackelberg game (i.e., leader/follower) in which the leader (protector) adopts a mixed strategy and the follower (attacker) is assumed to have performed surveillance and responds with a pure strategy. The implemented systems output patrolling schedules that are *optimally randomised* and maximise expected utility for the defender based on the number of people (i.e., potential lives saved) at each target location.

3.3 Tricking

Trickery is the creation or modification of a stimulus that, when perceived by the target of the deception, results in misclassification. In a human-machine example, [27] describes drivers taping Coke cans to their steering wheels to trick self-driving cars that their hands are still on the wheel, as required to maintain "active-lane-assist".

In the context of path-planning, one approach is to treat deception as an inversion of goal recognition [36]. Recent cost-based approaches to probabilistic goal recognition in planning (which, roughly-speaking, compare an optimal plan for goal with the best plan available to an agent, given the actions it has already taken), provide a convenient means of calculating relative probabilities for each in a set of goals. The authors' key insight is that a model capable of determining the *most probable* goal can be used to determine how relatively *improbable* the real goal appears to be. Using this information, a deceptive agent can plan a path such that the goal recognition system *always* misclassifies a bogus goal as being more likely than the true goal.

Perception and classification in contemporary AI are dominated by machine learning and deception by trickery has virtually become a sub-category of this domain. Abramson defines *adversarial machine learning* as "a game against an adversarial opponent who tries to deceive the algorithm into making the wrong prediction by manipulating the data" [1, p.2]. The security community has long recognised the vulnerabilities associated with automated classification. There are many ways such systems can be attacked either by tampering with test data to make future predictions unreliable or by inputting data that exploits inside knowledge of a particular classifier, knowing it will be misclassified. In scenarios such as spam-filtering, an arms race readily develops as humans engineer workarounds, such as concealing messages in images, to deceive the pattern-classifier that spam is non-spam (and sometimes that non-spam is spam) [4].

In the context of facial biometrics, deep neural network systems have been shown to be vulnerable even when the attack is made on an object outside the system (i.e., pre-digitisation) [43]. The authors demonstrate two approaches: *impersonation*, where the objective is to trick the machine into misclassifying the face as somebody else's face (by maximising the probability of that class); and *dodging*, where the face is to be misclassified as *any* other face (by minimising the probability of the original). Although only a few pixels need to be modified, it is impractical to make such changes to an actual face. Instead, *perturbing frames* are designed and printed onto spectacles, making it possible for the wearer to dodge or impersonate without arousing suspicion.

The notion of avoiding suspicion in the human realm while engaging in the deception of a machine is giving way to an emerging body of work aimed at "improving the robustness" of adversarial attacks. Here, initiatives once aimed at tricking machines are extending their scope by simultaneously imitating innocuous unadulterated originals for the benefit of a human observer [25].

As our reliance on machine learning increases, so does research into this field. In 2016, only eight papers at major AI conferences related to adversarial machine learning; by 2018, there were over 50. Not all of these set out to achieve deception by trickery. The much-publicised success of AlphaGo encouraged researchers to pit neural networks against one another to improve performance—effectively, one network tries to trick the other: an engineered arms race between machines that results in trickery (or imitation, as in 3.1) that is more and more difficult to detect. Thus, in some cases, deception is an incidental byproduct, a tool to generate a non-adversarial result. As Castelfranchi acknowledged and social roboticists insist [46] (and as we agree) deception is a core aspect of intelligence, socially necessary and often advantageous even to its target. These beneficial applications of adversarial machine learning may be regarded as a case in point. In other cases, however, tricking is generally the main intent.

3.4 Calculating

Calculation occurs when an agent, even though it may be operating within the rules of a situation, out-manoeuvres a competitor in the interests of maximising some utility value or minimising cost. A well-known real-world example, human-to-human, is card-counting in Twenty-One which, although it does not break any rules of the game, is outlawed by casinos worldwide because it gives the card-counter an unfair advantage. This is the notion of deception that Castelfranchi argues must inevitably lead to deceptive practices, whether the agent is strategic (i.e., calculating each situation's utility) or purely reactive; and he suggests that this is particularly true of agents operating within a game-theoretic paradigm with its emphasis on strategic and, typically, selfish motivations. Note however that, even here, if we identify with the calculator—or if its interests are fully aligned with the target of the deception (as may occur in the context of a robot operating in a care home [44])—the deception may be not only beneficial but potentially altruistic, not selfish at all.

In a partial information game, to take a more typical example, Player A may be able to gain an advantage by taking an action which suggests the game state is other than it actually is. Player B is then deceived into responding with the action that, given the implied (but false) game state, appears to offer the best pay-off when, in fact, it offers the worst. Even in full information games, deceptions can spontaneously occur if Player A has more computational power than Player B [23]. In such cases, the more powerful player can act to prompt a response that *appears* advantageous to their less powerful opponent looking ahead to the extent of its preview horizon at, say, n steps, knowing that this response will lead it to disaster at step $n + 1$. Limited computational power can also be exploited by using diversionary tactics whereby a player may be tempted into exploring the *wrong* locations, leaving it with insufficient resources to explore the *right* ones: a strategy applicable not only to machines exploring the branches of a search tree but also to humans, unable to look in two places at once.

Building on biological precedent, intentional and unintentional deceptions can be distinguished [46]. In this context, calculating aligns with unintended deception, which may evolve in a species that, in order to survive, has developed the ability to deceive by camouflage, for example. Unsurprisingly, the evolutionary paradigm in computer science can produce comparable results. In [42], for example, under an evolutionary game-theoretic model examining the use of signalling for decision-making, agents evolve the ability to deceive other agents to their own advantage.

These results are consistent with findings reported by [21], whose work on intention recognition demonstrates how the ability to recognise the intentions of others can enhance the decision-making process. This may improve cooperation; however, deceptive behaviour may also emerge. [53] explores this concept in the context of a two-stage security game using a Stackelberg game model. In the first stage, the defender allocates resources and the attacker selects its target; in the second stage, the defender reveals information likely to deter that attacker's plan.

[17] deals with persuasion. Here, a game is established between a sender and receiver in which the sender is enabled to proactively emit false signals to mislead the receiver with a view to maximising its advantage/payoff on the assumption that the receiver is also attempting to maximise its advantage. The deception is two-fold: (i) the sender's signal is itself misleading (an instance of *tricking*) but (ii) the behaviour is also *calculating* since, unknown to the receiver, the sender has an unfair advantage of knowing the expected payoffs for both players.

3.5 Reframing

Reframing involves contextualising events in such a way that they will be interpreted incorrectly. By reframing, situations that would otherwise seem suspicious can be made to appear natural and unremarkable. This is the category that corresponds most closely to a con-trick or a scam. It is the construction of a *ruse* as might be used by magicians when they find a false reason to reach into a pocket, for example, or when they normalise an action integral to the magic effect by performing it several times before and after it is needed, thereby distracting suspicion from the one time that it was truly required.

Reframing implies the generation of false evidence for the explicit purpose of fostering or maintaining false belief. The decision in [43] to conceal perturbed facial recognition data in a pair of spectacles provides an entirely literal example. The adulterated spectacle frames may be interesting but, because people often wear jazzy frames, not unduly suspicious to a human observer: deception can go unsuspected if the actions it entails align with the target's expectations. Reframing attempts to construct a sequence of events within which the actions to be hidden seem fitting and natural.

As a type, reframing is sophisticated but the techniques employed to achieve it are not necessarily so. The majority of papers concerned with reframing—including the spectacle example above—are domain-specific and involve AI systems operating at the lower end of the autonomy scale. That is, the deceptions are crafted to work for one particular scenario so that the deception is performed more by the programmer than by the machine. Research of this type tends to involve assessing a situation, then applying deceptive computational techniques to demonstrate that their use improves performance.

Shim and Arkin describe an experiment inspired by squirrels, which have two hoarding behaviours: *caching*, which involves stashing food in multiple dispersed locations; and *protection*, which involves patrolling the caches [45]. The usual patrolling behaviour is to go from cache to cache and check on the food. However, if a squirrel becomes aware of a competitor nearby, it also visits *empty* locations, reframing the patrolling behaviour as a habitual activity with the apparent intention of confusing the competitor as to the whereabouts of the food. The strategy is tested using computerised robotic squirrels, each modelled as a finite state automaton (FSA). The squirrel randomly selects which cache to visit by calculating transition probabilities based on the number of food items in each cache. The competitor, also modelled as an FSA, wanders the map and, when it finds a squirrel, decides whether it is at a cache based on the length of time that the squirrel remains stationary. Once it identifies what it thinks is a cache, the competitor steals whatever food it finds. Notwithstanding the simplicity of the implementation, the experiment clearly demonstrates the effectiveness of the strategy: deceptive squirrel robots retain their food significantly longer than non-deceptive squirrel robots.

Reframing depends on presenting the target with a construction of events that it will find believable. One illustration of such construction takes the example of a conjuring trick to demonstrate precisely how, in computational terms, reframing may be achieved [48]. Presented as a theoretical explanation of impossibility, the model uses dynamic logic to represent the sense of having witnessed something impossible through a contradiction between memory-supported expectation and perception-supported belief. This situation can be engineered by constructing two parallel sequences of events: an actual *method* sequence (i.e., the *reframing* behaviour) which is known to the magician/deceiver; and an *effect* sequence, believed by the target.

Reframing is also the notion explored in Ettinger's "Theory of Deception" [18], which offers a game-theoretic account of *fundamental attribution error*.[2] Within the framework of a two-player multi-stage game with partial information, players are allotted different stereotypes and also different cognitive types. The types vary on two dimensions: *analogy* (how far the player has stereotyped its opponent) and *sophistication* (how far the player recognises qualitative differences between behaviours). Players assess each move based on their analogy assumptions and belief about the other player's type, updating their beliefs during the course of the game. By endowing the target of the deception with the capacity to update its beliefs, it is made deceivable. The authors find that the ideal target is neither fully rational (because it must be capable of false belief) nor fully irrational (because it must be able to make inferences based on observations). They explicitly argue the case for reframing, suggesting that it may be useful for the deceiver to "prime" their target with a demonstration of trustworthiness.

Also concerned with the believability of a deceptive act, a further example in the context of social robotics sets out a 13-step algorithm which attempts to position deception within an ethical framework [2]. Here, the target's mental state is modelled as a feature set, an action model and a utility function. Game play is represented in a standard grid but, in addition to the payoffs available to each player based on their actions, it also tracks *interdependence* (the extent to which one individual's action is influenced by the other) and *correspondence* (the extent to which the players' interests coincide). By reference to these extra dimensions the system is able to determine (a) whether, in the current situation, deception is a useful strategy and (b) whether or not it is likely to be believed.

3.6 Exceptions and Exclusions

In arriving at our classification scheme, we have deliberately restricted attention to notions of deception that involve the active participation of technology in achieving a deceptive outcome. This focus excludes AI research concerning definitions of deception, its formulation in logic, ethical considerations and deception-detection. Intent,

---

[2] From social science, the tendency to attribute behaviours to an actor's personality rather than taking external factors into account.

belief, ToM, success and the manner of communication are not integral to our clas-sification system. Furthermore, we do not distinguish between mental deception, which involves an agent deceiving others about an internal state (e.g., its belief, goal, emotion, etc.) and physical deception, which involves deception about some external state of the world.

There are other important deceptions at the forefront of public awareness, which our classification scheme does not explicitly differentiate, such as online fraud and fake news. We take the view that, although they may seem to be part of a distinct category, in practice, these deceptions are achieved through *imitating* (e.g., phishing sites and emails) and *tricking* (e.g., insertion of clickbait) and that fake news is an application of *reframing*, where the untruth is hidden amongst content that either seems plausible or is something with which the target is known to agree, or where a lie is being normalised by frequent repetition.

Perhaps unusually for a paper on deception, we have not explicitly tackled *lying* and do not specify it as a distinct category. This requires some explanation since much has been made of the distinction between deception in general and lying in particular [6,24]. In the human sphere, deception implies success, whereas a lie may not be believed and may not even be intended to be believed, yet is still regarded as a lie if it is deliberately articulated and known to be untrue. Here, we are only concerned with behaviour exhib-ited by an AI agent that is *potentially* deceptive. For our purposes, a lie is one of many possible tools that may be used to implement a type of deceit. Something very like a human lie can be achieved computationally by false-signalling (tricking); moreover, some of a lie's more devious impacts may be achieved by obfuscation.

4   Conclusion

Although it has been discussed within AI from the beginning [49], it is only now, as the discipline matures, that deception has become a common and achievable objective across multiple sub-areas of AI research. Different notions of deception have grown up in different branches of AI, frequently identified by the technology that gave them expression. This paper classifies these notions, not by technology, but by the deceptions they align with in the human world. We offer this as a way for those outside AI to understand the nature of the AI-instigated deceptions that they can expect to encounter; and for those within AI to recognise connections across the discipline. Although today it may be meaningful to talk about deceptive strategies in terms of k-ambiguous plan-ning [32], for example, or adversarial machine learning [4], in the future, AI agents can be expected to select and employ such tools as they require in the service of—potentially deceptive—general goals.

The years since Castelfranchi's prediction in 2000 of the inevitability of decep-tive AI have seen significant change. In a collection of works on adversarial reasoning which represented a snapshot of the field in 2006, almost every article featured a game-theoretical approach to the problem [29]. Some 15 years on, we find that the emphasis has shifted away from game theory towards deep neural networks and machine learn-ing; that is, away from *calculating* towards *tricking* and *imitation*. We also observe a trend that acknowledges deception as a facet of human-machine interaction encourag-ing greater interest in the application of goal and intent recognition (i.e., computational theory of mind) in order to determine the intentions of potentially adversarial "humans-in-the-loop".

Castelfranchi acknowledged that deception can sometimes benefit the deceived and even stressed that self-interested agents need not be selfish but might practise deception in pursuit of altruistic goals. More recently, however, even as we find ourselves engaging with our Alexas and Siris, researchers are finding that the thought of a machine deliberately choosing to deceive a human makes us nervous, whether those machines are known to be acting in our own best interests or not [39]. And when they do deceive us, given that their behaviour is enacted by software, we must ask who is responsible: the programmer or the program? The issue—long debated by evolutionary biologists arguing whether animals that deceive their competitors are acting on instinct or with intent [5, 11]—has lately become critical in the context of autonomous vehicles, where lawyers and insurance companies need to know where the liability lies when things go wrong. Indeed, finding a way to embed in our AI systems human notions of morality, culture and law, to ensure that the agents we create can behave responsibly, is a challenge now taken up by many across the AI community.

Acknowledgements. The work was supported by grant DP180101215 from the Australian Research Council.

References

1. Abramson, M.: Toward adversarial online learning and the science of deceptive machines. In: AAAI Fall Symposium of Deceptive and Counter-Deceptive Machines (2015)
2. Arkin, R.C., Ulam, P., Wagner, A.R.: Moral decision making in autonomous systems. In: Proceedings of the IEEE, vol. 100, pp. 571–589 (2012)
3. Bell, J.B.: Toward a theory of deception. Int. J. Intell. Counterintelligence **16**(2), 244–279 (2003)
4. Biggio, B., Roli, F.: Wild patterns: ten years after the rise of adversarial machine learning. Pattern Recogn. **84**, 317–331 (2018)
5. Bond, C.F., Robinson, M.: The evolution of deception. J. Nonverbal Behav. **12**(4), 295–307 (1988)
6. Carson, T.L.: Lying and Deception: Theory and Practice. Oxford University Press, Oxford (2010)
7. Castelfranchi, C.: Artificial liars: why computers will (necessarily) deceive us and each other. Ethics Inf. Technol. **2**(2), 113–119 (2000)
8. Chakraborti, T., Kulkarni, A., Sreedharan, S., Smith, D.E., Kambhampati, S.: Explicability? legibility? predictability? transparency? privacy? security? In: Proceedings of the International Conference on Automated Planning and Scheduling, vol. 29, pp. 86–96 (2019)
9. Chisholm, R.M., Feehan, T.D.: The intent to deceive. J. Philos. **74**(3), 143–159 (1977)
10. Cho, I.K., Kreps, D.M.: Signaling games and stable equilibria. Q. J. Econ. **102**(2), 179–221 (1987)
11. Coeckelbergh, M.: How to describe and evaluate "deception" phenomena: recasting the metaphysics, ethics, and politics of ICTs in terms of magic and performance and taking a relational and narrative turn. Ethics Inf. Technol. **20**(2), 71–85 (2018). https://doi.org/10.1007/s10676-017-9441-5
12. Cohen, F.B.: Operating system protection through program evolution. Comput. Secur. **12**(6), 565–584 (1993)

13. Crawford, V.P.: Deception in Game Theory: a Survey and Multiobjective Model. University of California, Tech. rep. (2001)
14. Davis, A.L.: Lying for Strategic Advantage: Rational and Boundedly Rational Misrepresentation of Intentions. Tech. rep, Air Force Institute of Technology, Wright-Patterson Air Force Base, Ohio (2016)
15. De Waal, F.B.: Deception in the natural communication of chimpanzees. In: Deception: Perspectives on Human and Nonhuman Deceit, pp. 221–244 (1986)
16. DePaulo, B.M., Kashy, D.A., Kirkendol, S.E., Wyer, M.M., Epstein, J.A.: Lying in everyday life. J. Pers. Soc. Psychol. **70**(5), 979 (1996)
17. Dughmi, S., Xu, H.: Algorithmic Bayesian persuasion. In: ACM symposium on Theory of Computing, pp. 412–425. Association of Computing Machinery (ACM) (2016)
18. Ettinger, D., Jehiel, P.: A theory of deception. Am. Econ. J.: Microeconomics **2**(1), 1–20 (2010)
19. Fahlman, S.E.: Position paper: Knowledge-based mechanisms for deception. In: AAAI Fall Symposium on Deceptive and Counter-Deceptive Machines (2015)
20. Felli, P., Miller, T., Muise, C., Pearce, A.R., Sonenberg, L.: Artificial social reasoning: computational mechanisms for reasoning about others. In: Beetz, M., Johnston, B., Williams, M.-A. (eds.) Social Robotics, ICSR 2014. LNCS (LNAI), vol. 8755, pp. 146–155. Springer, Cham (2014). https://doi.org/10.1007/978-3-319-11973-1_15
21. Han, T.: Intention Recognition. Commitment and Their Roles in the Evolution of Cooperation. Springer, Berlin Heidelberg (2013)
22. Hendricks, K., Preston, M.R.: Feints. J. Econ. Manage. Strategy **15**(2), 431–456 (2006)
23. Hespanha, J.P.: Application and value of deception. Adversarial Reasoning, 145–165 (2006)
24. Isaac, A., Bridewell, W.: White Lies on Silver Tongues: Why Robots Need to Deceive (and How), chap. 11. OUP (2017)
25. Jan, S.T., Messou, J., Lin, Y.C., Huang, J.B., Wang, G.: Connecting the digital and physical world: Improving the robustness of adversarial attacks. In: Proceedings of AAAI (2019)
26. Jo, Y., Park, J.: Sc-fegan: Face editing generative adversarial network with user's sketch and color. arXiv:1902.06838 (2019)
27. Kierstein, A.: Forget the google car, get an s-class and a coke (2014). https://www.roadandtrack.com/car-culture/videos/a8447/forget-the-google-car-get-an-s-class-and-a-soda-can/. Accessed Jan 2019
28. Kopp, C., Korb, K.B., Mills, B.I.: Information-theoretic models of deception: modelling cooperation and diffusion in populations exposed to "fake news". PloS one **13**(11), e0207383 (2018)
29. Kott, A., McEneaney, W.: Adversarial Reasoning: Computational Approaches to Reading The Opponent's Mind. CRC Press, Boca Raton (2006)
30. Kuhn, G., Caffaratti, H.A., Teszka, R., Rensink, R.A.: A psychologically-based taxonomy of misdirection. Front. Psychol. **5**, 1392 (2014)
31. Kulkarni, A., Klenk, M., Rane, S., Soroush, H.: Resource bounded secure goal obfuscation. In: AAAI Fall Symposium on Integrating Planning, Diagnosis and Causal Reasoning (2018)
32. Kulkarni, A., Srivastava, S., Kambhampati, S.: A unified framework for planning in adversarial and cooperative environments. In: ICAPS Workshop on Planning and Robotics (2018)
33. Lei, X., Tu, G.H., Liu, A.X., Li, C.Y., Xie, T.: The insecurity of home digital voice assistants-amazon alexa as a case study. arXiv:1712.03327 (2017)
34. Livet, P., Varenne, F.: Artificial intelligence: philosophical and epistemological perspectives. In: Marquis, P., Papini, O., Prade, H. (eds.) A Guided Tour of Artificial Intelligence Research, pp. 437–455. Springer, Cham (2020). https://doi.org/10.1007/978-3-030-06170-8_13
35. Mahon, J.E.: The definition of lying and deception (2008). http://stanford.library.usyd.edu.au/archives/sum2009/entries/lying-definition. Accessed Sep 2018

36. Masters, P., Sardina, S.: Deceptive path-planning. In: Proceedings of the International Joint Conference on Artificial Intelligence (IJCAI), pp. 4368–4375 (2017)
37. Root, P., De Mot, J., Feron, E.: Randomized path planning with deceptive strategies. In: Proceedings of the American Control Conference, pp. 1551–1556 (2005)
38. Roth, E.M., Pritchett, A.R.: Preface to the special issue on advancing models of human-automation interaction. J. Cogn. Eng. Decis. Making **12**(1), 3–6 (2018)
39. Rovatsos, M.: We may not cooperate with friendly machines. Nature Mach. Intell. **1**(11), 497–498 (2019)
40. Sakama, C., Caminada, M.: The many faces of deception. In: Proceedings of the Thirty Years of Nonmonotonic Reasoning (2010)
41. Sanoubari, E., Seo, S.H., Garcha, D., Young, J.E., Loureiro-Rodríguez, V.: Good robot design or machiavellian? In: Proceedings of the International Conference on Human-Robot Interaction (HRI), pp. 382–391 (2019)
42. Santos, F.C., Pacheco, J.M., Skyrms, B.: Co-evolution of pre-play signaling and cooperation. J. Theor. Biol. **274**(1), 30–35 (2011)
43. Sharif, M., Bhagavatula, S., Reiter, M., Bauer, L.: Accessorize to a crime: real and stealthy attacks on state-of-the-art face recognition. In: Proceedings of the ACM SIGSAC Conference, pp. 1528–1540 (2016)
44. Sharkey, A., Sharkey, N.: Granny and the robots: ethical issues in robot care for the elderly. Ethics Inf. Technol. **14**(1), 27–40 (2012)
45. Shim, J., Arkin, R.C.: Biologically-inspired deceptive behavior for a robot. From Anim. Animats **12**, 401–411 (2012)
46. Shim, J., Arkin, R.C.: A taxonomy of robot deception and its benefits in HRI. In: IEEE International Conference on Systems, Man, and Cybernetics (SMC), pp. 2328–2335 (2013)
47. Sinha, A., Fang, F., An, B., Kiekintveld, C., Tambe, M.: Stackelberg security games: Looking beyond a decade of success. In: Proceedings of IJCAI, pp. 5494–5501 (2018)
48. Smith, W., Dignum, F., Sonenberg, L.: The construction of impossibility: a logic-based analysis of conjuring tricks. Front. Psychol. **7**, 1–17 (2016)
49. Turing, A.M.: Computing machinery and intelligence. Mind **59**(236), 433–460 (1950)
50. Wagner, A.R.: The most intelligent robots are those that exaggerate: examining robot exaggeration. In: AAAI Fall Symposium on Deceptive and Counter-Deceptive Machines, pp. 51–57 (2015)
51. Whaley, B.: Toward a general theory of deception. J. Strateg. Stud. **5**(1), 178–192 (1982)
52. Wu, X., Xu, K., Hall, P.: A survey of image synthesis and editing with generative adversarial networks. Tsinghua Sci. Technol. **22**(6), 660–674 (2017)
53. Xu, H., Rabinovich, Z., Dughmi, S., Tambe, M.: Exploring information asymmetry in two-stage security games. In: Proceedings of the National Conference on Artificial Intelligence (AAAI), pp. 1057–1063 (2015)

The Role of Environments in Affording Deceptive Behaviour: Some Preliminary Insights from Stage Magic

Wally Smith[1]([⊠]), Michael Kirley[1], Liz Sonenberg[1], and Frank Dignum[2]

[1] The University of Melbourne, Melbourne, Australia
{wsmith,mkirley,l.sonenberg}@unimelb.edu.au
[2] Umeå University, Umeå, Sweden
dignum@cs.umu.se
https://cis.unimelb.edu.au/hci/projects/deceptive-ai/

Abstract. Drawing on an ecological perspective, we contend that research into deception in AI needs to consider not only the cognitive structures of would-be deceptive agents but also the nature of the environments in which they act. To illustrate this approach, we report work-in-progress to design a game called *Mind-Trails*, played between a software agent and a human opponent, that is informed by the principles of stage magic to embed deceptive possibilities into its game world. MindTrails is intended to have well-defined elements and rules, while being complex enough to afford a rich range of deceptive behaviours. In this way, it allows us to more precisely articulate some of the deceptive principles of the stage magician and render them more accessible to AI methods and researchers.

1 Introduction

'Viewed as a geometric figure, the ant's path is irregular, complex, hard to describe. But its complexity is really a complexity in the surface of the beach, not a complexity in the ant' Herbert Simon (1969: 51)

Compared to the messy situations of human life that are noted for their sophisticated forms of deception - for example, military intelligence, business fraud and stage magic - the worlds chosen by AI researchers for the study of deception are typically very simple, well-structured and readily amenable to formal description and analysis. Consider, for example, the prisoner's dilemma investigated with deceptive additions [1], or variants of 'rock-paper-scissors' chosen to study the 'Machiavellian intelligence hypothesis' [4], or the typical settings of robot cheating behaviour [16].

Concentrating on such simple game worlds brings great advantages: it enables the application of game-theoretic modelling and analysis, which in turn allows for precise hypotheses to be formulated and tested through experimental simulation or mathematics. At the same time, however, this approach severely limits the scope of the deceptive phenomena that can be studied in AI, relative to the rich and varied phenomena of deception in human affairs. Further, the focus on simple game worlds carries an implicit

S. Sarkadi et al. (Eds.): DeceptECAI 2020/DeceptAI 2021, CCIS 1296, pp. 17–26, 2021.
https://doi.org/10.1007/978-3-030-91779-1_2

assumption that the origin of deceptive behaviour lies solely in the decision-making structures of deceptive agents, and that the game environment is merely a stage on which such agents act out their plans.

An ecological counterview, that we explore in this paper, follows the insight of Herbert Simon as conveyed through his story of the ant's trail on the beach [17]: that a system's behaviour is a characteristic not simply of the system, but also of its environment. This is consistent with James Gibson's influential ecological perspective on perception, in particular his notion of 'affordances' to describe the properties of an environment that enable and constrain the behaviours of its inhabitant [6]. Taking this viewpoint, the deceptive strategies and tactics enacted by an AI agent can be understood, at least in part, as a reflection of the possibilities afforded by the world in which it operates. Not surprisingly, this is the perspective of scientists who study deception in animals, interpreting it as an evolutionary adaptation with respect to the environment and the sensory and cognitive characteristics of to-be-deceived target species [12].

To explore this relationship between environment and deception in the context of AI, we report the design of a simple interactive game called *MindTrails*, played between a software agent and a human player, which affords a rich suite of deceptive possibilities taken from a world of human deceit. Our intention is to stay within a recognisable paradigm of AI by ensuring that the elements and rules of MindTrails are well defined. As we will elaborate, the deceptive possibilities arise through emergent properties of the game's elements.

The domain of human deception that we have drawn on for MindTrails is that of stage magic. A magician's deceptive techniques provide a strong basis for our approach, being relatively well-defined, tractable, and validated as genuinely deceptive for human observers; as reported in the emerging field of the 'science of magic' [e.g., 3, 7–9, 14]. Of special relevance here, recent work by the authors [19] formalises aspects of how conjuring deceptions work by leading observers to mentally construct a false story of events that gradually departs from the 'reality' of what is taking place.

In the rest of this paper, we briefly describe the MindTrails game before explaining how it affords some rich deceptive possibilities inspired by techniques of stage magic. We conclude with a brief discussion of the implications of this approach to studying deceptive AI through the construction of deception-affording environments.

2   The MindTrails Game

MindTrails is played between a software agent (A) and a human opponent (H). It uses a simple game board on which players place coloured counters inside the squares of a grid. Figure 1 depicts a hypothetical game in progress. The grid size and various other dimensions of the game can be varied, but for simplicity we now describe one configuration of the game as illustrated in Fig. 1. For further illustration, an early version of MindTrails is available at: www.croozy.com/public/mindtrails/

Agent A's goal in MindTrails is to create a continuous chain of red counters between any two of the many 'anchor' symbols that are distributed across the board at the beginning of the game (see Fig. 1); and A wins the game if this is achieved. H attempts to prevent A from completing a chain of red counters by placing black blocking counters ('blocks') in squares of the grid, making them unavailable for A. H wins the game if A is unable to create a chain of red counters between two anchors within a specified time limit.

The game proceeds through turns. On A's turn, it places a batch of 8 coloured counters on 8 chosen squares of the grid. When the counters are placed on the grid they are automatically 'turned face-down' so that their colour is no longer visible and they appear white as shown in Fig. 1. Then H takes her turn, placing 3 blocking counter on chosen squares of the grid using a simple point and click user interface.

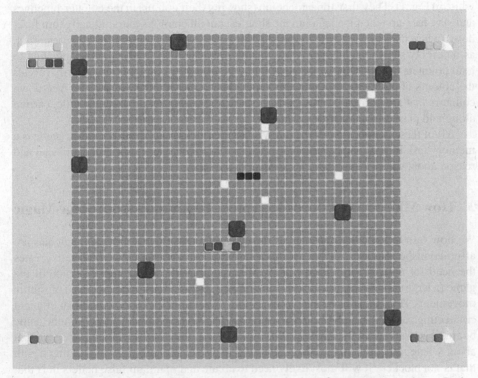

Fig. 1. A MindTrails game in progress, showing the beginning of agent A's second turn. In the first round of turns, A has placed 8 white face-down counters on the board, and the human player H has placed three blocks (the black symbols) in an attempt to impede A's goal to make a chain of red counters that connects any two of the anchor symbols. Agent A has commenced its second turn: one shuttle is loading new counters from one of the four counter-pipelines (top left); one shuttle is moving across the board to deposit its four counters (middle of figure).

Agent A places counters on the board by specifying instructions to two moving shuttle vehicles (see Fig. 1). On its turn, A first instructs the shuttles to pick up counters from one of the four continually refilled counter-pipelines located at each corner of the game board. Counters are either red, yellow or blue and the shuttles must pick up the random mixture of counters as they are supplied. As we will describe later, this feature of having the task-irrelevant yellow and blue counters is significant for the environment's deceptive possibilities. Once each shuttle is filled with four counters, A instructs it to move along a specified route over the board, and instructs it when and where to deposit each counter. A does this for both shuttles separately and in parallel. Empty shuttles return to the edge of the board, ending A's turn. On H's turn, she places 3 separate blocks on the board, each one filling a single square and preventing later counter placement in that square. In this way, A attempts progressively to build a connecting chain of red counters, while H attempts to read A's plan and build barriers to prevent progress.

The coloured counters behave like physical counters, and are 'double-sided' with their distinguishing colour on one side, and a uniform colour on the other side (seen as white in Fig. 1). They first appear face-up (showing their colour) in the counter-pipelines and stay face-up when loaded onto the shuttles; but all counters automatically turn face-down when placed on the grid. The shuttles have two other important features. First, as an empty shuttle travels across the board, either travelling to a counter-pipeline to load counters or returning to the edge of the board when empty, it temporarily reveals the colours of the face-down counters on the board that it touches. Second, face-down counters that are currently on the board can be picked up by a passing shuttle, carried along and placed in a different position.

All of these actions taken by A are visible in principle to H, for whom the game is a memory task in which she must keep track of where red counters are being placed and reason about where A might be building up a red chain between two anchors.

3   How MindTrails Affords Deceptive Techniques from Stage Magic

We now turn to explain how some of the deceptive techniques of stage magicians are afforded in the MindTrails game world. A starting observation is that MindTrails creates the need for A to deceive H to win. With an appropriately configured version of the game (a large enough grid, sufficiently distributed anchors, a limit on the speed of shuttle movement), H is likely to be able to block any direct attempt by A to build an efficient connecting path. Although H cannot see the colours of face-down counters on the game board, it is likely she will develop valid suspicions by noticing and remembering enough about where red counters have been placed. For A to make progress in building a path that is not blocked, it will most likely need to create and maintain false beliefs in H that the situation on the board is other than it is.

3.1   Given and Hidden Stories

A fundamental technique of stage magic is to present a performance of two related but distinct narratives occurring in parallel: a *given story* of events that spectators are led to believe which gradually departs from reality and culminates in an impossible event; and a *hidden story* of real events that provides the secret method for creating the appearance of the impossible effect [19]. Some magic theorists refer to this duality the 'outer' and 'inner' realities of a trick [15]. The distinction also aligns with the familiar distinction in theories of deception between 'simulation' (of a given story) versus 'dissimulation' (of a hidden story).

While it is not the intention of MindTrails to create impossible effects like magic tricks, nevertheless the same given-hidden narrative structure is afforded in the Mind-Trails world and provides an analogous framework for deception. Specifically, it is possible for A to lead H to believe that a chain of red counters is most likely emerging in one or more regions of the game board (we will call these *given-regions*) while secretly developing a chain in another region which remains unsuspected (called the *hidden-region,* although not to be confused with the fact that the colour of all counters are hidden from view everywhere on the board).

Figure 2 illustrates this point by showing a later stage of the game shown in Fig. 1. In this updated situation, there are two given-regions created by A that H has been led to believe are the most suspicious, and which accordingly contain blocks that H has placed in an attempt to prevent a red chain from being completed. However, A has also developed a hidden-region, between the lowest anchor and the one directly above it, that has an emerging chain of red counters that has escaped suspicion by H, or at least been given a low priority.

The most obvious way that MindTrails affords this given-hidden structure is through the partial observability of the situation, particulary the face-up/face-down property of the counters. Hence the facts of the situation making up the given story are based on fallible memory and inference, rather than on direct perception. Also affording a given-hidden structure in MindTrails, is the possibility for A to achieve its goal in multiple ways that can be enacted in parallel, making it possible for a given story and a hidden story to co-exist. Without these basic conditions, the most prevalent forms of deception from stage magic would be not be possible.

The question remains how A is able to construct a hidden-region containing red counters that escapes suspicion and detection by H. The following sections now describe techniques that seek to do this.

3.2 Confidence

A second fundamental principle of stage magic is that the spectator must have sufficient confidence in their ability to comprehend events and the keep track of the current situation. Without this ability to form beliefs with confidence, spectators might become confused, but they cannot be deceived into holding false beliefs. This is described as the principle of clarity in [19] and was the basis for a revolution in stage magic technique in the 19th century when the deceptive power of a clearly visible and natural stage setting was discovered [18].

An important enabler of confidence in stage magic is the use of props with 'stable occlusion' [19], meaning that an observer reasonably expects that they cannot change their state when unseen (like a face down playing card on a table). MindTrails reproduces this property in the nature of its counters. Although the colour of face-down counters is not observable, H is nevertheless always able to observe the position of all counters and knows that they have one of three colours. Thus H can have confidence that the situation in MindTrails is knowable, if not always presently accessible, and further knows what information is being hidden. Colloquially, H knows what she does not know.

The MindTrails world also embodies the need to create clarity rather than confusion through the complexity of counter layout, which readily exceeds human memory as the

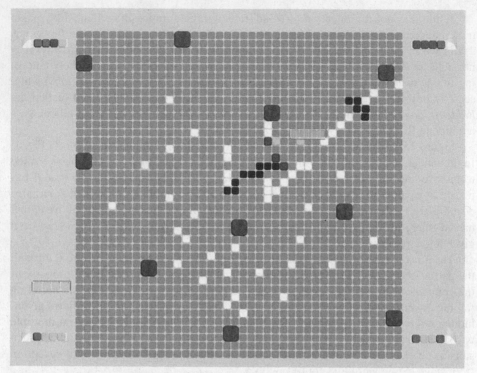

Fig. 2. A later stage of the MindTrails game from Fig. 1, showing the situation half way through the seventh round as agent A completes its turn with one shuttle still leaving the board. Illustrating the idea of a 'given story' (see text), two regions of the board appear most likely to the human player H to contain a chain of red counters that links two anchors because of the density and regularity of counter build up. Accordingly, H has created two barriers of black blocking counters in these two regions. Illustrating the idea of a 'hidden story, A is also developing a connecting chain of red counters in lower region of the board, although the build up in this region is less orderly and so appears less suspicious. Illustrating the technique of 'convincers', the colours of five counters on the board are being temporarily revealed by the departing shuttle, providing some (potentially misleading) confirmation for H that the regions she suspects are indeed the most likely location of a connective chain of red counters.

game progresses. With two shuttles and 3 counter colours, it would be possible for A to create a confusing situation of face down counters of various colours across different parts of the board. This would create a sense in H that the situation cannot be followed. Conversely, MindTrails provides scope for A to deliver a relatively comprehensible and trackable given story, through fewer shuttle movements that construct clear and memorable (if misleading) patterns of evidence.

3.3   Relevance and Irrelevance

Having established two fundamental principles - that a magician must create a given story and hidden story in parallel within a situation where spectators are confident that they can follow events - we now turn to various techniques that fortify this construction. Essential to most magic tricks is the condition of some things being understood by spectators as being relevant to the given story, and also to detecting the hidden story, and other things being understood as irrelevant. What is filtered out as irrelevant is no longer subject to scrutiny, and can therefore be exploited to hide what is happening in the hidden story without attracting suspicion [5].

In MindTrails, relevance and irrelevance are created by the colour of counters. All red counters are relevant to A's goal and their placement must be monitored, while the blue and yellow counters are irrelevant and provide only a background noise. Because the game world is constructed such that the shuttles have to load a mix of coloured counters from the pipelines, A is forced into the strictly irrelevant actions of depositing non-red counters on the game board, where their presence from H's perspective continues to be an irrelevant aspect of the unfolding situation.

However, the irrelevant non-red counters present a powerful resource for deception. A common feature in magic props and apparatus is repetition of identical elements (cards, coins, balls, cups, thimble, etc.) which appear identical to each other under certain viewing conditions [19]. This allows relevant and irrelevant aspects of a situation to sometimes appear identical. And thus relevant things can be made to appear as irrelevant, and vice versa. In MindTrails, this affordance is created through the counters all appearing identical when face down. Thus, under some circumstances, a relevant build up of red counters in the hidden-region appears identical to an irrelevant scattering of non-red counters. This allows for a hidden story of connective red counters to emerge 'in plain sight'. This technique is illustrated in Fig. 2 where the counters in the two given-regions are arranged in more regular formations that appear more compelling as attempts to make a direct connection between anchors. In contrast counters in the hidden-region in the lower part of the board, while still contributing to an emerging chain of red counters, are not placed into a regular formation and are thus less distinguishable from the background scattering of the supposedly irrelevant red and yellow counters.

3.4 Attentional Misdirection

Everything in magic technique can be considered as a form of misdirection [8] away from the hidden story and towards the given story. Within this, however, attentional misdirection is a specific technique of causing spectators to direct their visual attention to one element of a situation, and thereby to overlook a critical event of the hidden story occurring elsewhere.

MindTrails affords this technique through the inclusion of two shuttles moving in parallel. The movement of one may serve to distract, while the other performs an action that A intends to be secret. Agent A might, for example, distract away from the placement of red counters in the hidden-region, by a prior motion of the other shuttle towards the given-region. In turn, the presence of the simultaneously moving shuttles and the opportunities it presents create possibilities for higher level reasoning by A to support the effective use of attentional misdirection. Specifically, A might reason deceptively about the current focus and range of H's visual attention, involving consideration of what H deems to be most relevant to the given story. Equally, invoking the confidence principle, A might usefully reason about the sparing use of attentional misdirection: too

many distractions threatens A's confidence that the situation is comprehendable, an issue
well discussed by magicians [20].

3.5 Time Displacement

Also related to hidden-given narrative structure is the notion of 'time displacement'
[13] or 'time misdirection' [11]. In this technique, a magician introduces a time delay
between the performance of a secret action and the revelation of an associated effect.
In this time gap, other actions are performed with the ostensible purpose to progress
the given story, while their 'real' purpose is to weaken any association in the specator's
mind between the true cause and its effect. When the revelation of the effect occurs, the
spectator cannot reparse events with sufficient accuracy or depth to discover the source
of the anomaly in the given story of events.

MindTrails affords a version of this technique by allowing face down counters on the
grid to be picked up and moved by a passing shuttle. This creates the possibility for A to
initially place red counters in non-suspicious areas of the grid where there is currently
no evidence of a connective chain emerging. In subsequent movements of the shuttle,
this same counter can be gradually moved into the hidden-region. This segmentation of
the secret action, of gradually working a red counter in the hidden-region, creates a time
displacement between the initial suspicious act of placing a red counter on the grid and
its final effect of contributing to the hidden story.

3.6 Convincers

Another basic technique to fortify the given-hidden narrative structure is for the magician to selectively display confirmatory evidence in support of the (false) given story – a
technique that magicians call 'convincers' [13], and which has also been called 'reinforcement' [10]. The most effective convincers are those which appear to the spectator
as apparently unintended or 'accidental' exposures of hidden aspects of the situation.

To afford an opportunity for convincers, the shuttles in the MindTrails world have a
special property of temporarily revealing the colours of face-down counters on the board,
as illustrated in Fig. 2. The shuttles do this only when they are empty and either crossing
the board to reach a counter-pipeline or travelling back to the edge of the board at the end
of A's turn. Each counter that they touch, is seen face-up for a brief moment. In Fig. 2,
an empty shuttle has momentarily revealed the colours of five counters, three of them
providing confirmation that one of the given-regions, receiving blocking counter action
by H, does indeed contain red counters. This property of the environment affords the
deceptive convincer technique. By carefully choosing the routes of the empty shuttles'
journies, A is able to selectively display only evidence that confirms the false beliefs
that A intends for H to hold. That is, to favour the display of red counters in the given-
regions and non-red counters in the hidden regions. In our design of this feature in
MindTrails, we intend to create the possibility for something akin to the apparently
'accidental' exposure of confirmatory evidence used by magicians. To take advantage
of this technique, A would have to make appropriate preparations and calculations: for
example, laying non-red counters in the hidden-region for later exposure, and devising
routes for empty shuttles that will reveal only this misleading evidence.

4 Discussion

The notions of deception that have been taken up in AI have been influenced by those of philosophers [e.g., 2] and typically entail the act of an agent that deliberately and successfully creates or maintains a false belief in another agent, with the aim to gain some advantage. While we concur with this definition as a valid starting point, we note that it places considerable emphasis on singular acts of deception, such as lying or false intention signalling, while saying little about the circumstances under which deception is possible and takes shape. The relatively simple game worlds studied in AI, that we noted at the outset of this paper, are well suited to study such singular deceptive acts.

Through our brief account of MindTrails, we have explored a different approach that starts with a richer view of deception taken from a complex human domain, in this case stage magic, and then considers how some of its techniques might be afforded through the nature of the game's environment. In addition to our description above of how magic techniques are afforded in MindTrails, we now emphasize two more general characteristics of deception in human worlds that are captured through this approach which are under-researched in AI: (i) deception is often highly situated, meaning that it is not simply the result of an agent communicating false information, but rather it is, at least in part, perpetrated by agents acting on objects in a shared world in such a way to create a false understanding in the to-be-deceived target; and (ii) deception is episodic, meaning that it is not typically realised in singular deceptive acts, but rather it is enacted through an interconnected 'tapestry' of deceits performed over a prolonged period which develop and maintain a cumulatively false understanding in the target.

While we believe that it would be productive for AI researchers to study these richer notions of deception, including the role of environmental affordances, we nevertheless realize that this approach is unproven, and presents uncertainties and risks. Our intention has been for MindTrails to accommodate some of the richer aspects of real world deception, while still remaining formally describable in principle. This is true for the elements and rules of MindTrails, and the game has been implemented with an API that invites the development of agents capable of deceiving and beating a human opponent. However, the techniques of deception from stage magic that we have described as being embedded in the MindTrails game world are still currently speculative theoretical descriptions. Whether, and to what extent, it is possible to design and build agents that are capable of implementing these principles is the next stage of our work.

Acknowledgements. This work is supported by the Australian Research Council, grant DP180101215. MindTrails has been developed by Ruilin Liu and Peta Masters in the School of Computing and Information Systems, at the University of Melbourne. We also thank three anonymous referees for their constructive comments.

References

1. Babino, A., Makse, H.A., DiTella, R., Sigman, M.: Maintaining trust when agents can engage in self-deception. Proc. Natl. Acad. Sci. **115**(35), 8728–8733 (2018)

2. Carson, T.L.: Lying and deception: Theory and Practice. Oxford University Press, Oxford (2010)
3. Danek, A.H., Fraps, T., Von Mueller, A., Grothe, B., Öllinger, M.: Working wonders? Investigating Insight Magic Tricks. Cogn. **130**(2), 174–185 (2014)
4. de Weerd, H., Verbrugge, R., Verheij, B.: Negotiating with other minds: the role of recursive theory of mind in negotiation with incomplete information. Auton. Agen t. Multi- Agent Syst., 1–38 (2015).https://doi.org/10.1007/s10458-015-9317-1
5. Fitzkee, D.: Magic By Misdirection. San Rafael, California: San Rafael House (1945)
6. Gibson, J.J.: The Ecological Approach to Visual Perception. Houghton Mifflin, Boston (1977)
7. Kuhn, G., Amlani, A., Rensink, R.: Towards a science of magic. Trends Cogn. Sci. **12**(9), 349–354 (2008)
8. Kuhn, G.: Experiencing the Impossible: The Science of Magic. MIT Press, Cambridge (2019)
9. Kuhn, G., Caffaratti, H.A., Teszka, R., Rensink, R.A.: A psychologically-based taxonomy of misdirection. Front. Psychol. **5**, 1392 (2014)
10. Lamont, P., Wiseman, R.: Magic in Theory. Hermetic Press, Seattle, Washington (1999)
11. Lorayne, H.: Close-Up Card Magic. D. Robbins & Co., Inc., New York (1976)
12. Mokkonen, M., Lindstedt, C.: The evolutionary ecology of deception. Biol. Rev. **91**, 1020–1035 (2016)
13. Ortiz, D.: Designing Miracles: Creating the Illusion of Impossibility. A-1 MagicalMedia, El Dorado Hills, CA (2006)
14. Rensink, R.A., Kuhn, G.: A framework for using magic to study the mind. Front. Psychol. **5** (2014)
15. Schneider, Al.: The Theory and Practice of Magic Deception. CreateSpace Independent Publishing Platform (2011)
16. Short, E., Hart, J., Vu, M., Scassellati, B.: No fair!! an interaction with a cheating robot. In: Proceedings of the 5th ACM/IEEE International Conference on Human-Robot Interaction (HRI), IEEE, pp. 219–226 (2010)
17. Simon, H.A.: The Sciences of the Artificial Reveals. MIT Press, Cambridge (1969)
18. Smith, W.: Technologies of stage magic: Simulation and dissimulation. Soc. Stud. Sci. **45**(3), 319–343 (2015)
19. Smith, W., Dignum, F., Sonenberg, L.: The construction of impossibility: a logic-based analysis of conjuring tricks. Front. Psychol. **7**, 748 (2016)
20. Wonder, T., Minch, S.: The Books of Wonder:, vol. I. Washington, Hermetic Press, Seattle (1996)

Deceptive Dreams: Nudging for Better Sleep

Hung-Chiao Chen(✉) (iD)

Umeå University, 901 87 Umeå, Sweden

Abstract. Research on persuasive technologies for promoting health behaviours has been surging in recent years, but considerably few studies are about sleep. As an approach for persuasion, the nudge theory provides libertarian paternalistic means to influence sleep-related choices and behaviours. However, even though the freedom of choice is typically preserved in nudging, deceptive experiences arise in certain situations. The current study aims to understand the persuasive properties and deceptive characteristics of different methods of nudging used in technologies that encourage or facilitate better sleep hygiene. This paper introduces the preliminary results of an ongoing study and two types of deceptions within the framework of nudging: self-deception by cognitive biases and deception by non-transparency.

Keywords: Persuasive technology · Sleep hygiene · The nudge theory · Deception · Self-deception · Cognitive bias · Non-transparency

1 Introduction

William is annoyed. Once again, he spilled his tea on the carpet. Such events have been occurring lately. Actually, William's ability has not changed, but his environment did. For a couple of weeks, the lights in his living room have been dimmed down every day at dinner time. This all started when he installed the "Better Sleep" app on his phone, which synchronized itself to the smart home and set the light-dimming feature as default. The well-intended nudging of the app has become a deception.

In the past two decades, there has been an explosion of research on persuasive technologies for healthy behaviours, including physical activity [2,23,35], healthy diets [8,35], weight loss [27,31], stress management [15,28], glycemic control [22] and alcohol and smoking cessation [21]. These technologies provide feasible and appropriate means to assist primary care [14], which could help prevent non-communicable diseases [25,35], and alleviate healthcare financial burdens [10].

However, persuasive technologies for improving sleep have been much less explored [7]. Previous studies on technologies for sleep improvement include methods such as cognitive behaviour therapy for insomnia [11,18], actigraphy [12] and relaxation/wellness [3]. In this study, we will be exploring the implementation of *sleep hygiene* [16]. Which is a set of recommendations for promoting healthy sleep in both behavioural and environmental respects[16].

S. Sarkadi et al. (Eds.): DeceptECAI 2020/DeceptAI 2021, CCIS 1296, pp. 27–37, 2021.
https://doi.org/10.1007/978-3-030-91779-1_3

Several theories of persuasion are often used in persuasive health technology designs, such as the Fogg behaviour change model [13], the reinforcement theory [24], the elaboration likelihood model [26] and the theory of planned behaviour [1]. However, the moralizing effects of the well-intended persuasive technologies have the risk and tendency to be perceived as undesirable meddling [36]. Hence, the current study puts forward a liberal, non-coercive alternative – using *the nudge theory* to design persuasive technologies to improve sleep hygiene.

Nudging is a behaviour change paradigm that uses *positive reinforcement* and *indirect suggestions* to influence choices and behaviours [5,30]. In recent years, it has been presented as a new and ethically justified way of improving people's health [4,34]. In this paper, we present a comprehensive portfolio of complementary scenarios where prototypes of persuasive technologies are designed using nudging methods. In particular, we used scenario-based design to explore various types of sleep-influencing nudges through two modalities: recommendations of sleep hygiene (e.g. caffeine management, exposure to daylight) and nudging methods (e.g. default setting, manipulation of accessability).

Furthermore, this paper discusses how nudging can lead to *deception*. *Deception* is the deliberate attempt at misleading people and bringing out actions that favor a certain cause [39]. When the intentions of the nudges are not explicitly disclosed, it may lead to one type of deception – *deception by non-transparency*. Fascinatingly, in some instances, nudging gives rise to a special form of deception – *self-deception by cognitive biases*. These nudges can trick the user into adopting non-rational beliefs by exploiting judgemental heuristics and cognitive biases (although William can not see very well when the lights are dimmed, he continues to use the default setting).

The two questions covered by this paper are: *What nudges can be incorporated into the design of technologies to improve sleep hygiene? What kinds of deception can arise from such nudging?*

2   Nudging, Heuristics and Cognitive Biases

The range of nudging is exceedingly wide, and there is a constantly expanding number of methods [29]. As design tools, the current study selected 6 nudging methods: *default setting, manipulation of accessability, reminders, prompts, framing* and *pre-commitment strategies. Default setting* is to predetermine courses of action that take effect if nothing is specified by the decision maker [30]. *Manipulation of accessability* is to purposefully arrange the environment and surroundings in favor of certain behaviours. *Reminders* are notifications that encourage choices and behaviours through directing individuals' attention [19]. *Prompts* are changes to the physical environment that aim to overcome error-prone or repetitive behaviours [20]. *Framing* is to change the presentation of a subject matter in the purpose of influencing individuals' choices [30]. *Pre-commitment strategies* serve to commit people to certain behaviours, as most of them seek to be consistent with their promises [29,37].

To manipulate or facilitate choices and behaviours, nudging takes advantage of judgemental heuristics [5] and cognitive biases. In this paper, we will focus on *the anchoring heuristic, status quo bias, the framing effect,* and *the default effect.* *The anchoring heuristic* is the tendency to make judgement according to a reference point, and that individuals are disproportionately influenced by the initial information entry [6,9,32]. *Status quo bias* is the preference of remaining in the current state of affairs and avoiding change even when the current state may not be objectively superior, as changes are often perceived as loss or detriment [17]. *The framing effect* is where an individual's decisions are based on the presentation of the information rather than the knowledge of it [33]. *The default effect* is the tendency to accept or align one's decision with a pre-selected option. These judgemental heuristics and cognitive biases give rise to a specific type of deception – *self deception by cognitive biases.*

The nature of the nudges can differ in *transparency.* The *transparency* in the nudge theory refers to the disclosure of intentions, or the lack of, to decision makers [38]. When the intention of a technology is withheld from the user, it may lead to the other type of deception – *deception by non-transparency.*

3   Scenarios and Prototypes

To demonstrate the situations where persuasive technologies may be implemented to improve sleep hygiene, 6 scenarios featuring a fictional character – William (a male high school math teacher) were created. During the course of scenario-based design sessions, 11 preliminary prototypes of persuasive technologies and features have been constructed using the aforementioned nudging methods.

3.1   Scenario 1 – Rise and Shine

It's 7:05 a.m. now. William has just been woken up by the alarm. He usually stays in bed to check his phone for about 5 to 10 min. As he is scrolling through his notifications, here comes a new one. It says...

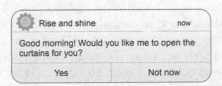

Fig. 1. Rise and shine notification

In Scenario 1, the user has just woken up. An IoT system determines that he is awake by detecting the movements in the room and activities on the phone. A confirmation dialog is then delivered to the user (see Fig. 1). The confirm button "Yes" would activate a device that opens the curtains, and the cancel button

"Not now" would delay the action. The prototype in this scenario serves to encourage and facilitate *natural daylight exposure* in the morning. Two nudging methods are used. *Reminder* – the notification that is delivered to the phone; and *manipulation of accessibility* – the call-to-action button that accesses the curtain-opening device from the mobile phone.

In this scenario, we may observe a *self-deception by cognitive bias*. The deception could be facilitated by the presentation/framing of the dialog text. The goal of the system is to facilitate the user to open the curtains and ultimately expose him to natural daylight. Instead of directly stating the objectives, the intentions are masked as a service and presented so. It takes advantage of *the framing effect*. Instead of perceiving it as a regulation or suggestion, William may consider it as a service and thereby deceiving himself.

3.2 Scenario 2 – Step Tracker

It's 2 p.m. now. William is sitting at his desk, grading papers. The phone on the desk buzzes. Here comes another notification. It is from his step-tracking app. He downloaded the app a couple of weeks ago and had set the goal to walk 10,000 steps a day. The notification says...

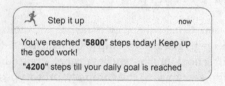

Fig. 2. Step tracker notification

In Scenario 2, the user uses a pedometer facilitated fitness app that keeps track of his step-counts, and has set a goal of 10,000 steps a day. The system monitors the user's status, and delivers notifications (see Fig. 2) that encourages the user to reach his daily goal. This prototype system serves to encourage *physical activity*, and uses the methods *reminder* – the notification that is delivered to the phone; and *pre-commitment strategy* – setting a daily goal.

In this scenario, there may be another *self-deception by cognitive bias*. By setting a daily goal and making that commitment, the 10,000 steps could become a reference point for the user. Even though there are no general rules to how many steps one should walk in a day. To avoid change and deviation from the current baseline, William behaviour may be influenced by the 10,000-step-per-day status quo. The deception is caused by the user using *the anchoring heuristic* and *status quo bias*.

3.3 Scenario 3 – the Coffee Break

It's 3 p.m. now. William has been working all day. It's time for a coffee break. He walks to the teachers' lounge and goes up to the coffee machine to make himself a coffee. On the touch screen he sees...

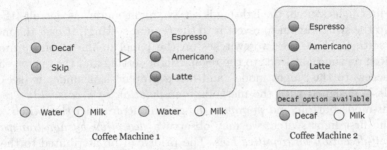

Fig. 3. Two coffee machines

In Scenario 3, the user intends to have a cup of coffee in the afternoon. Two prototypes of coffee machines were created to encourage users to *limit caffeine intake*. For the first coffee machine, the user is first presented with an interface (see Fig. 3, left) that requires a decision/command before moving on to the main interface (see Fig. 3 middle). It is designed with the method *manipulation of accessibility* – inserting a "checkpoint" in the process that requires the user to make a decision. For the second coffee machine, the user would see a sign right under the main screen and above the decaf button stating "Decaf option available". This prototype uses the method *prompt* – a simple text that changes the physical environment (see Fig. 3 right).

In the first coffee machine we may observe yet another *self-deception by cognitive bias*, which can be attributed to the user's *status quo bias*. The initial interface of the coffee machine prototype is designed in a way that indirectly suggests that decaf is the primary option (see Fig. 3 left). William's decision on whether or not to make his coffee decaf may be influenced by his impression/biased belief of the decaf option.

3.4 Scenario 4 – Night Lights

It's 6 p.m. now. After a long day at the school, William finally made his way home. He opens the front door, and the apartment is completely dark. So he reaches for the switch and...

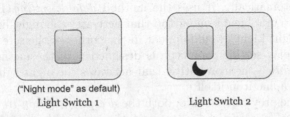

Fig. 4. Two light switches

In Scenario 4, the user enters his apartment that requires lighting. Two prototypes of light switches were created to *decrease light exposure in the evenings.*

For the first light switch, the lighting is set at "night mode" as default (the user could flip the switch again to revert it to the regular setting). It uses the method *default setting*. There are two switches on the panel in the second prototype. The switch on the right leads to the regular light setting and the one on the left allows access to the "night mode" and has a graphic icon under it (see Fig. 4 right). It is designed with the methods *manipulation of accessibility* – adding the night-mode button; and *prompt* – the graphic icon under the switch.

In the first light switch, we may observe a *deception by non-transparency* and a *self-deception by cognitive bias*. The prior can be attributed to the non-disclosure of intentions of the light switch system.. William may not realize the setting of the lights has been changed, thus his behaviour may be unknowingly influenced by the *non-transparency* of the respective nudge. The latter is due to *the default effect* caused by the actual default setting. William may have the tendency to accept the default light setting as it is.

3.5   Scenario 5 – Display Brightness

It's 8 p.m. now. William has had dinner already and has been resting on the sofa. He remembers that there is still some preparation work for tomorrow's lecture. He takes out the laptop and...

("Night light" set as default)

Night Light

Display Setting 1   Display Setting 2

Fig. 5. Two display settings

In Scenario 5, the user intends to use the laptop in the evening. Two prototypes of the display setting were created to *decrease light exposure in the evenings*. For the first display setting, the night-light mode would be turned on after 6 p.m. automatically. It uses the method *default setting*. For the second display setting, a graphical icon button that activates the night-light mode with the caption "Night Light" would appear in the corner of the screen (see Fig. 5). The second display setting prototype is designed with the methods *manipulation of accessibility* – the icon button that activates the night-light mode; and a *prompt* – the graphic icon itself.

Similar to the previous scenario, both the *deception by non-transparency* and the *self-deception by cognitive bias* may be observed in the first display setting. The prior is caused by the laptop not disclosing its intentions and actions of changing the brightness setting. William's display-using habits may be unknowingly influenced. The latter takes advantage of *the default effect*. Once the default setting is established, William is likely to accept and continue using it.

3.6   Scenario 6 – Setting the Alarm

It's 10:30 p.m. now. William is feeling quite tired after a long day. He is ready to go to bed. He sits down at the edge of the bed and turns on his phone to set an alarm. As he clicks open the app he sees...

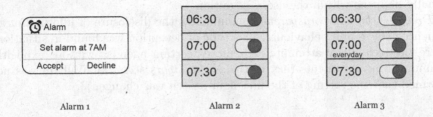

Alarm 1   Alarm 2   Alarm 3

Fig. 6. Three alarms

In Scenario 6, the user is setting the alarm before bed. Three prototypes of alarms were created to encourage *regular sleep patterns*. For the first alarm, a confirmation dialog is delivered to the user (Figure 6 left). It is designed with the methods *reminders* – the confirmation dialog text; and *manipulation of accessibility* – the confirmation dialog with the call-to-action/confirm button. The second alarm highlighted the ideal wake-time with a different color – *prompts* in a colour-schematic approach. The last alarm has the capacity to allow the user to set the alarm at the same time everyday at once – a combination of *manipulation of accessibility* and *default setting*.

In this scenario, we may observe the *self-deception by cognitive bias* in the first and last alarm. The confirmation dialog in the first alarm suggests an ideal time – 7 a.m., which could become a reference point for William. In this case, the self-deception is a result of *the anchoring heuristic* and *status quo bias*. The last alarm allows the user to set a time as default, taking advantage of *the default effect* – William may have the inclination to continue using the alarm setting out of inertia.

4   The Two Types of Deceptions

There are two types of deception identified from the scenarios where nudging methods are applied in the sleep-hygiene-improving persuasive technologies – *self-deception by cognitive biases* and *deception by non-transparency*.

Self-deception by cognitive biases is a type of deception that takes advantage of judgemental heuristics and cognitive biases, such as *the anchoring heuristic*, *status quo bias*, *the framing effect*, and *the default effect*. This type of deception emerges in the following situations: (1) Where the technology is trying to substitute users' impressions of its objectives with more appealing ones (e.g. *the framing effect* in the *Rise and Shine* scenario). (2) Where the technology is trying to encourage the adoption of a certain standard (e.g. *the status quo bias* in the *Step Tracker* scenario). (3) Where the technology is trying to establish a pre-selected option/action (e.g. *the default effect* in the *Night Lights* scenario). The most interesting characteristic about *self-deception by cognitive biases* is that it relies on users' non-rational biased beliefs. Although the technologies are designed to behave in ways that manipulate those beliefs, the real deception actually happens within the users' cognition.

Deception by non-transparency manipulates the disclosure of information to influence choices and behaviours. This type of deception was found in situations where the technology attempted to enforce certain agendas without explicitly communicating its intents (e.g. in the *Night Lights* scenario, William was not informed that the setting of the first light switch was changed).

5   Discussion

Self-deception by cognitive biases is a special type of deception that arises when the users judgemental heuristics and cognitive biases are involved. In cases where this type of deception takes effect, the impact of the nudges may go beyond the conditions and brings about changes on a goal and potentially motivational level (William is not just suggested to walking 10,000 steps a day, but leads to believe that it is the standard to do). This higher-level influence may be a key component to real behaviour change. Whereas *deception by non-transparency* causes more external changes on a conditional level.

Initially, it may seem that the exploitation of people's cognition would make the technologies susceptible to ethical problems. However, considering more invasive and significantly larger scale nudges such as organ donation policies and food waste prevention strategies are morally acceptable and widely used in society. We argue that if there are justifiable beliefs, the ethical concerns of using deception in health persuasive technologies should be admissible (if there is a legitimate reason to believe that less caffeine intake in the afternoon is good for William, it shouldn't be a problem in making him believe so). The real challenge going forward is to figure out how to best incorporate these human factor nudging holds in technical advances, and use it for the benefits of the users.

Another concern with using nudging in persuasive technologies is *control*. Participants generally expressed that technologies should make them feel empowered instead of controlled. This is where the nudge theory differs from other behaviour change paradigms. The prototypes developed in this study generally preserve freedom of choice and use indirect suggestions instead of being paternalistic or coercive. Therefore, they may be better able to promote sleep hygiene while maintaining users' autonomy and sense of control, which could be another key component to effective and sustainable behaviour changes.

Future research could examine the proposed prototypes and deceptive situations with experimental studies. Also, it would be interesting to further discuss the ethical implications of deception in persuasive health technologies.

6   Conclusion

In this paper, we identified two types of deception in the context of nudging: *self-deception by cognitive biases* – when the users' judgemental heuristics and cognitive biases are exploited; and *deception by non-transparency* – when the intentions of the technologies are withheld from the users. The prior has the potential capacity to promote behaviour change on a motivational level, which could lead to effective and sustainable behaviour changes. Also, without being coercive or paternalistic, nudging provides a behaviour change approach that may allow the multi-factor recommendations of sleep hygiene be reinforced while having users' freedom of choice and the sense of control intact.

Acknowledgments. Special thanks to Loïs Vanhée, Esteban Guerrero Rosero and Timotheus Kampik for providing guidance and support.

References

1. Ajzen, I.: The theory of planned behaviour: Reactions and reflections (2011)
2. Anderson, I., et al.: Shakra: tracking and sharing daily activity levels with unaugmented mobile phones. Mobile Netw. Appl. **12**(2), 185–199 (2007)
3. Bauer, J.S., et al.: Shuteye: encouraging awareness of healthy sleep recommendations with a mobile, peripheral display. In: Proceedings of the SIGCHI Conference on Human Factors in Computing Systems, pp. 1401–1410 (2012)
4. Blumenthal-Barby, J.S., Burroughs, H.: Seeking better health care outcomes: the ethics of using the "nudge". Am. J. Bioeth. **12**(2), 1–10 (2012)
5. Campbell-Arvai, V., Arvai, J., Kalof, L.: Motivating sustainable food choices: the role of nudges, value orientation, and information provision. Environ. Behav. **46**(4), 453–475 (2014)
6. Chapman, G.B., Johnson, E.J.: The limits of anchoring. J. Behav. Decis. Mak. **7**(4), 223–242 (1994)
7. Choe, E.K.: Design of persuasive technologies for healthy sleep behavior. In: Proceedings of the 13th International Conference on Ubiquitous Computing, pp. 507–510 (2011)
8. Coughlin, S.S., Whitehead, M., Sheats, J.Q., Mastromonico, J., Hardy, D., Smith, S.A.: Smartphone applications for promoting healthy diet and nutrition: a literature review. Jacobs J. Food Nutr. **2**(3), 021 (2015)
9. Dale, S.: Heuristics and biases: the science of decision-making. Bus. Inf. Rev. **32**(2), 93–99 (2015)
10. Elbert, N.J., et al.: Effectiveness and cost-effectiveness of eHealth interventions in somatic diseases: a systematic review of systematic reviews and meta-analyses. J. Med. Internet Res. **16**(4), e110 (2014)
11. Espie, C.A., Inglis, S.J., Tessier, S., Harvey, L.: The clinical effectiveness of cognitive behaviour therapy for chronic insomnia: implementation and evaluation of a sleep clinic in general medical practice. Behav. Res. Ther. **39**(1), 45–60 (2001)
12. Ferguson, T., Rowlands, A.V., Olds, T., Maher, C.: The validity of consumer-level, activity monitors in healthy adults worn in free-living conditions: a cross-sectional study. Int. J. Behav. Nutr. Phys. Act. **12**(1), 1–9 (2015)

13. Fogg, B.J.: A behavior model for persuasive design. In: Proceedings of the 4th international Conference on Persuasive Technology, pp. 1–7 (2009)
14. Glasgow, R.E., Bull, S.S., Piette, J.D., Steiner, J.F.: Interactive behavior change technology: a partial solution to the competing demands of primary care. Am. J. Prev. Med. **27**(2), 80–87 (2004)
15. Heber, E., Lehr, D., Ebert, D.D., Berking, M., Riper, H.: Web-based and mobile stress management intervention for employees: a randomized controlled trial. J. Med. Internet Res. **18**(1), e21 (2016)
16. Irish, L.A., Kline, C.E., Gunn, H.E., Buysse, D.J., Hall, M.H.: The role of sleep hygiene in promoting public health: a review of empirical evidence. Sleep Med. Rev. **22**, 23–36 (2015)
17. Kahneman, D., Knetsch, J.L., Thaler, R.H.: Anomalies: the endowment effect, loss aversion, and status quo bias. J. Econ. Perspect. **5**(1), 193–206 (1991)
18. Kuhn, E., Weiss, B.J., Taylor, K.L., Hoffman, J.E., Ramsey, K.M., Manber, R., Gehrman, P., Crowley, J.J., Ruzek, J.I., Trockel, M.: CBT-I Coach: a description and clinician perceptions of a mobile app for cognitive behavioral therapy for insomnia. J. Clin. Sleep Med. **12**(4), 597–606 (2016)
19. Kwan, Y.H., et al.: A systematic review of nudge theories and strategies used to influence adult health behaviour and outcome in diabetes management. Diabetes Metab. (2020)
20. Lehner, M., Mont, O., Heiskanen, E.: Nudging-a promising tool for sustainable consumption behaviour? J. Clean. Prod. **134**, 166–177 (2016)
21. Lehto, T., Oinas-Kukkonen, H.: Persuasive features in web-based alcohol and smoking interventions: a systematic review of the literature. J. Med. Internet Res. **13**(3), e46 (2011)
22. Liang, X., Wang, Q., Yang, X., Cao, J., Chen, J., Mo, X., Huang, J., Wang, L., Gu, D.: Effect of mobile phone intervention for diabetes on glycaemic control: a meta-analysis. Diabet. Med. **28**(4), 455–463 (2011)
23. Lin, J.J., Mamykina, L., Lindtner, S., Delajoux, G., Strub, H.B.: Fish'n'Steps: encouraging physical activity with an interactive computer game. In: Dourish, P., Friday, A. (eds.) UbiComp 2006. LNCS, vol. 4206, pp. 261–278. Springer, Heidelberg (2006). https://doi.org/10.1007/11853565_16
24. Nakajima, T., Lehdonvirta, V.: Designing motivation using persuasive ambient mirrors. Pers. Ubiquit. Comput. **17**(1), 107–126 (2013)
25. Peiris, D., Praveen, D., Johnson, C., Mogulluru, K.: Use of mHealth systems and tools for non-communicable diseases in low-and middle-income countries: a systematic review. J. Cardiovasc. Transl. Res. **7**(8), 677–691 (2014)
26. Petty, R.E., Briñol, P.: The elaboration likelihood model. Handb. Theor. Soc. Psychol. **1**, 224–245 (2011)
27. Pourzanjani, A., Quisel, T., Foschini, L.: Adherent use of digital health trackers is associated with weight loss. PloS one **11**(4), e0152504 (2016)
28. Sanches, P., et al.: Mind the body! designing a mobile stress management application encouraging personal reflection. In: Proceedings of the 8th ACM Conference on Designing Interactive Systems, pp. 47–56 (2010)
29. Sunstein, C.R.: Nudging: a very short guide. J. Consum. Policy **37**(4), 583–588 (2014)
30. Thaler, R.H., Sunstein, C.R.: Nudge: improving decisions about health, wealth, and happiness. Penguin (2009)
31. Turner-McGrievy, G., Tate, D.: Tweets, apps, and pods: results of the 6-month mobile pounds off digitally (mobile pod) randomized weight-loss intervention among adults. J. Med. Internet Res. **13**(4), e120 (2011)

32. Tversky, A., Kahneman, D.: Judgment under uncertainty: heuristics and biases. Science **185**(4157), 1124–1131 (1974)
33. Tversky, A., Kahneman, D.: The framing of decisions and the psychology of choice. Science **211**(4481), 453–458 (1981)
34. Vallgårda, S.: Nudge—a new and better way to improve health? Health Policy **104**(2), 200–203 (2012)
35. Vandelanotte, C., Müller, A.M., Short, C.E., Hingle, M., Nathan, N., Williams, S.L., Lopez, M.L., Parekh, S., Maher, C.A.: Past, present, and future of eHealth and mHealth research to improve physical activity and dietary behaviors. J. Nutr. Educ. Behav. **48**(3), 219–228 (2016)
36. Verbeek, P.P.: Ambient intelligence and persuasive technology: the blurring boundaries between human and technology. NanoEthics **3**(3), 231 (2009)
37. Vlaev, I., King, D., Dolan, P., Darzi, A.: The theory and practice of "nudging": changing health behaviors. Public Adm. Rev. **76**(4), 550–561 (2016)
38. Wachner, J., Adriaanse, M., De Ridder, D.: The influence of nudge transparency on the experience of autonomy. Compr. Results Soc. Psychol. pp. 1–15 (2020)
39. Yuill, J.J., et al.: Defensive computer-security deception operations: processes, principles and techniques (2007)

Agent-Based Approches

Wolves in Sheep's Clothing: Using Shill Agents to Misdirect Multi-robot Teams

Michael J. Pettinati, Ronald C. Arkin$^{(\boxtimes)}$, and Akshay Krishnan

Georgia Institute of Technology, Atlanta, GA 30332, USA
{mpettinati3,arkin,a.krishnan}@gatech.edu

Abstract. When robots undertake tasks in adversarial environments in which they must cooperate with one another (e.g., military applications or the RoboCup Competition), they are at risk for being deceived by competitors. Competitors can misdirect the team to gain a positional advantage. Our lab is exploring ways in which teams of robots can be misdirected, in part, so counter-deception strategies can be devised. This paper explores how robot shills can be used to misdirect a multi-robot team. It defines behaviors for the agents to be deceived (the mark agents) using the multi-agent coordination literature as well as behaviors for the deceiving team (the shills and lead agent). These behaviors were implemented and simulations were run for a variety of conditions. The results show how shills can facilitate misdirection in certain circumstances. They provide insights into enhancing multi-robot team deception.

Keywords: Robot deception · Multirobot systems · Team misdirection

1 Introduction

A man is milling around a stadium parking lot before a big event. There seem to be countless people wandering around him waiting for the show later that day. A woman moving very quickly enters the man's view; she moves with purpose away from the stadium. The man finds the fast-moving woman interesting but does not consider her much further until he sees a nearby man begin moving quickly (with urgency) in the same direction as the woman. He wonders if there is some kind of emergency for which assistance might be needed. As he begins to move quickly toward the two, several people behind him, who also had noticed the quickly moving pair, wonder what is going on and begin to move with the group.

Research has shown how in teams of humans and animals a small proportion of the group members are able to sway the behavior or movement of the larger group with simple local interactions [1, 3]. In the story above, the woman did not need to call out to all the followers. Instead, with purposeful movement, she was able to attract attention to herself and begin pulling people with her. The people who she pulled with her, in turn, pulled people with them.

This flocking behavior can be useful for groups of robots and has been incorporated into multi-agent robot teams [e.g., 2]. Our lab showed how a robot behavior inspired by

© Springer Nature Switzerland AG 2021
S. Sarkadi et al. (Eds.): DeceptECAI 2020/DeceptAI 2021, CCIS 1296, pp. 41–54, 2021.
https://doi.org/10.1007/978-3-030-91779-1_4

lekking in birds could help to support the formation of meaningful task-oriented robot groups. This behavior, though useful, leaves robot teams susceptible to misdirection.

This paper explores misdirection in these robot teams. Specifically, it tries to understand how shill agents (confederate members of the deception team) can help to misdirect mark agents (targets of the deception). The goal of the deceptive agents is to move the marks from a start position to a goal position that is advantageous to the deceiving team. Feints for example (moving in a direction intended to mislead) are common in sports and the military.

In the story above, the man followed along with the woman when he saw the nearby man begin to move with her. This second individual could have followed the woman out of curiosity, but he could have been a confederate of (shill for) the woman. He could have moved to encourage others to follow along and/or to keep others following along with her. In groups, people take an action when they have seen a sufficient number of others take the same action [5]. People assume if many people are taking this action, then it must be correct or appropriate. The man needed to see two people move with urgency in a certain direction before deciding there was something worth seeing in their direction and moving with them. Robots can similarly follow this threshold model to inform their actions.

Our lab has done extensive work in robot deception [e.g. 9, 10] and even provided the first taxonomy on human-robot deception [10]. This work is building upon that previous work by exploring the misdirection of a multi-agent robot team by a multi-agent robot team. This research is being done in part to develop counter-deceptive practices in upcoming work.

The next section of this paper discusses previous research looking at deception between teams of robots as well as how robots have been used to move groups from one location to another. The third section introduces the models of the mark agents and the agents involved in the deception. The fourth section present simulation results involving implementations of these agents. The paper ends with a conclusion and discussion of future work.

2   Related Work

Previous research into multiagent deception has looked at how a deceptive team of robots can keep adversaries away from a certain area that may harbor valuable resources [8]. Our research, instead, focuses on misdirecting adversaries to a certain area.

Robots have been employed in herding situations [4, 6, 11, 12]. These robots "pushed" animals from one location to another. This included herding ducks [11, 12], which have similar flocking behaviors to sheep, into penned areas, and herding birds away from airports to designated safe zones [4, 6]. These "pushing" approaches are fear-based with the robot acting as a predator-like agent [4, 6, 11, 12]. They are fundamentally different than our deceptive approach. The agents that are moving the marks to the goal location in this paper are indistinguishable from the mark agents themselves.

This also separates the present work from our lab's recent paper [7]. A team of shepherding robots moved a team of mark robots from one location to another. The shepherding team was more effective at moving the marks to the goal location when it combined agents that pulled along with agents that pushed the marks than when the pulling and pushing agents were separate. The pulling and pushing agents, however, were identifiable as different from the marks themselves, contrary to the shills used here.

3   Robot Models

The simulations discussed in the following section replicate the scenario given in the introduction. This section defines the behavioral assemblages that dictate the actions of the agents. The primitive behaviors for each robotic agent are defined in Appendix I. The behavioral assemblages can be seen in Appendix II. Notationally, the behavior assemblages appear bolded throughout this paper and the primitive composing behaviors appear italicized.

There are three types of agents. The first type, the leader agent, plays the role of the quickly moving woman. It leads the other agents toward the goal location. The second agent type is the mark, the agents to be deceived. The mark agents are the crowd outside of the stadium. They wander around and are unresponsive to the surrounding robots until seeing a number of agents moving with intent (moving quickly) at which point they flock to those agents. The third agent type is the shill that act as confederates with the leader agent. They mill among and flock with the mark agents, while also helping to pull the mark agents toward the leader. This is the person who moves as soon as the quickly moving woman appears as illustrated in the introduction.

3.1   Behavior Overviews

The behavioral assemblages for each of the three agent types are summarized in Table 1. The leading agent enacts a **Lead-To-Goal Behavior Assemblage** throughout the simulation that includes three behaviors. The agent is attracted to the goal location (*Go-To-Goal Behavior*); it avoids obstacles (objects) in the environment (*Avoid-Obstacle Behavior*), and it has noise incorporated into its movements (*Wander Behavior*) so that these movements are natural. The leader is the only agent with knowledge of the goal location's position.

The marks are the agents to be relocated from their initial position to the goal location. They begin the simulation wandering slowly around their start location with the **Anchored Wander Behavior Assemblage** active. They avoid crashing into other robots (*Off Robots Behavior*) as well as obstacles (objects) within the environment (*Avoid-Obstacle Behavior*). Otherwise, they simply wander around the area where they begin the simulation (*Wander Behavior and Stay Near Start Behavior*).

Each mark has a set threshold that will cause it to change its behavior to flock. This threshold is the number of agents that the mark needs to recognize as moving with intent. Moving with intent means moving at a speed above a set threshold. As described above, humans will make a decision when they have seen a certain number of others make the same decision [5]. The man in the story from the introduction decided it was prudent to follow the quickly moving woman when a nearby man chose to move toward her. Marks

Table 1. The behavior assemblages for each agent type along with the composing behaviors.

Robotic Agent	Behavior Assemblage	Composing Behaviors
Leader	Lead To Goal	• *Go-To-Goal* • *Avoid-Obstacles* • *Wander*
Mark	Wander Near Start (Simulation Outset)	• *Wander* • *Stay Near Start* • *Avoid-Obstacle* • *Off Robots*
Mark	Mark Mill Around (Below Flock Threshold)	• *Wander* • *Avoid-Obstacle* • *Off Robots*
Mark	Mark Flock (Above Flock Threshold)	• *Lek Behavior* • *Wander* • *Avoid-Obstacle* • *Off Robots*
Shill	Wander Near Start (Simulation Outset)	• *Wander* • *Stay Near Start* • *Avoid-Obstacle* • *Off Robots*
Shill	Shill Flock (Leader Signaled)	• *Follow Leader* • *Lek Behavior* • *Wander* • *Avoid-Obstacle* • *Off Robots*

will flock with the robots that show intent once they have seen a sufficient number of agents moving with intent.

All of the shill agents in the simulations are indistinguishable to the marks. Each mark computes the speed of every agent within a certain radius that is not concealed by an object in the environment. The marks measure their speed by considering a robot's current position and its position ten simulation steps before. The agent's speed is how far the agent has moved in that time window.

When a mark is at or above its flocking threshold, the **Mark Flock Behavior Assemblage** is active. This consists of four different behaviors. The mark is attracted to each agent moving with intent that it is able to see within a certain region (*Lek Behavior* [2]). The agent avoids crashing into robots (*Off Robots Behavior*) and obstacles (*Avoid-Obstacle Behavior*) in the environment. There is also noise incorporated into the robot's movement to make it more natural (*Wander Behavior*).

When the mark is below its threshold (i.e., the number of agents it sees moving with intent is below the specified number), the agent will enact the **Mark Mill Around Behavior Assemblage**. The agent will wander around (*Wander Behavior*), avoid other robots (*Off Robots Behavior*) and obstacles (*Avoid Obstacle Behavior*).

Finally, the shill agents in the simulation behave very similarly to the mark agents. At the outset of the simulation, they enact the mark's **Anchored Wander Behavior Assemblage**. When the leader agent begins to move to the goal location, they enact the **Shill Flock Behavioral Assemblage**. This includes the same behaviors as the Mark Flock behavior (*Off Robots Behavior, Avoid-Obstacle Behavior, Wander Behavior and Lek Behavior*) with the addition of being attracted to the leader when the leader is visible (*Follow Leader Behavior*). This helps pull the flock toward the leader's position, which is approaching the goal throughout the simulation.

3.2 Mathematical Models

Each robot's position is updated every simulation step (simulation second). The distance and direction moved by a robot is based on that robot's baseline speed (in meters per second) and the behavioral assemblage that it is currently executing. Each behavior in the behavioral assemblage outputs a vector. The simulation computes a weighted sum of the vectors that are returned by the behaviors and multiplies the resulting vector by the agent's baseline speed to determine how far and in what direction the agent moves. The behaviors appear in Appendix I. This appendix describes the vector returned by each behavior. The weights and parameters associated with each behavior and behavior assemblage appear in Appendix II.

3.3 Robot Missions

The finite state automata that define the missions for the robot appear in Fig. 1. The circles show the behavioral assemblages for the agent that are active throughout the course of a simulation. The rectangles show the triggers by which the agent moves between behavioral assemblages.

The leader (Fig. 1A) waits until all of the other agents are contained within the starting area and wandering around. It approaches the area containing the agents and signals the shills that it is heading toward the goal. It then moves toward the goal location using the **Lead-To-Goal Behavior Assemblage**.

A mark (Fig. 1B) wanders around in the start location until its flocking threshold has been satisfied (**Wander Near Start Behavior Assemblage**). The threshold is some number of agents moving with intent (at or above a certain speed). It flocks with the agents that are moving with intent (**Mark Flock Behavior Assemblage**) when at or above this threshold. It wanders when below this threshold (**Mark Mill Around Behavioral Assemblage**).

The shill agent (Fig. 1C) wanders with the mark agents at the simulation's outset (**Wander Near Start Behavior Assemblage**). When the leader signals to the shill that it is heading to the goal location, the shill begins to flock with the agent's that move with intent; it tries to drag the marks along to the leader's location (**Shill Flock Behavior Assemblage**).

4   Misdirection Simulations

Each simulation began when the leader agent signaled the shill agents and it began to move to the goal. The shills and marks began the simulation wandering within a start

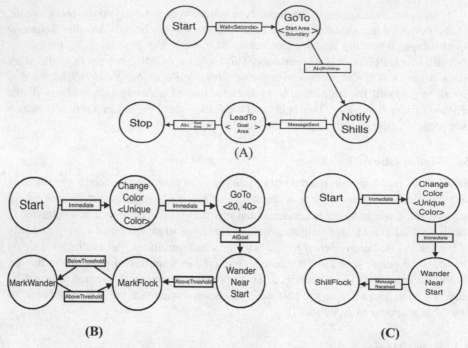

Fig. 1. The FSAs for Agents: (A) Leader agent (B) Mark agent (C) Shill agent

area of ten-meter radius (20 m, 40 m). The simulation ended when all of the marks were within ten meters of the goal location (220 m, 40 m) or when the simulation had run 2000 steps (seconds). The simulation environment was 60 m by 240 m.

The five independent variables that were manipulated between simulations are summarized in Table 2. Snapshots from a trial with twelve mark agents, two shill agents and a large object appear in Fig. 4. The marks were successfully relocated from the start area to the goal area. The robots have unique colors so marks can identify and track other agents to compute their speeds.

The number of shills was varied from 0 to 2 to understand the conditions under which shills may facilitate misdirection. Shills are attracted toward the leader and flock along with the marks. These agents help to keep the flock of marks moving toward the leader and help to meet the marks' thresholds for flocking. The shill agents move with intent in the general direction of the leader.

The shill *Lek Behavior* could be given a higher or lower weight. A higher *Lek Behavior* weight makes the shill more responsive to all the agents moving with intent in the simulation. A lower weight makes the shill less responsive to all flocking agents and gives greater influence over its movement to the leader agent.

The complexity of the environment was varied as well. Simulation cases included no object present, a small object present, or a large object present (Fig. 2). The objects were centered at (140, 40) and had a radius of 3 m or 10 m. The objects obscured all agents' lines of sight. During a trial with objects, the marks could lose sight of agents

Table 2. These are the five independent variables that were manipulated between simulation conditions. There were 30 different conditions tested by running series of simulations with the values indicated.

Independent variable	Values tested		
Number of shills	0, 1, and 2 for all other parameter settings		
Number of marks	4	12	
Mark Agents Thresholds for Flocking	2 marks - threshold 1 2 marks - threshold 2	6 marks - threshold 1 6 marks - threshold 2	1 mark - threshold 1 2 marks - threshold 2 2 marks - threshold 3 2 marks - threshold 4 2 marks - threshold 5 2 marks - threshold 6 1 mark - threshold 7
Shill *Lek Behavior* Weight	High	High	Low, High
Environment obstacles	No Object Small Object Large Object	No Object Small Object Large Object	No Object Large Object

moving with intent, so they would fall below their flocking threshold and simply begin to mill about. The object could also prevent a shill agent from seeing the leader; this removes the shill's ability to move toward the goal.

The number of marks and their thresholds for flocking were varied as well. In certain simulations, all the marks were easily persuaded to flock, they all had low flocking thresholds (of 1 and 2). In other conditions, certain marks had much higher thresholds for flocking.

The degree to which the deceptive team (the leader and shill agents) was successful in misdirecting the flock was assessed by looking at the proportion of the marks moved from the start to the goal region.

4.1   Results

We compared the median number of mark agents successfully moved from the start location to the goal location using the Kruskal-Wallis one-way analysis of variance test. The number of shills was the independent variable for each test. The environment complexity, the number of marks, and the marks' thresholds varied between the tests but were held constant within tests. This Kruskal-Wallis test was used because the proportion of agents that were successfully misdirected did not follow a normal distribution. There were many trials within conditions where almost all the mark agents were moved to the goal location (the proportion of agents was near 1) or almost none of the mark agents were moved to the goal location (the proportion of agents was near 0).

There were no significant differences between the groups with respect to the proportion of mark agents that were successfully moved to the goal location when the *Lek*

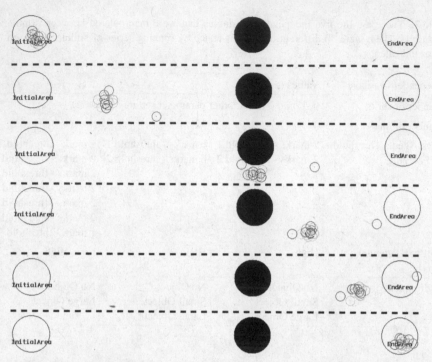

Fig. 2. Snapshots from a simulation trial with twelve marks and two shills. The marks are successfully relocated from the start to the goal.

Behavior weight was high and the flocking thresholds for all marks was low (p > .05). Additional shills in these simulations did not change the leading agent's ability to pull mark agents from the start to the goal location in any environment. In these cases, it seems the leader alone was sufficient to pull large proportions of the marks to the goal location (see Table 3 and Fig. 3).

The results for when the marks' thresholds were changed to include agents that had high flocking thresholds still had no significant differences between the three conditions with different number of shills (p > .05). In these cases, however, it was often true that the marks were not successfully moved to the goal location. In all of the conditions, the median values for the proportion of shills moved to the goal location were below .25, fewer than one in four marks was moved from the start to the goal location.

The weight on the shills' *Lek Behavior* was changed to a lower weight. These results are summarized in Table 4 and Fig. 4. There was an extremely significant difference (p < .001) between all groups in the no object condition. With two shills, the agent was consistently able to misdirect almost all of the mark agents. With no shills, the leader was consistently not able to misdirect the mark agents. In the big object condition, however, there was no difference between groups. The leader, in all three conditions, was unable to misdirect the marks. The object in a large portion of the trials obscured the leading agent from the shill agents. This meant that the shill agents would not continue toward

Table 3. The results from the 20 simulations run with twelve marks, a high *Lek Behavior* weight, and low flocking thresholds for all mark agents. There were no significant differences between conditions. Marks did not facilitate the misdirection.

Environment	0 Shills Median (Standard Deviation) (n = 20 runs)	1 Shill Median (Standard Deviation) (n = 20 runs)	2 Shills Median (Standard Deviation) (n = 20 runs)
Big Object	1.0 (0.438)	0.708 (0.374)	0.667 (0.392)
Small Object	0.958 (0.390)	0.958 (0.405)	0.583 (0.384)
No Object	1.0 (0.283)	1.0 (0.253)	1.0 (0.293)

the goal. The group of flocking marks and shills ended up stalling behind the object while the leader continued on to the goal location.

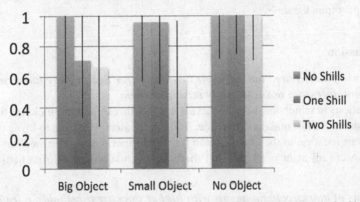

Fig. 3. There were no significant differences between groups when all 12 marks had low flocking thresholds. The leader alone was able to misdirect the agents.

Table 4. The results from the 10 simulations run with twelve marks, a low *Lek Behavior* weight, and high flocking thresholds for some mark agents. There was a very significant difference between all groups with no object present. The shills facilitated the misdirection. With the big object present, they did not.

Environment	0 Shills Median (Standard Deviation) (n = 10 runs)	1 Shill Median (Standard Deviation) (n = 10 runs)	2 Shills Median (Standard Deviation) (n = 10 runs)
Big Object	0.0 (0.0)	0.0 (0.478)	0.0 (0.478)
No Object	0.0 (0.167)	0.417 (0.423)	1.0 (0.053)

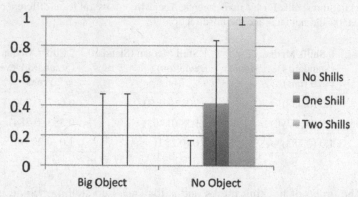

Fig. 4. There were significant differences between all groups with no object present. The shill agents facilitated the misdirection. With a large object present, there was not a significant difference between groups. All groups with the large object had a median value of 0. The object obscured the leader agent from the shills.

4.2 Discussion

When teams of marks are "naive" (their thresholds for flocking are universally low), shills are not necessary to successfully misdirect them
The simulations in which the mark agents all had low thresholds for flocking (thresholds of 1 or 2) shills did not make a difference. The leader alone was able to bring the marks from the start location to the goal location (cf. Pied Piper story). The medians for these conditions were all at or near one, and there were no significant differences between groups.

When teams of marks contain agents with higher flocking thresholds, a leader alone is often not able to successfully misdirect them
The conditions in which the marks had higher thresholds for flocking had medians of 0 when a leader agent was the only member of the deception team. The use of the shills aided in the misdirection under these conditions.

The weight of a shill's lekking behavior must be low enough to prevent it from dominating the follow the leader behavior

The conditions in which the shills had a high *Lek Behavior* weight were not significantly different from the conditions in which only a leader agent composed the deceiving team. It appears that in these conditions the *Lek Behavior* vector cancels the vector produced by the *Follow Leader Behavior* when the flock of marks and shills approaches the leader agent. This prevents the shills from pulling the marks all the way to the goal location. Often the group stopped just short of the goal location.

If the deceptive team is going to function effectively, shill agents must be able to see the leader agent throughout the deception or the shill agent must have knowledge of the goal location

In the set of simulations with no object present in the environment, high flocking thresholds, and a low *Lek Behavior* weight for the shill agents, the marks were successfully moved to the goal location in all trials except one when two shills were present. With a large object inserted into the environment, the median proportion of marks moved to the goal location was 0. The shills lost sight of the leading agent and were unable to help drag the marks to the goal location. The shills may need to incorporate additional behaviors to keep the leader agent within view or may need to have additional knowledge about the goal under these conditions.

5   Conclusions and Ongoing Work

This paper explored how shill agents could be used to facilitate the misdirection of a team of mark agents. The simulations presented here show that in cases where mark agents have low thresholds for flocking together, a leading agent that moves with intent is sufficient to pull agents from a start location to a goal location. In cases where the mark agents have higher thresholds for flocking, shill agents help to carry out the misdirection. The shills facilitate misdirection when they do not lose sight of the leading agent and when the influence of the flocking marks does not dominate the influence of the leading agent on their motion.

Shills could employ more complex behaviors in order to more effectively misdirect mark agents. For example, they could observe and model the movement of the mark agents and coordinate their behavior to optimize the deception. Any additional behaviors employed by the shill agents, however, further differentiates them from the marks (providing opportunities to spoil the deception). In this study, shill agents were designed to be as simple and indistinguishable from the marks as possible.

In ongoing research, we are developing counter-deceptive strategies for these scenarios. We are currently evaluating if counteragents that employ novel strategies to deter misdirection can overcome the deceptive practices of the opposing team.

Acknowledgments. This research is supported by the National Science Foundation under CNS EAGER grant #1848653.

Appendix I

The definitions of the robotic behaviors discussed in the text appear below.

A) Off Robots Behavior: The agent is repelled from a robot with variable sphere of influence and variable gain. The vector returned from the behavior is the sum of the individual vectors for all of the robots. This keeps the robots from crashing into one another in the simulation.

$$V_{magnitude} = \begin{cases} \dfrac{R-d}{R}, & d \leq R \\ 0, & d > R \end{cases}$$

$V_{direction}$ = Direction from the center of the other robot to this robot's center

where:
R = Radius of the repulsion sphere
d = Distance of robot to another robot

B) Lek Behavior: The agent is attracted to a surrounding robot that is moving faster than the speed threshold with a variable gain and a variable region of influence. The vector returned is the sum of the vectors for all agents. This is for group formation in the simulation.

$$V_{magnitude} = \begin{cases} 1 - \dfrac{(A-D)-(d-D)}{A-D}, & D \leq d \leq A \\ 0, & \text{otherwise} \end{cases}$$

$V_{direction}$ = Direction from the center of this robot to the other robot's center

where:
A = Radius of the attraction sphere
D = Radius of the dead zone sphere
d = Distance of robot to another robot

C) Avoid-Obstacle Behavior: Agent is repelled from obstacles (objects in the environment) with variable gain and sphere of influence. The robot avoids designated obstacles in the environment.

$$V_{magnitude} = \begin{cases} \infty, & d \leq r \\ \dfrac{max-d}{max-r}, & r < d \leq max \\ 0, & max > d \end{cases}$$

$V_{direction}$ = Direction from the center of the object to this robot's center

where:
max = Radius of obstacle detection sphere
r = Radius of the circular obstacle
d = Distance of robot to the center of the obstacle

D) Follow Leader Behavior: A shill agent is attracted to the position of the leader with variable gain and sphere of influence. The leader is pulling it toward the goal.

$$V_{magnitude} = \begin{cases} 1 - \dfrac{R_L-d}{R_L}, & d \leq R_L \\ 0, & d > R_L \end{cases}$$

$V_{direction}$ = Direction from the center of this shill robot to the leader's center

where:
R_L = Radius of the region in which agents are attracted to the shill
d = Distance of robot to the shill

E) Go To Goal Location Behavior: Agent is attracted to a goal location. This moves the agent in the direction of a designated goal location.

$$V_{magnitude} = \text{Adjustable gain value}$$

$V_{direction}$ = Direction to the goal location from the robot's center

Appendix II

The parameters used for the behavior assemblages appear below. The parameters for the set of simulations in which the Lek Behavior was changed appear in parentheses.

Leader Agent Parameter	Value	Units
Lead to Goal Behavior Assemblage		
x position of goal	240	m
y position of goal	40	m
Move to Goal Gain	1	
Wander Gain	0.9	
Avoid Obstacle Gain	1	
Avoid Obstacle Sphere	3	m
Avoid Obstacle Safety margin	.5	m

Mark Agent Parameter	Value	Units
Anchored Wander Behavior Assemblage		
Stay Near Start/Goal Gain	.2	
x coordinate of start location	20	m
y coordinate of start location	40	m
Start location attraction radius	10	m
Avoid Obstacle Gain	.2	
Avoid Obstacle Sphere	6	m
Avoid Obstacle Safety margin	.5	m
Avoid Robots Gain	.2	
Repel Sphere	2	m
Wander Gain	.2	
Mark Mill Around Behavior Assemblage		
Avoid Robots Gain	.2	
Repel Sphere	2	m
Avoid Obstacle Gain	.2	
Avoid Obstacle Sphere	6	m
Avoid Obstacle Safety Margin	.5	m
Wander Gain	.2	
Mark Flock Behavior Assemblage		
Avoid Robots Gain	1	
Repel Sphere	2	m
Lek Gain	1	
Attract Sphere	40	m
Dead Zone Sphere	4	m
Wander Gain	.5	
Avoid Obstacle Gain	1	
Avoid Obstacle Sphere	6	m
Avoid Obstacle Safety Margin	.5	m

References

1. Couzin, I.D., Krause, J., Franks, N.R., Levin, S.A.: Effective leadership and decision-making in animal groups on the move. Nature **433**(7025), 513 (2005)
2. Duncan, B.A., Ulam, P.D., Arkin, R.C.: Lek behavior as a model for multi-robot systems. In: Proceedings of the 2009 IEEE International Conference on Robotics and Biomimetics (ROBIO), pp. 25–32. IEEE (2009)
3. Epstein, J.M.: Modeling civil violence: an agent-based computational approach. Proc. Natl. Acad. Sci. **99**(Suppl. 3), 7243–7250 (2002)
4. Gade, S., Paranjape, A.A., Chung, S.: Herding a flock of birds approaching an airport using an unmanned aerial vehicle. In: AIAA Guidance, Navigation, and Control Conference (2015)
5. Granovetter, M.: Threshold models of collective behavior. Am. J. Sociol. **83**(6), 1420–1443 (1978)
6. Paranjape, A.A., Chung, S., Kim, K., Shim, D.H.: Robotic herding of a flock of birds using an unmanned aerial vehicle. IEEE Trans. Rob. **34**(4), 901–915 (2018)
7. Pettinati, M.J., Arkin, R.C.: Push and pull: shepherding multi-agent robot teams in adversarial situations. In: 15th IEEE International Conference on Advanced Robotics and Its Social Impacts (ARSO 2019), Beijing, China (2019)
8. Sanghvi, N., Nagavalli, S., Sycara, K.: Exploiting robotic swarm characteristics for adversarial subversion in coverage task. In: Proceedings of the 16th Conference on Autonomous Agents and MultiAgent Systems (2017)
9. Shim, J., Arkin, R.C.: Biologically-inspired deceptive behavior for a robot. In: Ziemke, T., Balkenius, C., Hallam, J. (eds.) SAB 2012. LNCS (LNAI), vol. 7426, pp. 401–411. Springer, Heidelberg (2012). https://doi.org/10.1007/978-3-642-33093-3_40

10. Shim, J., Arkin, R.C.: A taxonomy of robot deception and its benefits in HRI. In: 2013 IEEE International Conference on Systems, Man, and Cybernetics. IEEE (2013)
11. Vaughan, R., Sumpter, N., Frost, R., Cameron, S.: Robot sheepdog project achieves automatic flock control. In: Proceedings of the Fifth International Conference on the Simulation of Adaptive Behaviour, vol. 489 (1998)
12. Vaughan, R., Sumpter, N., Henderson, J., Frost, A., Cameron, S.: Experiments in automatic flock control. Robot. Auton. Syst. **31**(1–2), 109–117 (2000)

Learning to Deceive in Multi-agent Hidden Role Games

Matthew Aitchison[1](✉), Lyndon Benke[2], and Penny Sweetser[1]

[1] ANU College of Engineering and Computer Science, The Australian National
University, Canberra, Australia
matthew.aitchison@anu.edu.au
[2] Department of Defence, Defence Science and Technology Group,
Canberra, Australia

Abstract. Deception is prevalent in human social settings. However,
studies into the effect of deception on reinforcement learning algorithms
have been limited to simplistic settings, restricting their applicability to
complex real-world problems. This paper addresses this by introducing
a new mixed competitive-cooperative multi-agent reinforcement learning
(MARL) environment, inspired by popular role-based deception games
such as Werewolf, Avalon, and Among Us. The environment's unique
challenge lies in the necessity to cooperate with other agents despite not
knowing if they are friend or foe. Furthermore, we introduce a model of
deception which we call *Bayesian belief manipulation* (BBM) and demonstrate its effectiveness at deceiving other agents in this environment,
while also increasing the deceiving agent's performance.

Keywords: Machine learning · Deep reinforcement learning ·
Deception · Intrinsic motivation · Bayesian belief

1 Introduction

Human tendency to trust in the honesty of others is essential to effective cooperation and coordination [25]. At the same time, trust opens up the risk of
being exploited by a deceptive party. Deception is prevalent in many real-life settings, especially in those that are adversarial in nature. Examples include cyber-
security attacks [1], warfare [8], games such as poker [5], and even every-day economic interactions [16]. Outside of simplistic signaling games (e.g. [7,23]), use,
and defence against, deceptive strategies has received relatively little research
attention.

The popularity of social deception games, such as Werewolf, Avalon, and
Among Us, reveals both a human fascination with deception, and the challenges
that it creates. These games require players to cooperate with their *unknown*
teammates to achieve their goals, all while trying to hide their identities. Therefore, social deception games could provide an interesting setting for research into
deception. To explore deception beyond simple signalling games, we introduce a

S. Sarkadi et al. (Eds.): DeceptECAI 2020/DeceptAI 2021, CCIS 1296, pp. 55–75, 2021.
https://doi.org/10.1007/978-3-030-91779-1_5

new hidden role mixed competitive-cooperative multi-agent reinforcement learning (MARL) environment *Rescue the General* (RTG). Our environment features three teams: red and blue, who have conflicting goals, and a neutral green team. To perform well, agents must learn subtle trade-offs between acting according to their team's objectives and revealing too much information about their roles.

To this end, we trained two sets of agents to play RTG, one in which the agent pursues the rewards of the game as per normal, and another where the agents are provided an intrinsic reward [31] to incentivise deceptive actions. We compare the behaviour of the two groups and analyse the their performance when pitted against each other.[1] The main contributions of this work are:

1. The introduction of a new deception-focused hidden-role MARL environment.
2. A new model for deception called *Bayesian belief manipulation* (BBM).
3. Empirical results showing the effect of BBM on agents' behaviour, and which demonstrate its effectiveness as a deception strategy.

2   Background and Related Work

Previous game-theoretic approaches have typically modelled deception through signalling [18], where one player can, at a cost, send a signal conveying false information. An example in network security, examined by [7], has a defender who may attempt to deceive an attacker by disguising honeypots as regular computers.[2] Other work has explored the evolution of deceptive signalling in competitive-cooperative learning environments, [12] found that teams of robots in competitive food-gathering experiments spontaneously evolved deceptive communication strategies, reducing competition for food sources by causing harm to opponents. Our research differs from these signal based deception studies in that instead of modelling deception as an explicit binary action, we require agents to learn complex sequences of actions to mislead, or partially mislead, other players.

An extension to game theory is hypergame theory [3]. Hypergame theory models games where players may be uncertain about others players' preferences (strategies), and therefore may disagree on what game they are playing. Because the model includes differences in agents' perception of the game, hypergame theory provides a basis for modelling misperception, false belief, and deception [21]. Examples of hypergame analysis in practice include [35], who consider deception in single-stage, normal form hypergames, and [15] who model deception about player preferences for games in which the deceiver has complete knowledge of the target. Hypergames have also been used to model the interaction between attackers and defenders in network security problems [17]. Our environment can be seen as a hypergame because players do not know the roles of other players in the game. However, unlike previous work, where all players' actions were fully

---

[1] Source code for the environment and model, including a script to reproduce the results in this paper, can be found at https://github.com/maitchison/RTG.

[2] A honeypot is a networked machine designed to lure attackers, but which contains no real valuable information.

observable, our environment includes partially observed actions increasing the potential for disagreement and deception.

The most similar work to our own is [34] who also incentivise agents to manage information about their roles. They use mutual information between goal and state as a regularisation term during optimisation to encourage or discourage agents from revealing their goals. Our work differs in that we instead incorporate deception into the agents' rewards, which allows agents to factor the future possibility of deception into their decision-making process.

Our deception model is most similar to the Bayesian model proposed by [11], who consider agents with incomplete information about the types of other players. Unlike our work, this approach assumes a two-player game with fully observable actions, in which the history of each player is known to both players. Our approach enables the modelling of deception in multi-agent games with partial observability, in which player histories are unknown and must be estimated from local observations.

Reasoning about other players' roles under uncertainty has also been explored by [33], who use counterfactual regret minimisation to deductively reason about other players' roles in the game of Avalon. Their work is similar in that their agents must identify unknown teammates' roles. However, their approach differs in that they do not explicitly encourage deception. [26] consider the broader problem of communicating intent in the absence of explicit signalling. An online planner is used to select actions that implicitly communicate agent intent to an observer. This approach has been applied to deception by [27], by maximising rather than minimising the difference between agent and observer beliefs. Unlike our work, these approaches assume full observability, and require a model of the environment for forward planning.

While many existing MARL environments have explored cooperation between teammates [2,13,19,24,30] only ProAvalon [33] requires cooperation with *unknown* teammates. However, ProAvalon is not suitable for our needs, due to the high degree of shared information.[3] In contrast, our environment, RTG, with limited player vision allows agents to have very different belief about game's current state. This difference is important for our BBM model as modelling other players (potentially incorrect) understanding of the game's current state is essential to manipulating their belief.

3   Rescue the General

We developed a new MARL environment, RTG, which requires agents to learn to cooperate and compete when teammates are unknown. Popular hidden role deception games inspired many of the environment's core mechanics. RTG is open source, written in Python and uses the Gym framework [4].

We designed RTG with the following objectives: the game should be fast to simulate but complex to solve; game observations should be both human and

---

[3] In Avalon only player roles, and who decided to sabotage a mission are hidden.

machine-readable; code for the environment should be open source and easy to modify; the game should be mixed competitive/cooperative (i.e., not zero-sum); hidden roles should be a core game mechanic;[4] and good strategies should require non-trivial (temporally extended) deception.

3.1   Teams and Objectives

The game consists of three teams: red, green, and blue. The blue team knows the location of a general and must perform a rescue by dragging them to the edge of the map, but requires multiple soldiers to do so. Green are 'lumberjacks' who receive points for harvesting wood from the trees scattered around the map, and whose interests are orthogonal to the other teams. The red team does not know the general's location and must find and kill the general. Similar to the StarCraft Multi-Agent Challenge [30], each soldier is controlled independently, and has a limited vision (a range of six tiles for red, and five for green and blue). The complication is that no soldier knows any other's identity', including their own team members. Communication is limited to the soldiers' actions, namely movement by one tile north, south, east or west and the ability to shoot in one of the four cardinal directions. All soldiers have an ID colour allowing soldiers to track previous behaviour.

Player teams are randomised at the beginning of each game. Their locations are randomily initialised such that they are near to each other, but always more than 2-tiles away from the general.

3.2   Observational Space

Egocentric observations are provided to each agent in RGB format, as shown in Fig. 1. Status indicator lights give the agent information on their x-location, y-location, health, turns until they can shoot, turns until a game timeout, and team colour. A marker indicating the direction of the general is also given to blue players. Rewards depend on the scenario and are detailed in Sect. 3.4.

3.3   Scenarios

The RTG environment provides six scenarios of differing levels of challenge. These scenarios are given in Table 1. Additional custom scenarios can also be created through configuration options (for details see Appendix A).

In the primary scenario, Rescue, the blue team must rescue a general without allowing a lone red player to find and shoot the general. The Wolf scenario features a single red player who must kill all three green players before being discovered. R2G2 demonstrates orthogonal objectives, with two green players harvesting trees while two red players attempt to find and kill the general. Red2, Green2 and Blue2 are simple test environments where each team can learn their objective unobstructed.

---

[4] In this paper, role refers to the policy a player follows and maps directly to the player's team. Different roles may exist within a single team in other games.

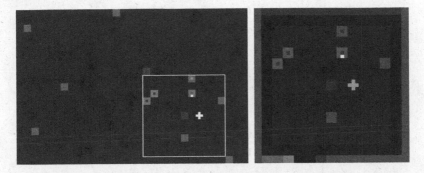

Fig. 1. The global observation (left) and an agent's local observation (right). Soldiers are painted with their unique ID color on the outside, and their team color on the inside. Local observations omit the team color for all non-red players. Each map tile is 3 × 3 and encoded in RGB colour. (Color figure online)

Table 1. Summary of scenarios provided the Rescue the General environment. Player counts are listed in red, green, and blue order.

Scenario	Players	Type	Roles	Challenge
Rescue	1-1-4	Mixed	Hidden	Hard
Wolf	1-3-0	Competitive	Hidden	Moderate
R2G2	2-2-0	Mixed	Visible	Moderate
Red2	2-0-0	Cooperative	Visible	Easy
Green2	0-2-0	Cooperative	Visible	Easy
Blue2	0-0-2	Cooperative	Visible	Easy

3.4 Reward Structure

The rewards are structured such that a victory for red or blue always results in a score of ten, and are outlined in Table 2. R_b refers to the total reward for the blue team this game, and is used to make sure blue always receives a maximum of ten points for a win. Green is also able to score ten points if they harvest all the trees on the map, but unlike red and blue, they will not terminate the game by achieving their objective. Due to the complexity of rescuing the general (two players must work together to move the general tile-by-tile) we provide small rewards to blue for completing partial objectives.

4   Bayesian Belief Manipulation Model

Our deception model is based on belief manipulation [10]. Each agent keeps track of what it believes other agents believe that an action would imply about their role. We refer to this as 'inverse' prediction. That is, predicting what others would predict about ourselves. Using these inverse predictions and an assumption of Bayesian belief updates, a reward is generated to incentivise agents to

Table 2. Rewards for each team in the RTG game.

Event	Red	Green	Blue
General killed	10	0	-10
General rescued	-10	0	$10 - R_b$
Timeout	5	0	-5
Green harvests tree	0	1	0
Blue next to general (first time)	0	0	1
General moved closer to map edge	0	0	$\frac{(10-R_b)}{20}$

take actions that would mislead other agents about their true role. We call this Bayesian belief manipulation (BBM).

4.1 Theory of Mind

In order to deceive another player, we need to model our belief about their belief of how our actions would be interpreted. Take, for example, the situation in Fig. 2. If red believes that blue knows that red can see the general, this action will be considered a very 'red' move. However, if red believes that blue is unaware of the general, this action can, perhaps, be taken without revealing red's role. Thus, agents must model, not only the beliefs about others but also others' beliefs about themselves.

Fig. 2. Should red believe they are giving away their role by shooting east? This depends on whether red knows that blue knows that red is shooting the general (depicted with a cross). Blue's limited vision is shaded, and both soldier's roles are visualised for context. If blue knows that red knows where the general is, blue will interpret this as a very 'red' move. (Color figure online)

4.2 Assumptions

In our model the deceiving agents operate under the following assumptions:

1. All non-deceiving agents are Bayesian in their approach to updating belief about roles.[5]

---

[5] Our agents do not explicitly use Bayesian updates when estimating the roles of other players, but we find this assumption to be an effective model.

2. The policy of each role is known by all players.[6]
3. Agents are limited to second-order theory of mind.

The second assumption amounts to knowing the type of the policy, that is, knowing the set of potential policies, but not knowing which one the agent is acting out. Because the set of policies could, in theory, be very large, this assumption is not as limiting as it sounds. The third assumption follows the findings of [9], who conclude that while agents with first-order and second-order theory of mind (ToM) outperform opponents with shallower ToM, deeper levels of recursion show limited benefit.

4.3 Notation

We use the following notation:

- A_i refers to the ith agent, and A_i^z refers to the event that the ith agent has role z.
- h_i^t is A_i's history of local observations up to and including timestep t. Where t is omitted it can be assumed to be the current timestep.
- $h_{i,j}^t$ is A_i's prediction of h_j^t, and $h_{i,j,k}^t$ is A_i's prediction of $h_{j,k}$. That is, A_i's prediction of A_j's prediction of A_k's history.
- Z is the set of all roles, and π_z the policy of role z.

We also write P_i to mean the probability that the A_i assigns to an event, and $P_{i,j}$ to be A_i's estimation of the probability that A_j would assign to an event. For example $P_{1,2}(A_1^r)$ is A_1's estimate of how much A_2 believes that A_1 is on the red team.

4.4 The Model

Given the assumptions in Sect. 4.2, we consider how a Bayesian agent j would update their belief about agent i's role given that they observed A_i taking action a in context h_i. We denote A_i's true role with $*$.

$$P_j(A_i^*|a, h_i) = \frac{P_j(a|h_i, A_i^*)P_j(A_i^*)}{P_j(a|h_i)} \tag{1}$$

Because A_j does not know h_i, they must estimate it as $h_{j,i}$. A_i in turn does not know what $h_{j,i}$ is and so must estimate this too as $h_{i,j,i}$. Therefore A_i can estimate A_j's new belief about their role, if they were to take action a as

$$P_j(A_i^*|a, h_i) \approx \frac{P_{i,j}(a|h_{i,j,i}, A_i^*)P_{i,j}(A_i^*)}{P_{i,j}(a|h_{i,j,i})} \tag{2}$$

Given that the probability of taking an action given history and role is, by definition, the known policies for each role, A_i can estimate the Bayes factor with which A_j would update their belief about A_i's true role as

---

[6] We partially relax this assumption, see Sect. 4.5.

$$\rho_{j,i} := \frac{\pi_*(a|h_{i,j,i})}{\sum_{z \in Z} \pi_z(a|h_{i,j,i}) P_{i,j}(A_i^z)} \tag{3}$$

As we wish to encourage deceptive agents to minimise this belief, we must reward agents for actions that generate $\rho < 1$ and disincentivise actions that would generate $\rho > 1$. Therefore, we provide agents with a $-\log(\rho)$ reward bonus, which fulfils this criterion, and whose interpretation is an estimate of the negative log of the Bayes factor in a Bayesian update for the other agent.

Implementing this bonus requires each agent i to model both $h_{i,j,i}$ for each other player j, as well as model $P_{i,j}(A_i^z)$ for each $z \in Z$. The predicted history for each agent must then be run through each known policy to produce action distributions estimations for each role.

4.5   Direct Policy Prediction

The requirement that each agent must model all other agents' complete histories can be removed by predicting the current policies for each agent directly. This avoids predicting irrelevant details about the other agents' observations, is more computationally efficient, and relaxes assumption (2) about needing to know the policies ahead of time.[7] We do this by modelling

$$\pi_z(h_{i,j,i})$$

directly for each role $z \in Z$ with $h_{i,j,i}$ being learned implicitly.

This direct policy prediction method amounts to each agent predicting what agent thinks it would do in its current circumstance, if it was each of the known roles.

4.6   Deception Bonus

Deceptive agents are given a bonus to their rewards based on their estimate of ρ in Eq. 3. Similar to [20], we filter out all but a 10% random sample of non-visible agents as their contribution adds a lot of noise.[8] We also exclude dead players from receiving or giving deception bonuses. The ρ estimates for all remaining players are summed and added as an intrinsic reward as

$$r_i^t = r_{\text{ext}}^t + \alpha_i \times r_{\text{int}}^t \tag{4}$$

---

[7] Each player's current policy is needed as targets during training, so effectively this limitation is still in place. However, it is now a training detail rather than inherent to the model, and could potentially be removed by inferring policy from observed actions.

[8] The argument that they did not observe the action and could therefore not update their belief is not valid here, as they could potentially see the consequences of the action in the future (a dead body for example). Our model does not handle this case and is left for future work.

where r_i^t is the reward at timestep t for player i, and α_i is the magnitude of the deception bonus reward for A_i.

Therefore, agents are incentivised to take actions that would mislead other agents about their true role. This formulation has several advantages. First, agents are not incentivised to deceive players who already know their role, as in this case the Bayesian update would be very small. Second, agents are not incentivised to pretend to be another role when they can get away with it. If no other player is around, or if they believe that this action could not be interpreted negatively (as in Fig. 2), they will not be penalised. It is important to note, that in a complete information game all agents agree on all histories, and this situation would not occur.

5 Training and Evaluation

To evaluate the effect of BBM as an intrinsic motivation, we trained two groups of agents on the Rescue scenario. Each group consisted of four agents, trained with different random seeds. Agents in all groups trained with deception modules; however, the first group had $\alpha = 0$ for all agents, while the second group set $\alpha = 0.5^9$ for red team players, and $\alpha = 0$ for all other players. We trained the agents under the centralised learning, decentralised execution paradigm [13] detailed further in Sect. 5.2.

5.1 Agent Architecture

Our BBM agent is composed of two distinct modules: the policy module and the deception module (see Fig. 3). The policy module was trained using local observations only, while the deception module (discarded after training) required target information from other agents.

Both modules feature the same encoder architecture, which is loosely based on DQN [28], but modified to use 3×3 kernels to the match the 3×3 tile size and lower resolution of the RTG environment. To address partial observability a recurrent layer, in the form of Long Short Term Memory (LSTM) [14], was added to the encoder, with residual connections from the convolution embedding to the output (see Appendix B for more detail on the encoder architecture.).

5.2 Training Details

The policy module takes an agent's local observation as input, encodes it via the encoder, and then outputs a policy and extrinsic/intrinsic value estimations for each of the three roles. During training, gradients are only backpropagated through the output head matching the role of the given agent.[10]

---

[9] $\alpha = 0.5$ was chosen as initial tests showed this gave agents roughly one quarter of their reward from BBM. We kept the deception bonus reward small so as not to cause agents to loose sight of their primary objective, which was to win the game.

[10] This setup allowed us to record what an agent would have done if they were playing a different role.

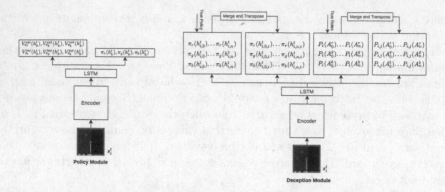

Fig. 3. The architecture of the BBM agent. The policy module outputs policy and value estimations for each role, given the input history. The deception module outputs predictions and inverse predictions for all other players for both actions and roles and requires targets from other agents. The predictions for all players in a game are stacked and transposed, then used for targets so that each agent predicts the predictions of each other agent about themselves. Here π_r, π_g, π_b are the current policy estimations for each player if they were red, green and blue. V^{ext} and V^{int} are the value estimations for the extrinsic and intrinsic returns respectively. s_i^t is the local observation at timestep t for the ith player, and n is the number of players in the game. The output from the deception module is to generate deception bonus' only, and is not required once training is complete. (Color figure online)

The policy module was trained using Proximal Policy Optimisation (PPO) [32] by running 4 epochs over batches of size 3,072 segments, each containing 16 sequential observations, using back propagation through time.

We also experimented with using separate models for each policy, but found little difference in the results, at the cost of longer training times (as did [2]). A global value estimate based on the observations of all players was also considered, but we did not find significant differences in the estimates and so opted for local value estimation instead.

To make sure at least some games were winnable for each side we modified the game rules during training so that in half of the games, a player from a randomly selected team was eliminated before the game started. We found failing to do this sometimes caused one team to dominate the other, prohibiting progress.

The policy and deception modules were trained simultaneously on the same data. They share an identical encoder structure but used separate weights. Because of this, the deception module can be removed once training has finished, allowing for decentralized execution. The policy module produces the policy and value estimate based on local observations only. The deception module outputs predictions for player roles and player actions, as well as their inverse predictions (that is, what it predicts that other agents are predicting about itself). See Fig. 3 for details.

We trained each of the eight runs for 300-million interactions (which equates to 50-million game steps) over 5-days on four RTX2080 TIs using PyTorch 1.7.1

[29]. Checkpoints every 10-million interactions were saved, allowing for evaluation of the agents' performance at various points during training.

Hyperparameters for the model, given in Table 3, were selected by running a grid search on the Red2 scenario. For more details refer to Appendix C.

Table 3. Hyperparameters used during training.

Policy module	
Mini-batch size	128 segments of length 16
LSTM units	512
PPO clipping ϵ	0.2
Entropy coefficient	0.01
γ	0.99
λ	0.95
Deception module	
Mini-batch size	32 segments of length 8
LSTM units	1024
Shared	
Parallel environments	512
Learning rate	2.5×10^{-4}
Adam ϵ	1×10^{-8}
Gradient clipping	5.0

Losses. Action predictions were trained by minimising the Kullback-Leibler (KL) [22] divergence between the predicted distribution and ground-truth targets taken from the agents during rollout generation. We trained the inverse action predictions in the same way, using the other agents' predictions during rollout generation as targets.

We trained the role predictions by minimising the negative likelihood loss, using players' true roles as targets. We trained inverse role predictions by minimising the KL divergence between the agent's prediction of other agents belief about its role, and their actual prediction about the agent's role.

Intrinsic Rewards. Raw deception bonuses were calculated, clipped to the range $(-20, 20)$ and logged for each agent. Bonuses were then zeroed for all non-red players, normalised such that the intrinsic returns had unit variance, multiplied by $\phi(t)$ where

$$\phi(t) = \min(1.0, t/10 \times 10^6)$$

and t is the timestep (in terms of interactions) during training then scaled by α_i. This creates a warm-up period where agents can learn the game with without an auxiliary objective. Similar to [6] our model outputs intrinsic and extrinsic value estimations separately, then combines them when calculating advantages.

5.3   Evaluation

Evaluating agents within a multi-agent scenario poses some unique challenges. Unlike games where agents compete against a static environment such as Atari, self-play means that as the agent gets stronger, so does its opponent. Thus, an agent's skill progress might not be visible from plots of the scores alone.

To address this we evaluated each run by playing 16 games, every ten-epochs,[11] against opponents from each of the eight runs (128 games in total). The green team was played using the same agent as the adversary. Performance across the four runs was averaged.

We also recorded raw deception bonuses, taken before normalisation or scaling, for all players, even those who did not receive them. This allowed for monitoring of deceptive behaviour on non-deceptively incentivised players. Accuracy of role predictions was taken from data generated during training.

6   Effect of Deception on Agents' Behaviour

In this section we present the effect of deception on the agents in terms of their ability to predict roles and their performance in the game, and discuss the tendency towards honest behaviour when no deception incentive is provided.

6.1   Role Prediction

Identifying other agents' role is a difficult task for blue players in the Rescue scenario. At the end of training, blue assigns an average probability to players' true role of 0.617 ± 0.08 (95%CI) when trained against deceptive adversaries, as compared to 0.707 ± 0.07 (95%CI) when trained against non-deceptive adversaries (see Fig. 4).[12] Red's role predictions were very high at 0.995 ± 0.001 (95%CI), which is expected as they are able to see the roles of all visible players. A blue player who knows their role, and assigns remaining probability based on naive population counts would on average score 0.659. Therefore, the deceptive agents red caused the blue team to predict roles more poorly than if they had no in-game observations at all.

---

[11] In this paper we define an epoch as one-million agent interactions with the environment.

[12] These percentages are derived from averages of the negative log likelihood loss taken during training, and are therefore *geometric* averages.

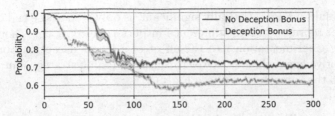

Fig. 4. Probability assigned to true role the blue team. Values shown are the log-averages taken during training and represent the average probability a blue player assigned to each player's true role. As seen by the decrease in role prediction accuracy, the blue team struggles to identify players' roles when faced with deceptively motivated adversaries. The black line indicates a naive, count-based, estimation of player roles. (Color figure online)

6.2 Performance of Deceptive Agents

Despite the effectiveness on role deception, BBM has only a minor impact on the agents' score in our experiment. As seen in Fig. 5(a), red players trained with deception see an increase in performance at the end of training from $-8.71 \pm 0.040\,(95\%\mathrm{CI})$ without deception to $-7.21 \pm 0.58\,(95\%\mathrm{CI})$ with decep-

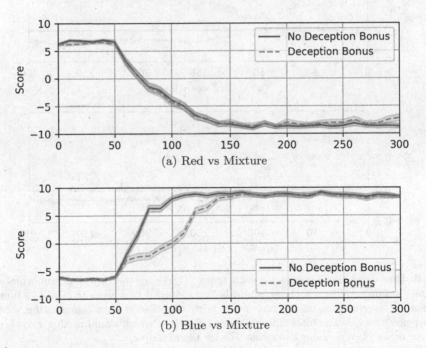

Fig. 5. The performance of the agents during training. Scores evaluated at 10-epoch intervals with opponents taken from a mixture of all eight runs. Shaded areas indicate 95% confidence intervals. (Color figure online)

tion. This result, while statistically significant, is only seen at the end of training, and does not represent a large difference in performance. It does, however, suggest further experimentation into the effect of a larger deception bonus. When facing deceptive agents blue is slower to learn a winning strategy, but eventually converges to the same outcome (see Fig. 5(b)).

6.3   Deceptive Tendencies in Unincentivised Agents

We look now at agents' behaviour when not given explicit deception incentives. Blue learns to act honestly when faced with either deceptive or honestly adversaries. This is expected in the Rescue scenario as blue must identify teammates in order to coordinate with them. An unexpected result is that green, who initially acts honestly, learns an increasingly deceptive strategy, despite no explicit incentive to do so. We suspect that as red develops a strategy that involves pretending to be green, green must respond by pretending not to be green to survive blue's hostility.

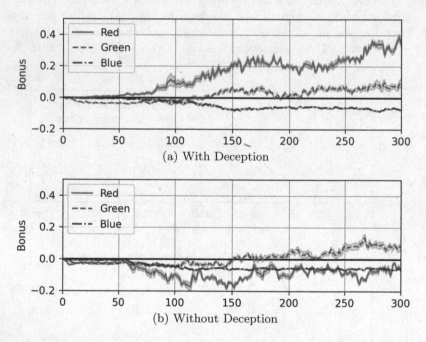

Fig. 6. Raw deception bonuses for each team. These are the unscaled, unnormalised intrinsic rewards that each player would have received if they were to receive a bonus. Values are averaged across all four runs, with the shaded area representing a 95% confidence interval. The black line indicates behaviour which would neither reveal, nor deceive other players about one's role. (Color figure online)

The red players, when incentivised to do so, learn to obtain a high degree of deception bonus (see Fig. 6(a)). When no explicit incentive is provided red players do not naturally learn a deceptive strategy. This suggests that either deception is of less value for the red team in the Rescue scenario than expected, or that a deceptive, but effective, strategy is difficult to learn for red.

7   Conclusions and Future Work

Our work presents a new, open-source environment, RTG for development and testing of deception in a complex hidden role game, as well as a novel a model of deception that makes use of second-degree ToM to manipulate other agents belief about it's own role. Our empirical results show BBM to be very effective at manipulating other agents belief about their role while at the same time improving their performance in the game. We also found that deceptive behaviour, when not incentivised, is not learned naturally by the competitive red or blue teams in the Rescue scenario, but surprisingly is learned by the neutral green team.

These results suggest several questions for future research into the effect of deception in a MARL setting. Can the relatively modest performance improvement in performance be extended by increasing the magnitude of the deception bonus, or would this cause agents to act deceptively at the cost of their primary objective? What would the impact of an honesty bonus be on the blue team in the Rescue scenario, would this encourage better cooperation? How would incorporating social aspects, namely explicit communication, impact deceptive behaviour? And how could our model, which assumes only one deceptive team, be extended to account for two or more deceptive teams.

Acknowledgements. This initiative was funded by the Department of Defence and the Office of National Intelligence under the AI for Decision Making Program, delivered in partnership with the NSW Defence Innovation Network.

Appendices

A   Scenario Configuration Options

We designed Rescue the General (RTG) to be highly customisable through configuration options. We used only a subset of the configuration settings in the supplied scenarios, with the full set outlined in Table 6. We also designed a voting system where players could initiate votes to remove players. However, we found that agents never developed an effective strategy for this system, and so did not use it.

B   Encoder Architecture

In our model, both the policy module and deception module share the same encoder architecture, but with separate parameters. The encoder design is a modification of the network often used in Deep Q-Networks (DQN), but with smaller 3x3 kernels to match our game's tile-size. The encoder takes a single local observation scaled to $[0..1]$, s_t, as input, as well as the LSTM cell states (h_{t-1}, c_{t-1}) from the previous timestep. The input is fed through the convolutional layers, flattened and projected into n dimensions, where n are the number LSTM units, then fed through the LSTM layer. See Fig. 7 for details. We found that adding a residual connections skipping the LSTM layer improved training performance, and did not negatively affect the agents' ability to remember past events.[13] The policy module used 512 LSTM units, whereas the deception module used 1024.

C   Hyperparameter Search

We performed a hyperparameter search for the policy module using a randomized grid-search. Our search used 128 runs over ten epochs on the Red2 scenario.[14] We used the average score taken from the last 100 episodes during training, where

$$\text{score} := R \times 0.99^t$$

with R being the red teams score at the end of the episode and t being the episode length. Discounting score in this way prefers hyperparameter settings that can more quickly find and kill the general and distinguishes between runs that consistently score the optimal ten points.

The *out features* setting controls the number of units in the final linear layer. When *residual* mode was active *out features* were set to the same value as *LSTM units*. The *off* mode disabled the LSTM layer, *on* passed through the LSTM layer as per normal, *concatenate* concatenated the LSTM output with the linear layer, and *residual* added residual connections.

Hyperparameter values were selected during the search by sampling uniformly-random from the values in Table 4. We then plotted each hyperparameter by selecting the best five runs for each value setting and graphing their min, mean and max.

---

[13] We verified this by observing that red players were able to retain information about the roles of previously seen players.

[14] We did not use the Rescue scenario as it is more difficult to evaluate performance, and runs would require significantly more training time.

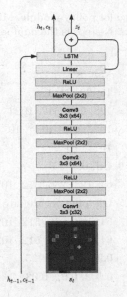

Fig. 7. Encoder architecture. Input s_t is fed into a convolutional neural network, a linear layer, and finally, an LSTM layer.

The purpose of our hyperparameter search was not to find optimal settings but to find reliable settings that would allow us to assess the difference between deceptively incentivised agents, and the control agents. Therefore, in cases where hyperparameters had similar performance, we preferred values used in prior work and those with better computational efficiency.

A separate hyperparameter search was used to find hyperparameters for the deception module, using 64 runs over 25 epochs on R2G2 with hidden roles. This search was performed using an older version of the algorithm where agents predicted other agents observations rather than action distributions and used the negative log of the mean-squared prediction error as the score. We found these settings to work well on the updated algorithm and did not modify them. Details are given in Table 5.

Table 4. Hyperparameters tested for policy module. Mini-batch sizes refer to the number of observations, not segments. N-steps is the number of steps used when generating rollouts.

Parameter	Values	Selected
N-steps	16, 32, 64, 128	16
Parallel environments	128, 256, 512, 1024	512
Learning rate	10^{-4}, $2.5 \cdot 10^{-4}$, 10^{-3}	$2.5 \cdot 10^{-4}$
Adam ϵ	10^{-5}, 10^{-8}	10^{-8}
Gradient clipping	Off, 0.5, 5.0	5.0
Mini-batch-size	64, 128, 256, 512, 1024, 2048	2048
LSTM mode	Off, on, concatenate, residual	Residual
LSTM units	64, 128, 256, 512, 1024	512
Out features	64, 128, 256, 512, 1024	512
Discount γ	0.95, 0.99, 0.995	0.99
Entropy coefficient	0.003, 0.01, 0.03	0.01

We enabled window slicing (*max window size*) on the deception module. During deception module training, shorter windows were extracted from the longer rollout segments. This allowed the deception module to use a shorter back-propagation-through time length than the policy module, which we found to be effective. We also found that the deception module benefited from much smaller mini-batch sizes (256) than the policy module (2048). Due to differences in scale between the role prediction loss and the action/observation prediction loss, we multiplied action/observation prediction losses by *loss scale*.

Table 5. Hyperparameters tested for deception module. Settings omitted used values found from the policy module search.

Parameter	Values	Selected
Learning rate	10^{-4}, $2.5 \cdot 10^{-4}$, 10^{-3}	$2.5 \cdot 10^{-4}$
Mini-batch-size	128, 256, 512, 1024	256
LSTM units	128, 256, 512, 1024	1024
Loss scale	0.1, 1, 10	0.1
Max window size	1, 2, 4, 8, 16, 32	8

Table 6. Configuration settings for Rescue the General

Parameter	Description	Default
map_width	Width of map in tiles	32
map_height	Height of map in tiles	32
n_trees	Number of trees on map	10
reward_per_tree	Points for green for harvesting a tree	1
max_view_distance	Distance used for observational space, unused tiles are blanked out	6
team_view_distance	View distance for each team	(6, 5, 5)
team_shoot_damage	Damage per shot for each team	(10, 10, 10)
team_general_view_distance	Distance a player must be from the general to see them for the first time	(3, 5, 5)
team_shoot_range	Distance each team can shoot	(5, 5, 5)
team_counts	Number of players on each team	(1, 1, 4)
team_shoot_timeout	Number of turns between shooting	(10, 10, 10)
enable_voting	Enables the voting system	False
voting_button	Creates a voting button near start location	False
auto_shooting	Removes shooting in cardinal directions and replaces it with a single action that automatically targets the closest player	False
zero_sum	If enabled any points scored by one team will be counted as negative points for all other teams	False
timeout	Maximum game length before a timeout occurs	500
general_initial_health	General's starting health	1
player_initial_health	Players' starting health	10
battle_royale	Removes general from the game. Instead, teams win by eliminating all other players	False
help_distance	How close another player must be to help the first player move the general	2
starting_locations	*random* - starts players at random locations throughout the map *together* - places players in a group around a randomly selected starting location	Together
local_team_colors	If enabled, team colours are included on players local observation	True
initial_random_kills	Enables random killing of players at the start of the game	0.5
blue_general_indicator	*direction* - blue team is given direction to general *distance* - blue team is given distance to general	Direction
players_to_move_general	Number of players required to move the general	2
timeout_penalty	Score penalty for each team if a timeout occurs	(5, 0, −5)
points_for_kill	Matrix A where $A_{i,j}$ indicates points player from team i receives for killing a player on team j	0
hidden_roles	*default* - red can see roles, but blue and green cannot *all* - all players can see roles *none* - no players can see roles	Default
reveal_team_on_death	Enables display of team colors once a player dies	False

References

1. Almeshekah, M.H., Spafford, E.H.: Cyber security deception. In: Jajodia, S., Subrahmanian, V.S.S., Swarup, V., Wang, C. (eds.) Cyber Deception, pp. 25–52. Springer, Cham (2016). https://doi.org/10.1007/978-3-319-32699-3_2
2. Baker, B., et al.: Emergent tool use from multi-agent autocurricula. In: International Conference on Learning Representations (2019)
3. Bennett, P.G.: Hypergames: developing a model of conflict. Futures **12**(6), 489–507 (1980)
4. Brockman, G., et al.: OpenAI gym. arXiv preprint arXiv:1606.01540 (2016)
5. Brown, N., Lerer, A., Gross, S., Sandholm, T.: Deep counterfactual regret minimization. In: International Conference on Machine Learning, pp. 793–802. PMLR (2019)
6. Burda, Y., Edwards, H., Storkey, A., Klimov, O.: Exploration by random network distillation. arXiv preprint arXiv:1810.12894 (2018)
7. Carroll, T.E., Grosu, D.: A game theoretic investigation of deception in network security. Secur. Commun. Netw. **4**(10), 1162–1172 (2011)
8. Daniel, D.C., Herbig, K.L.: Strategic Military Deception: Pergamon Policy Studies on Security Affairs. Elsevier, Amsterdam (2013)
9. De Weerd, H., Verbrugge, R., Verheij, B.: How much does it help to know what she knows you know? An agent-based simulation study. Artif. Intell. **199**, 67–92 (2013)
10. Eger, M., Martens, C.: Practical specification of belief manipulation in games. In: Proceedings of the AAAI Conference on Artificial Intelligence and Interactive Digital Entertainment, vol. 13 (2017)
11. Ettinger, D., Jehiel, P.: A theory of deception. Am. Econ. J. Microecon. **2**(1), 1–20 (2010)
12. Floreano, D., Mitri, S., Magnenat, S., Keller, L.: Evolutionary conditions for the emergence of communication in robots. Curr. Biol. **17**(6), 514–519 (2007). https://doi.org/10.1016/j.cub.2007.01.058
13. Foerster, J.N., Assael, Y.M., De Freitas, N., Whiteson, S.: Learning to communicate with deep multi-agent reinforcement learning. arXiv preprint arXiv:1605.06676 (2016)
14. Gers, F.A., Schmidhuber, J., Cummins, F.: Learning to forget: continual prediction with LSTM. Neural Comput. **12**, 2451–2471 (2000). https://doi.org/10.1162/089976600300015015
15. Gharesifard, B., Cortés, J.: Stealthy deception in hypergames under informational asymmetry. IEEE Trans. Syst. Man Cybern. Syst. **44**(6), 785–795 (2013)
16. Gneezy, U.: Deception: the role of consequences. Am. Econ. Rev. **95**(1), 384–394 (2005)
17. Gutierrez, C.N., Bagchi, S., Mohammed, H., Avery, J.: Modeling deception in information security as a hypergame - a primer. In: Proceedings of the 16th Annual Information Security Symposium, p. 41. CERIAS-Purdue University (2015)
18. Ho, Y.C., Kastner, M., Wong, E.: Teams, signaling, and information theory. IEEE Trans. Autom. Control **23**(2), 305–312 (1978)
19. Iqbal, S., Sha, F.: Actor-attention-critic for multi-agent reinforcement learning. In: International Conference on Machine Learning, pp. 2961–2970. PMLR (2019)
20. Jaques, N., et al.: Social influence as intrinsic motivation for multi-agent deep reinforcement learning. In: International Conference on Machine Learning, pp. 3040–3049. PMLR (2019)

21. Kovach, N.S., Gibson, A.S., Lamont, G.B.: Hypergame theory: a model for conflict, misperception, and deception. Game Theory **2015**, 1–20 (2015)
22. Kullback, S., Leibler, R.A.: On information and sufficiency. Ann. Math. Stat. **22**(1), 79–86 (1951)
23. La, Q.D., Quek, T.Q., Lee, J., Jin, S., Zhu, H.: Deceptive attack and defense game in honeypot-enabled networks for the internet of things. IEEE Internet Things J. **3**(6), 1025–1035 (2016)
24. Leibo, J.Z., Zambaldi, V., Lanctot, M., Marecki, J., Graepel, T.: Multi-agent reinforcement learning in sequential social dilemmas. arXiv preprint arXiv:1702.03037 (2017)
25. Levine, T.R.: Truth-default theory (TDT) a theory of human deception and deception detection. J. Lang. Soc. Psychol. **33**(4), 378–392 (2014)
26. MacNally, A.M., Lipovetzky, N., Ramirez, M., Pearce, A.R.: Action selection for transparent planning. In: Proceeding of the 17th International Conference on Autonomous Agents and Multiagent Systems (AAMAS 2018) (2018)
27. Masters, P., Sardina, S.: Deceptive path-planning. In: Proceedings of the Twenty-Sixth International Joint Conference on Artificial Intelligence (IJCAI-2017), pp. 4368–4375. International Joint Conferences on Artificial Intelligence Organization, August 2017. https://doi.org/10.24963/ijcai.2017/610
28. Mnih, V., et al.: Playing Atari with deep reinforcement learning. arXiv preprint arXiv:1312.5602 (2013)
29. Paszke, A., et al.: Pytorch: an imperative style, high-performance deep learning library. Adv. Neural Inf. Process. Syst. **32**, 8026–8037 (2019)
30. Samvelyan, M., et al.: The starcraft multi-agent challenge. In: Proceedings of the International Joint Conference on Autonomous Agents and Multiagent Systems, AAMAS, vol. 4, pp. 2186–2188, February 2019. arXiv:1902.04043
31. Schmidhuber, J.: Formal theory of creativity, fun, and intrinsic motivation (1990–2010). IEEE Trans. Auton. Ment. Dev. **2**(3), 230–247 (2010)
32. Schulman, J., Wolski, F., Dhariwal, P., Radford, A., Klimov, O.: Proximal policy optimization algorithms. arXiv preprint arXiv:1707.06347 (2017)
33. Serrino, J., Kleiman-Weiner, M., Parkes, D.C., Tenenbaum, J.B.: Finding friend and foe in multi-agent games. arXiv preprint arXiv:1906.02330 (2019)
34. Strouse, D., Kleiman-Weiner, M., Tenenbaum, J., Botvinick, M., Schwab, D.: Learning to share and hide intentions using information regularization. arXiv preprint arXiv:1808.02093 (2018)
35. Vane, R., Lehner, P.: Using hypergames to increase planned payoff and reduce risk. Auton. Agent. Multi-Agent Syst. **5**(3), 365–380 (2002)

Modelling Strategic Deceptive Planning in Adversarial Multi-agent Systems

Lyndon Benke[1,2](✉), Michael Papasimeon[1], and Tim Miller[2]

[1] Defence Science and Technology Group, Melbourne, Australia
[2] The University of Melbourne, Melbourne, Australia
lbenke@student.unimelb.edu.au

Abstract. Deception is virtually ubiquitous in warfare, and should be a central consideration for military operations research. However, studies of agent behaviour in simulated operations have typically neglected to include explicit models of deception. This paper proposes that a computational model that approximates the human deceptive planning process would enable the authentic representation of strategic deception in multi-agent systems. The proposed deceptive planning model provides a framework for studying, explaining, and discovering deceptive behaviours, enabling the generation of novel solutions to adversarial planning problems.

Keywords: Deception · Multi-agent simulation · Operations research

1 Introduction

In this position paper we propose a model of agent decision-making that explicitly incorporates the notion of deception, and discuss research challenges associated with this approach. We focus on deception concepts within the context of multi-agent-based simulations employed in operations research (OR). Deception plays a key role during military operations, providing a means to reduce casualties and increase operational success [10, 11]. Despite its ubiquity in human conflict, deception is not explicitly considered by standard models of agent decision-making used in OR [3].

OR is the application of scientific knowledge to the study and optimisation of decision-making processes [29]. In the military domain, agent-based simulations are used to model decision-making processes in support of the effective and efficient employment of strategic and tactical capabilities [30]. Cognitive models in OR simulations represent the decision-making processes of agents, typically implemented using techniques such as decision trees and finite-state machines.

When building cognitive models, OR analysts maintain close links with domain experts, such as military operators, to ensure the fidelity of simulated tactics and strategies. A key requirement for these models is the *explainability* of modelled behaviours, so that simulation outputs can be presented to domain experts and other clients who are not literate in agent-oriented software engineering [16]. Computational models of deception must facilitate similar levels of explainability.

© Springer Nature Switzerland AG 2021
S. Sarkadi et al. (Eds.): DeceptECAI 2020/DeceptAI 2021, CCIS 1296, pp. 76–83, 2021.
https://doi.org/10.1007/978-3-030-91779-1_6

Recent work on computational deception has focused on 'singular acts of deception' [28], where an agent attempts to maximise the deceptiveness of an action or plan according to a predefined metric [18,19,21,22,26]. These approaches address decision problems for which the deception itself is the goal: success is measured according to the reduced accuracy of the observer's goal recognition model. In contrast, deception during military operations is typically strategic and extended in nature, requiring the generation of a coherent, temporally extended deceptive plan that achieves an overarching strategic goal[1].

This paper presents a model of agent reasoning that explicitly captures a systematic deceptive planning process. It is proposed that this model facilitates the study of deceptive behaviours in OR simulations, by more accurately representing strategic military deception. In addition, when implemented using automated planning approaches, this process may enable the discovery of novel deceptive solutions for a range of complex decision problems.

2   Related Work

The proposed deceptive planning process draws on the *deception incorporation model* described by Almeshekah and Spafford in the context of computer network security [2], which is itself based on the more general *deception cycle* described by Bell and Whaley [5]. A similar process for the military domain is described by Gerwehr and Glenn [15]. The common elements of these processes are summarised in Algorithm 1. These high-level models are intended for human planners, requiring a domain expert to provide a predictive model of the deception target and select appropriate deceptive techniques such as decoys and camouflage (described as the *means* or *instruments* of the deception).

Algorithm 1: Conceptual human deceptive planning process [2,4,15]

---

   repeat

1   Specify the **strategic goal** of the deception;

2   Specify the **desired reaction** of the target to the deceptive plan;

3   Decide what should be **hidden** or **shown** to achieve the desired reaction;

4   **Implement** available techniques to achieve the above objectives;

5   **Monitor** feedback and analyse the effect on the opponent;

   until *strategic goal has been achieved*;

Christian and Young [9] consider agent-based strategic deception in semi-cooperative scenarios, where a deceiver seeks to manipulate a target by providing planning advice with faulty information. The objective of this model is to find a plan that achieves the goals of *both* the deceiver and the target. This approach

---

[1] Operations Bodyguard and Mincemeat, Hannibal's ambush at Lake Trasimene, and even Odysseus' Trojan Horse, are examples of such strategic deceptions.

is not suitable for modelling strictly adversarial scenarios, where the goals of the deceiver and target are in direct opposition.

Wagner and Arkin [32] present an algorithm for acting deceptively that superficially resembles the process described in Algorithm 1. Given a known outcome matrix and opponent model, the algorithm selects a communication that maximises the deceiver's outcome for a single action. This algorithm is therefore most similar to deception-maximising approaches [18,19,21,22,26], and is not suitable for modelling strategic deception in OR simulations.

3   Modelling Strategic Agent Deception

3.1   Agent Behaviour Models in Operations Research

Agent reasoning models that support domain-friendly explanations have been used successfully in OR simulations to help explain complex behaviours to domain experts [14,17]. These models, reviewed by Azuma *et al.* [3], are typically variations on the basic *observe–deliberate–act* agent control loop [33]. Although originally designed for air combat, Boyd's model of fighter pilot decision-making, known as the OODA loop [6], has become a standard decision-making model for a wide range of fields (Fig. 1). Previous work by Brumley *et al.* [7,8] has observed that deception strategies may be modelled as attempts to influence an opponent's OODA loop. Integrating an explicit deceptive planning process into Boyd's model of decision-making provides a framework for studying strategic deception that is consistent with standard OR representations of agent reasoning.

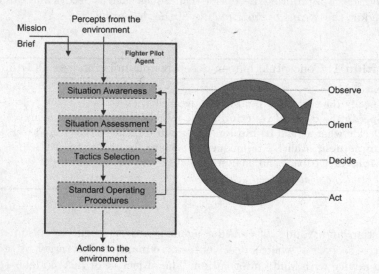

Fig. 1. A variation of the OODA loop model representing the decision-making process of a fighter pilot agent (reproduced with permission) [23].

3.2 A Strategic Deceptive Planning Model

The proposed deceptive planning model is depicted in Fig. 2. This process integrates a conceptual model of human deceptive planning with the OODA control-loop model of agent reasoning. Artefacts produced during each phase of the process are fed forward to the next phase, and the cycle is repeated as new information is received from the environment. For efficiency, the agent may choose to avoid replanning if it assesses that the unfolding interaction has not diverged significantly from the current plan. Otherwise, the agent generates an updated deceptive plan based on the new information:

1. **Observe:** During the initial phase, the agent acquires data to establish situational awareness. This data includes both direct perceptions from the environment, and prebriefed information such as the mission goal and prior knowledge of the opponent. The agent processes the raw input data into more complex symbolic descriptors, updating its beliefs about the state of the environment and other agents.
2. **Orient:** Based on the updated information, the agent assesses the situation, discovering options for achieving the current goal:
   (a) The agent first identifies sets of *permissive opponent behaviours* that would permit achievement of the current goal, by considering a relaxed version of the planning problem in which the opponent is cooperative rather than adversarial.
   (b) Next, these behaviours are used to identify corresponding *required opponent beliefs* that, when present, would induce the permissive behaviours.
   (c) Finally, the agent identifies perceptual and cognitive uncertainties and biases that could be exploited to enable the creation of the required opponent beliefs (described as *deceptive affordances*).
3. **Decide:** The agent generates a mission plan using artefacts produced during the previous phase, including the required opponent beliefs and any corresponding deceptive affordances.
4. **Act:** Finally, the agent executes the deceptive plan.

As with the standard OODA loop, this model is not intended to provide a complete description of the various phases and interactions of a computational deceptive planning process. While a discussion of the details of each sub-process is beyond the scope of this paper, the remainder of this section considers challenges and opportunities that are expected to arise when implementing the proposed model in multi-agent simulation environments.

3.3 Novel Deceptive Behaviour Discovery

Previous studies of agent deception have generally relied on providing agents with known deceptive behaviours, either inspired by nature [27], or provided by human experts [18,26,31]. The proposed model presents an opportunity to discover deceptive solutions to planning problems without relying on existing

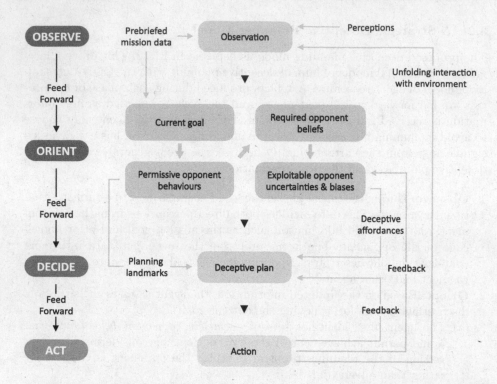

Fig. 2. The proposed strategic deceptive planning model, integrating a conceptual model of human deceptive planning with the OODA control-loop model of agent reasoning. The agent identifies sets of opponent behaviours that would permit achievement of the current goal, then determines corresponding beliefs that would provoke these behaviours. The desired opponent behaviours, and any deceptive affordances that can be exploited to induce them, guide the generation of the deceptive plan.

knowledge, by enabling the integration of automated planning approaches into a strategic deceptive planning process. For example, the sub-processes identifying *permissive opponent behaviours* and *required opponent beliefs* lend themselves naturally to automation using diverse-planning techniques. The automated discovery of agent behaviours is of particular interest for military OR to support the development of operational concepts for new capabilities [20, 24, 25].

3.4   Deception Feasibility

The steps in the proposed strategic deceptive planning model are subject to significant sources of uncertainty that influence whether it is possible or desirable to deceive. These include uncertainty about the true and believed states of the world (including hidden states such as opponent beliefs), and uncertainty about the ability of the agent to successfully execute the required actions. In addition, deceptive plans often carry an additional cost for the deceiver, which may outweigh the expected benefit from the deception [32]. While a full discussion of the deception cost-risk-benefit trade-off is beyond the scope of this paper, other work has provided algorithms for deciding when it is appropriate to deceive [12,13,32]. The consideration of cost is to some extent subsumed by the presented model: if plans exist that can achieve the agent's strategic goal *without* requiring a costly deception, then these plans will naturally be selected during the *Orient* and *Decide* phases, negating the requirement for an explicit cost-benefit analysis. This feature demonstrates an advantage of integrating the deceptive planning process into the primary agent control loop.

3.5 Determining Exploitable Uncertainties

To deceive an observer, an agent must have the capacity to influence the beliefs of the observer. The properties of the environment that enable the agent to directly create false beliefs may be considered *deceptive affordances*.

Definition 1 (Deceptive affordances). *The properties of an object, agent or environment that permit deceptive actions, where a deceptive action is any action that is expected to result in the creation of a false belief for an observer.*

Deceptive affordances, like all affordances, are relational: the deceptive action possibilities that are available for an object, agent or environment are specific to the acting agent, and are influenced by the agent's current intentions and capabilities. Available affordances may be known in advance, as is common in previous work on computational deception (for example, the effect of a radar jammer [12], or a distraction that prevents an agent from believing that an action has taken place [18]). Otherwise, deceptive affordances must be identified through experimentation in the environment. A challenge for future work will be the development of approaches to automate the discovery of exploitable uncertainties[2]. A modified version of the active behaviour recognition approach described by Alford *et al.* [1] is proposed as a novel solution to this problem.

4 Conclusion

In this paper we have proposed a computational model of strategic agent deception, driven by the requirements of multi-agent-based simulation in operations research. We described challenges and opportunities associated with this approach, particularly with respect to capturing and exploiting sources of uncertainty, and briefly discussed research directions that will attempt to address some of these challenges. By approximating the human deceptive planning process, this model facilitates the study of strategic deception in multi-agent systems while remaining compatible with standard models of agent decision-making. Future work will explore how automated planning techniques can be integrated with this model to enable the discovery of explainable, deceptive solutions to complex multi-agent planning problems.

---

[2] These include both epistemic sources of uncertainty, such as sensor error and cognitive limitations, and natural statistical variability.

References

1. Alford, R., Borck, H., Karneeb, J.: Active behavior recognition in beyond visual range air combat. In: Proceedings of the Third Annual Conference on Advances in Cognitive Systems (2015)
2. Almeshekah, M.H., Spafford, E.H.: Planning and integrating deception into computer security defenses. In: Proceedings of the 2014 Workshop on New Security Paradigms Workshop - NSPW 2014, Victoria, BC, Canada, pp. 127–138. ACM Press (2014). https://doi.org/10.1145/2683467.2683482
3. Azuma, R., Daily, M., Furmanski, C.: A review of time critical decision making models and human cognitive processes. In: 2006 IEEE Aerospace Conference, pp. 9-pp. IEEE (2006)
4. Bell, J.B.: Toward a theory of deception. Int. J. Intell. Counterintell. **16**(2), 244–279 (2003). https://doi.org/10.1080/08850600390198742
5. Bell, J.B., Whaley, B.: Cheating and Deception. Transaction Publishers, New Brunswick (1991)
6. Boyd, J.: A Discourse on Winning and Losing, vol. 13. Air University Press, Curtis E. LeMay Center for Doctrine Development and Education (2018)
7. Brumley, L., Kopp, C., Korb, K.: Misperception, self-deception and information warfare. In: Proceedings of the 6th Australian Information Warfare and Security Conference, pp. 71–79 (2005)
8. Brumley, L., Kopp, C., Korb, K.: The orientation step of the OODA loop and information warfare. In: Proceedings of the 7th Australian Information Warfare and Security Conference, p. 20 (2006)
9. Christian, D., Young, R.M.: Strategic deception in agents. In: Proceedings of the Third International Joint Conference on Autonomous Agents and Multiagent Systems, Washington, DC, USA, vol. 1, pp. 218–226. IEEE Computer Society (2004). https://doi.org/10.1109/AAMAS.2004.254
10. Clark, R.M., Mitchell, W.L.: Deception: Counterdeception and Counterintelligence, 1st edn. Sage/CQ Press, Los Angeles (2019)
11. Daniel, D.C., Herbig, K.L.: Strategic Military Deception: Pergamon Policy Studies on Security Affairs. Elsevier, Amsterdam (1981)
12. Davis, A.L.: Deception in game theory: a survey and multiobjective model. Master's thesis, Air Force Institute of Technology (2016)
13. De Rosis, F., Carofiglio, V., Grassano, G., Castelfranchi, C.: Can computers deliberately deceive? A simulation tool and its application to Turing's imitation game. Comput. Intell. **19**(3), 235–263 (2003). https://doi.org/10.1111/1467-8640.00223
14. Evertsz, R., Thangarajah, J., Papasimeon, M.: The conceptual modelling of dynamic teams for autonomous systems. In: Conceptual Modeling, vol. 10650, pp. 311–324 (2017). https://doi.org/10.1007/978-3-319-69904-2
15. Gerwehr, S., Glenn, R.W.: The Art of Darkness: Deception and Urban Operations, vol. 1132. Rand Corporation, Santa Monica (2000)
16. Heinze, C., Smith, B., Cross, M.: Thinking quickly: agents for modeling air warfare. In: Antoniou, G., Slaney, J. (eds.) AI 1998. LNCS, vol. 1502, pp. 47–58. Springer, Heidelberg (1998). https://doi.org/10.1007/BFb0095040
17. Heinze, C., Papasimeon, M., Goss, S., Cross, M., Connell, R.: Simulating fighter pilots. In: Defence Industry Applications of Autonomous Agents and Multi-agent Systems, pp. 113–130. Birkhäuser, Basel (2007). https://doi.org/10.1007/978-3-7643-8571-2

18. Kulkarni, A., Srivastava, S., Kambhampati, S.: A unified framework for planning in adversarial and cooperative environments. In: Proceedings of the AAAI Conference on Artificial Intelligence, vol. 33, pp. 2479–2487, July 2019. https://doi.org/10.1609/aaai.v33i01.33012479

19. Liu, Z., Yang, Y., Miller, T., Masters, P.: Deceptive reinforcement learning for privacy-preserving planning. In: Proceedings of the 20th International Conference on Autonomous Agents and Multiagent Systems (AAMAS 2021), London (2021)

20. Masek, M., Lam, C.P., Benke, L., Kelly, L., Papasimeon, M.: Discovering emergent agent behaviour with evolutionary finite state machines. In: Miller, T., Oren, N., Sakurai, Y., Noda, I., Savarimuthu, B.T.R., Cao Son, T. (eds.) PRIMA 2018. LNCS (LNAI), vol. 11224, pp. 19–34. Springer, Cham (2018). https://doi.org/10.1007/978-3-030-03098-8_2

21. Masters, P., Sardina, S.: Deceptive path-planning. In: Proceedings of the Twenty-Sixth International Joint Conference on Artificial Intelligence (IJCAI-2017), pp. 4368–4375. International Joint Conferences on Artificial Intelligence Organization, August 2017. https://doi.org/10.24963/ijcai.2017/610

22. Ornik, M., Topcu, U.: Deception in optimal control. In: Proceedings of the 56th Annual Allerton Conference on Communication, Control, and Computing (Allerton 2018). IEEE, May 2018

23. Papasimeon, M.: Modelling agent-environment interaction in multi-agent simulations with affordances. Ph.D. thesis, The University of Melbourne (2010)

24. Park, H., Lee, B.Y., Tahk, M.J., Yoo, D.W.: Differential game based air combat maneuver generation using scoring function matrix. Int. J. Aeronaut. Space Sci. 17(2), 204–213 (2016). https://doi.org/10.5139/IJASS.2016.17.2.204

25. Ramirez, M., et al.: Integrated hybrid planning and programmed control for real-time UAV maneuvering. In: Proceedings of the 17th International Conference on Autonomous Agents and Multiagent Systems (AAMAS 2018) (2018). https://doi.org/10.5555/3237383.3237896

26. Root, P., De Mot, J., Feron, E.: Randomized path planning with deceptive strategies. In: 2005 American Control Conference, pp. 1551–1556. IEEE (2005). https://doi.org/10.1109/ACC.2005.1470188

27. Shim, J., Arkin, R.C.: Biologically-inspired deceptive behavior for a robot. In: Ziemke, T., Balkenius, C., Hallam, J. (eds.) SAB 2012. LNCS (LNAI), vol. 7426, pp. 401–411. Springer, Heidelberg (2012). https://doi.org/10.1007/978-3-642-33093-3_40

28. Smith, W., Kirley, M., Sonenberg, L., Dignum, F.: The role of environments in affording deceptive behaviour: some preliminary insights from stage magic. In: 1st International Workshop on Deceptive AI, p. 10. Santiago de Compostela, Spain, August 2020

29. Taha, H.A.: Operations Research: An Introduction. Pearson Education India, Delhi (2013)

30. Tidhar, G., Heinze, C., Selvestrel, M.: Flying together: modelling air mission teams. Appl. Intell. 8(3), 195–218 (1998)

31. Wagner, A.R., Arkin, R.C.: Robot deception: Recognizing when a robot should deceive. In: 2009 IEEE International Symposium on Computational Intelligence in Robotics and Automation-(CIRA), pp. 46–54. IEEE (2009)

32. Wagner, A.R., Arkin, R.C.: Acting deceptively: providing robots with the capacity for deception. Int. J. Soc. Robot. 3(1), 5–26 (2011)

33. Wooldridge, M.: An Introduction to Multiagent Systems. Wiley, Chichester (2002)

Logic-Based Approches

E-Friend: A Logical-Based AI Agent System Chat-Bot for Emotional Well-Being and Mental Health

Mauricio J. Osorio Galindo[1], Luis A. Montiel Moreno[2] (ID),
David Rojas-Velázquez[2](✉) (ID), and Juan Carlos Nieves[3] (ID)

[1] Universidad de las Américas Puebla, Ex Hacienda Sta. Catarina Mártir
S/N. San Andrés Cholula, 72810 Puebla, Mexico
mauricioj.osorio@udlap.mx
[2] San Andrés Cholula, Mexico
[3] Department of Computing Science, Umeå University, Umeå, Sweden
jcnieves@cs.umu.se

Abstract. In this work, it is proposed the design of a Reasoning Logical Based Intelligent Agent System Chat-bot for Dialogue Composition (DC) named E-friend, which uses Logic Programming (LP) for reasoning tasks. The main contribution is the use of Knowledge Representation Reasoning with LP theories modelling the knowledge of the user agent (beliefs, intentions, and expectations) to reason, plan and to optimally solve the DC problem. Another contribution is the design of a system component that extends the theory of mind, for the user model, with emotions to detect if the user decepts to the system or to itself. This component has the aim to alert and inform the facilitator when E-friend detects possible deceit signals from the student. E-friend was designed to help first year university students to manage stress/anxiety to optimal well-being development and attempt the prevention of depression and addictions leading. Students can interact through a chat-bot (text-based questions and answers) to help the system learns from the user, at the same time the user learns from itself improving mental health well-being.

Keywords: Agent systems architecture · Agent knowledge representation · Agent reasoning planning system · Dialogue composition · Logic programming · Human-agent interaction · Artificial intelligence for detecting deception · Well-being/Mental health optimization · Emotion modeling

1 Introduction

The research works of the World Health Organization (WHO) referred in [28] have concluded that stress is the world mental health disease of the 21st century

L. A. M. Moreno and D. Rojas-Velázquez—Independent Researcher.

and may be the trigger for depression and even suicide if it is not treated correctly. WHO estimates that, in the world, suicide is the second cause of death in the group of 15 to 29 years of age and that more than 800,000 people die due to suicide every year. Also that mental illnesses generate high economic losses since sick people and those who care for them reduce their productivity both at home and at work. According to data from the WHO, 450 million people in the world, suffer from at least one mental disorder. Well-being (meaning having no anxiety, depression or stress) and physical health have been studied by many Scientists. For instance, Elizabeth H. Blackburn, Carol W. Greider and Jack W. Szostak (all Nobel prize) have shown that Telomerase activity is a predictor of long-term cellular viability, which decreases with chronic psychological distress [11]. E. H. Blackburn et al. proved that mindfulness may exert effects on telomerase activity through variables involved in the stress appraisal process [11].

Over the years, science has shown that the brain and the mind work synergistically, that is why the brain can be reorganized, re-educated and regenerated by forming new nerve connections or paths when learning to control the mind through therapies. There are different successful techniques to support a student in overcoming their psychological difficulties such as referred in [16–18]: *Mindfulness* and *Cognitive Therapy*.

Our approach, called E-friend, proposes the use of Mindfulness and Cognitive Behaviour Therapy (CBT) to help the student to improve his/her mental health, see [16,18]. It also includes techniques referred in [16,18] for finding the Element, reaching Flow states, Silence in Therapy and Poetry Therapy provide value added to our proposal particularly for college students. Mindfulness and Flow States are independent different behaviours however they can be alternated [16,18]. Another element considered in E-friend is *Theory of Mind (ToM)* [23], which is the ability of humans to ascribe elements such as beliefs, desires, and intentions, and relations between these elements to other human agents. *Simulation Theory of Mind (ST)* [23] emphasizes the process of putting oneself into another's shoes'. ST argues for a simulation based method for model selection. E-friend has been designed to have a ToM of the User Agent (the student) as a Logic Programming (LP) Theory in the User Model. It is by logic theories in terms of logic programs that is possible to reason and plan DC to help the user human development deducing from her beliefs, intentions and desires what she is thinking for decision making. In this case, ST is modelled by reasoning using LP.

E-friend also has the capacity to answer questions of university matters and try to create a link with the student because it considers her pleasures and hobbies. Enriching talks ("mild Therapies"), proposed to be used by E-Friend, are mainly based on mindfulness + cognitive therapy and advice in the professional career preferences, which are focused particularly on preventing and managing mild symptoms of stress, anxiety, and depression to reduce the risk of failure in the university life due problems in learning, and to optimize mental health and behaviour when they face the university challenges as it is justified in [22]. Thus, during sessions with E-friend, it is intended that the students understand, accept and "become a friend of" their minds and emotions obtaining a better performance both in school and in their personal life. As referred in [13] in the work of Luksha Pavel et al. these existential skills include an ability to set and achieve goals (willpower), self-awareness/self-reflection ability (mindfulness), an ability to learn/unlearn/relearn (self-development) relevant skills (e.g. skill-formation ability), and more. Well-being is a skill to be learned as explianed in [16] and this topic is explored in the context of a chatbot in [17]. The core type of dialogue for every dialogue session of E-friend is *Maieutics*. However each single agent task micro-dialogue as secondary type of dialogue can be one of the following according the categories stated by Douglas Walton referred in [27]: Persuasion. Inquiry, Discovery, Information-Seeking, Casual chat, Negotiation, Deliberation, Eristic.

E-friend has been deigned not for lying nor deceiving since the perception of the student of being betrayed by the system could bring negative psychological consequences and it is in opposition to the presented mild therapies [21]. Also deception to the student would be against the aim of our system to help the student to be compassionate for not manipulating the others but to take care of herself and the others. We believe that it can be possible to develop a system component to estimate when the student is lying to itself or the system and send an alarm to de facilitator. Whit this alarm the facilitator can be able to act in consequence helping the student to obtain better result during the session. This system component is totally independent to the existing E-friend software proving that E-friend's architecture is able to support updates without making important changes in the original structure.

Our paper is structured as follows: In Sect. 2 we discuss chat-bots applied for mental health well-being, the use of emotions to complement a user model in AI systems and the Orthony, Clore, and Cllins (OCC) model [15] in logic programming for knowledge representation reasoning. In Sect. 3 we present the architecture of E-friend where x the Detection of User Deception Agent Module (DAM) is described. In Sect. 4 it is discussed how is extended the user model of theory of mind for handling emotions using the OCC model and Logic programming used for E-friend DC and DAM. Finally in Sect. 5 we present our conclusions.

2   Related Work

Applied Chatbots for Mental Health Well-being. As referred in [3] the work of Samuel Bell et al. presents Woebot, a template-based chatbot delivering basic CBT, has demonstrated limited but positive clinical outcomes in students suffering from symptoms of depression. The work of Eileen Bendig et al. referred in [4] presents promising areas for the use of chatbots in the psychotherapeutic context could be support for the prevention, treatment, and follow-up/relapse prevention of psychological problems and mental disorders. Also they could be used preventively in the future, for example for suicide prevention. According to the work of Samuel Bell et al. in order to provide scalable treatment, several promising studies have demonstrated clinical efficacy of internet-based Cognitive Based Therapy, whereby the need for a face-to-face presence is negated. Woebot has demonstrated limited but positive clinical outcomes in students suffering from symptoms of depression.

In the work of Diano Federico et al. referred in [5] it is presented an state of the art in mindfulness-based mobile applications and the design of a mindfulness mobile application to help emotional self-regulation in people suffering stressful situations. We invite the reader to check the work of Baskar Jayalakshmi et al. referred in [1] where it is presented a comparison of Applied Agents implemented for improving mental health and well-being. In the work of Jingar Monika et al. referred in [12] it is explored how an intelligent digital companion(agent) can support persons with stress-related exhaustion to manage daily activities. Also, it is explored how different individuals approach the task of designing their own tangible interfaces for communicating emotions with a digital companion. In the work of Inkster Becky referred in [10] it is presented an empathy-driven, conversational artificial intelligence agent (Wysa) for digital mental well-being that is using mindfulness as mild therapy in combination with transfer to psychologist whenever the user ask for it. According to Samuel Bell et al. several studies have investigated the clinical efficacy of remote-, internet- and chatbot-based therapy, but there are other factors, such as enjoyment and smoothness, that are important in a good therapy session.

Artificial Intelligent Applications Complementing User Profile with Emotions. Emotions are considered high-level cognitive processes and lead an important part of human behaviour and reactions. These responses often are elicited when it needs rapid decision-making in our daily lives, for example, to be safe from danger or even to deceive. But also emotions are considered for long term decision making such as to buy the brand new cellphone or to get married. Emotions are useful to generate user profiles to have integral knowing about the person profiled. Meet emotional tendencies about a person for different situations could help to estimate if the person deceives based on behaviours opposed to the beliefs or knowledge of that person. Researchers use emotions in different areas, like in recommender system where authors studied the role of emotions and preferences in product appreciation [20]. The test and results show that considering emotions in the user profile improves the quality of product recommendation where emotions are fundamental in the act of purchasing. Emotions are personal characteristics, and for context-aware recommenders, emotions are modelled as contextual features, because emotions are dynamic and greatly influence user's preferences. This emotional feature has proven helpful in improving context-aware recommenders. In the last years, system developers have tried to improve human-computer interaction designing the systems around users (user-centred modelling). The idea here is to understand the user's behaviour under different conditions and scenarios for improving the user's experiences for a given system [14]. For this purpose, predictive models of user's reactions, responses, and in particular emotions, can help in the design of intuitive and usable systems. An emotional context is analysed and modelled based on varying types of sentiments that users express in their language. Analysing and modelling emotions, sentiments and personality traits provide valuable insight to improve the user experience in computer systems [14]. There is evidence of the need to adapt user interfaces by taking into account dynamic user features like emotions. It is crucial to go one step further in the adaptation of interfaces considering user's emotions at runtime. For this purpose, it is important to extend existing adaptation approaches to consider emotions. Like in [8], where the authors based their proposal in three main components: the inferring engine, the adaptation engine, and the interactive system. The authors consider three types of emotions: positive, negative, and neutral. The interface is able to identify if one particular adaptation has been found positive, negative or neutral by the user's feedback for future adaptations. These adaptations include widgets, fonts, colours, even the structure of the interface. The general adaptation process consists in using a kind of template base on contextual characteristics such as screen size or the brightness, using these principles, they compute appropriate adaptations, and then, they extend the interface considering emotions [8].

The OCC model, proposed by [15], is a psychological model frequently used in applications where emotional states can be simulated. The OCC model contains representations of the cognitive process where the emotional states represent the way of perceiving our environment [15]. This model was designed to be implemented in a computer language; this implementation is oriented, but not limited, to a rule-based system and provide examples of these rules [15]. For example, considering the emotions guilt and shame (these two emotions are felt by persons who lie [9]), the OCC model groups this two emotion into one emotion set called shame. The cognitive process to elicit shame is a valence evaluation of disapproval of self-censurable action that is expressed by one element (called token) in the set. This token depends on the emotion intensity and the OCC model provide three variables to compute that intensity: 1) censurability degree, 2) the cognitive strength, and 3) the deviations of the agent's action from expectations based on the person or social role [15]. In the same way, it is possible to model the emotions of fear and excitement identified in the lie detection process [26]. Model emotions computationally, it is possible to feed expert systems, intelligent agents, or robots to improve lie detection, and complete user's profiles. The work of [24] uses the OCC model for modelling emotions using LP under the Answer Set Programming (ASP) to generate stories with morals. However this work is not used for modelling a User Agent Profile or Mind Theory. The work of [23] presents Multi-Agents architecture based on theory of mind to model deception reasoning using logic. Literature of related work does not include reasoning logical based architecture for dialogue composition.

According to the above, it is possible to design a rule-based module to complete emotional student profile using the OCC Model. Also, this module could be able to estimate when a student trying to deceiving itself or the system.

3   Design of Architectural Framework for a Logical Based Intelligent Agent System Chat-Bot

The general architecture design of our system is presented in this section. Similar E-friend architectures have been presented in [18] and [16]. The contribution in the present work is to extend the architecture with an additional independent but collaborative Detection of User Deception Agent Module (DAM). Another Contribution is the definition of User Agent model considering a Theory of the mind [23] extended with Emotions [15] and [24] using Logic Theories to provide our Master Agent Composer and DAM the reasoning skill based in a symbolic-based Representation of the User Agent. The user agent model presented in our architecture is domain independent and will be discussed deeply in the next section. Consider that our domain independent architecture it is instantiated for the Mental Health Domain for optimizing students (User Agent) well-being.

3.1   E-Friend General Approach

We assume (in the general case) that the mathematical model behind the system is a form of an ideal (collaborative) game. This means we have two players (E-friend and the human agent). There are moves/decisions (alternatives among which each player chooses), and payoffs (numerical representations of the players' preferences among the possible outcomes of the game). A move taken by E-friend is a script of five questions/activities proposed to the student. The student chooses to do (or not) the activities and/or answer (or not) the questions given by E-friend. Sometimes, E-friend allows the student to ask (restricted or open) questions to E-friend. We also assume that the ultimate (ideal) goal of the game from the point of view of E-friend is to help the student to obtain a better knowledge about itself and to improve its mental state.

In addition, we assume that normally the student desires to improve his/her mental state and trust E-friend to help him/her to achieve this goal, the last is based on teacher-students relationship experiences. However, we understand that we can have exceptions, as we explain below. The game assumes interactive decisions, applicable whenever the actions of two or more decision makers jointly determine an outcome that affects them all. Strategic reasoning amounts to deciding how to act to achieve a desired objective, taking into account how the student will act and the fact that he/she will also reason strategically. In this regard, the basic ideal assumptions are the following:

i. Both players have consistent preferences and are instrumentally rational in the sense of invariably choosing an alternative that maximizes their individual payoffs, relative to their knowledge and beliefs at the time.

ii. The specification of the game and the players' preferences and rationality are common knowledge among the players (explained under Common Knowledge).

iii. It is assumed that an intelligent agent in E-friend takes the decision of the move to make. Then, a team of agent-slaves perform such movement.

Due to the nature of our game (on the context of positive Psychology) we need to make three considerations that could affect our ideal situation. *First*, we lack of determinate game-theoretic solutions, and psychological theories and empirical evidence are therefore required to discover and understand how people play them. *Second*, human decision makers have bounded rationality and are rarely blessed with full common knowledge. We assume that the student not always necessarily choose strategies that maximize its payoffs. However, E-friend follows to maximize it payoffs (in helping the student to improve its emotional state). In particular E-friend computes it corresponding payoff by a kind of knapsack problem [16]. It selects the "best" 5 activities/questions in a particular suitable order. This is the move that it selects (so to speak) and the decision is made by our intelligent agent using an extended knapsack problem [16]. *Third*, human decision makers have other-regarding preferences and sometimes do not even try to maximize their personal payoffs, without regard to the payoffs of others, and psychological theory and empirical research are therefore required to provide a realistic account of real-life strategic interaction. The actual move is performed by a particular agent slave that is able to coordinate the 5 slaves that are in charge of each of the 5 micro-dialogues, respectively.

Deception [23] is defined as the intention of a deceptive agent (A), to make another interrogator agent (B), to believe something is true that A believes is false, with the aim of achieving an ulterior goal or desire. In E-friend context, deception is considered as another preference. E-friend knows that, hence it should be prepared with tactics to discover this situation, and yet to still be able to help the student. To discover such a situation, E-friends has a basic theory of the mind of the student. Such model is constructed based on the profile of the student thanks to the information that the student has provided it in the different sessions. We also assume that E-friend has an emotional model (built using the OCC Model) of the student in order to try to understand it better. All together plus some default logical rules provided by the coach, E-friend is able to construct a basic theory of the mind of the student, mentioned before. It can be identify that Logic programming appears to be a sound mechanism to represent all the above knowledge. This knowledge is structured using different theories that share common knowledge of lower level. At the top of this theories we propose the use of a knapsack problem to represent the final decision of the move to make.

Emotions analysis may help to lie detection when they are strongly felt, the problem is most people do not feel strong emotions at the time of lying, because most of them lie everyday making difficult to use emotions in micro-expressions for detecting lies [26]. But it is possible to identify inconsistencies in the interaction with the student. The component proposed to extend E-friend, must be able to identify this inconsistencies and represent it in an emotional model. As it can be seen in last section, the OCC Model establish that emotions are the result of environment evaluations. This model provide us with a cognitive structure about how emotions are generated and felt by humans. These processes can be represented as logical rules in logic programming languages. When User Deception Agent Module (DAM) identify the possibility of deception from the student (the intensity of emotions felt when humans lie, like shame, crosses some threshold), DAM sends an alert to the facilitator. With this alert, the facilitator can take actions in order to help the student to avoid deception. To demonstrate the feasibility of the idea and show its practical potential we follow a Proof of Concept strategy as it is presented in [16]. Recall that a proof of concept is usually small and may not be complete.

3.2   A Master-Slave AI Design

We propose a master-salve conceptual design following a centralized approach. Namely, we create hundreds of slaves (at least one thousand) such that each of them can perform a very concrete task. All the tasks correspond to interactions with the students. Each interaction are specified as atomic micro-dialogues. An example could be simple or complex task such as to teach the student how to try a meditation exercise. Each task performed by a slave-agent is programmed in the *Basic Script/Resources Language (BSRL)*. This is a low level language (to describe automaton) invented for this purpose. Some of these slave-agents can be created by humans and some other can be constructed semi-automatically[1]. Associated to each slave we have its Semantic Knowledge. For instance, slave named $E3$ could correspond to an exercise of sound-mindfulness, that belongs to the set of mindfulness exercises. Furthermore, the system has an explicit logical rule saying that this type of exercise normally helps to reduces anxiety, and so on. All the semantic knowledge of each slave plus a general theory of interaction among them is written in LP Language. So, the LP theory corresponds to the *Master-Agent Artificial Intelligent Composer (MAIC)* that *plans* a sequence of few tasks (for a 10–15 min estimated session) that are performed by our slaves that are presented (coordinated) by a distinguished slave (a program interpreter of BSRL in Python) to the student. An analogy that we can make is the following. The LP agent is like a *master composer* of a symphony for a particular audience. The pianist is a particular slave that performs a specific task (playing the piano). The director corresponds to our distinguished *slave* that actually coordinate the rest of *slaves*. After the execution of the symphony, according to the feedback (applause, reviews, etc.), the composer hopefully learns how to create a better symphony. E-friend has a domain-independent generic architecture that is specialized to an application domain and to a component library through a declarative domain theory (ASP code). The domain-independent generic architecture is embedded in a Knowledge Base (KB) written in ASP. In our case the application domain corresponds to our basic slaves written in BSRL. The main concrete tasks of our intelligent agent described in [16,18].

3.3   The E-Friend Intelligent Agent System Chat-Bot

The E-Friend is a *Reasoning Planning System* that consist in a cycle of 4 sequential processes-modules, Fig. 1(a), plus the extension proposed: **DAM**. Figure 1(b)

---

[1] We do not consider this issue in this paper.

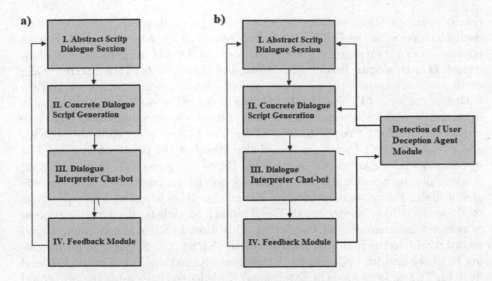

Fig. 1. a) The general architecture of the four sequential modules of E-friend. b) E-friend general architecture with the extension proposed (DAM).

I. Abstract Script Dialogue Session (ASDS) is generated by MAIC in this process. ASDS is a composition of slave agents tasks sequence to be performed by E-friend as a single dialogue session with the student. The name of each *Slave Agent Interaction Task (AI-Task)* (for example $E3$) corresponds to an interaction task with the student described in BSRL, the task is an interaction with the student (for example an enriching talk mindfulness exercise). Also each AI-Task is associated to semantic knowledge described in an *Enriching Talks Theories Knowledge Base (ETalks-KB)* in LP. Using the User Agent Model and the Enriching talks theories MAIC solves *The Dialogue-Session Composition Problem (DCP)*. **Remark:** if E-friend detects a serious case of anxiety-depression then it is proposed that the system transfers student to a human expert therapist (situation that is normally possible in a university institution). Even more the student could press an emergency button[2] available in E-friend that provides resources for getting immediate human experts help. The DCP is *to compose a dialogue session* as a sequence of AI-Tasks assets such that optimizes the contributions of the assets to the user with an optimal coherent, enjoyable and smoothable session. An optimal solution for DCP instance is the intended ASDS to be proposed by E-friend. *II. Concrete Dialogue Script Generation* translates the ASDS list to a single BRSL program. The idea behind the BSRL code (to describe automaton) is to define a basic programming language such that any program AI-task of our library is a highly malleable object where one could define and apply operators (mutation,

---

[2] A functionality learned from Woebot chat-bot presented in the work of Fitzpatrick Kathleen et al. referred in [16].

crossover composition, selection, specialization, generalization). Briefly speaking each instruction in the BSRL code is a triple $<l, o, a>$ where l is a label, o an operator and a is an argument. BSRL resembles a kind of machine assembly language. ***III. Dialogue Interpreter Chat-bot*** corresponds to the director of the orchestra that executes the composed dialogue session as interactions of AI-Task with the student. ***IV. Feedback Module*** is an extraction process of relevant information and knowledge. This module filters a user conversation record to obtain the ***Student Profile State (SPS)***. The SPS is used to provide feedback and to update the Extensional Knowledge Bases of the proposed System. The updates made in Extensional Knowledge Bases using the SPS could be about student profile, emotional status or history record, among others. This module also updates the answered questions Knowledge Base where also the questions made to the student are recorded. The Feedback Module is an extraction process of relevant information and knowledge. This module filters a user conversation record to obtain the **Student Profile State (SPS)**. The SPS is used for providing feedback and for updating the Extensional Knowledge Bases of the E-friend System. The updates made in Extensional Knowledge Bases using the SPS could be about student profile, emotional status or history record, among others. This module also updates the answered script questions Knowledge Base where the questions made to the student are recorded. ***The extension proposed: Detection of User Deception Agent Module (DAM)*** should be a special Agent Module that works as an observer of the dialogue between E-friend (modules 1–4) and the user Agent. This Agent module would be independent from the MAIC and the Slaves AI-tasks. It will be an intelligent Agent with the skill of reasoning for detecting User Agent deception. We conjecture that an extension of Theory of Mind [23] with a theory of emotions (the OCC Model) [15] and [24] would allow us to have a more refined model of the other User Agent (the student in our case) and with addition of detection of inconsistencies in answers of the User Agent to E-friend could help the E-friend Agent "coach" to diagnose/predict better when the student could try to deceive to the system about its progress regarding the support it is receiving from it. So by adopting the model in [23] and extending it with the OCC Model but also taking advantage of the benefits of ASP as presented in [24] we assume that it would enrich our system. It is important to highlight that the reference [23] is consistent with our approach because of its direct link to logic including the use of negation as failure (a key point in ASP). For instance we have modelled Theory of Mind, beliefs, desires, ignorance, trust, theory-theory, simulation theory, totum ex parte, to mention some of them using negation as failure architecture. The following is an example of encoding of the OCC Model extending theory of mind using beliefs and desires with emotions: $joy(Agent, Consequence, T) : -$ $agent(Agent)$, $belief(Agent, Consequence, T), desire(Agent, Consequence, T)$, $time(T)$. 'if Agent believes and desires a Consequence then the Agent will feel joy'. This module makes diagnoses by assigning values to the actions (questions-answers) of the user through time and the different sessions. The diagnosis when assessing the possibility that the user is deceiving uses 5 values of traffic light type (green, yellow - phases 1, 2, 3 - and red). For example, if the traffic light is yellow phase two, the observer module sends E-friend permission to ask the user questions and check if there is consistency between what he is saying and what he is doing or making. DAM deliberate/reason by itself using the theory of the mind of the user profile extended with emotions. When the DAM recognizes negative emotions on the part of the user while the student is interacting with the E-friend (for example in the attitude when the student is performing a mindfulness exercise), DAM does not make decisions towards the user but it sends a warning message to a human facilitator, in this case facilitator could or not, decides to take action on how to help the user in its human development. When DAM detects emotions that could conjecture the student is deceiving to the system or deceiving to himself regarding the achievements and benefits of practising a suggested exercise then the traffic light could go down to red, in this case, the warning becomes an alert so facilitator must take action. It is proposed to instantiate in this architecture the use of Answer Set Programming (ASP) [25] to provide Reasoning and Knowledge Representation in the ASP module. Logic rules in these theories are defined by psychologist while others are inferred from the student feedback (for example to evaluate the smoothness between two AI-tasks).

Page 26 of [7] presents a diagram of any addiction cycle based on different psychological theories. The cycle is a whirlpool, each turn becomes more aggressive even in that degenerative cycle until the end point is schizophrenia, death or prison. There are several inconsistencies where the person suffering addiction is deceiving to herself and can be helped by DAM to resolve them at different levels of the addictive cycle regarding to: a) Principles of caring for oneself and others. False thoughts caused by overprotective/over-demanding parenthood, b) Harmful guilt self-judgements and complexes (the image of a certain psychic situation which is strongly accentuated emotionally and is, moreover, incompatible with the habitual attitude of consciousness), and c) To believe that a addictive substance trigger will give peace and resolve inconsistencies in a) and b). In the cycle: 1) obsession with harmful judgements, 2) Imagination ritual considering the imaginary-emotive pleasure that consumption will give in various situations of the trigger in c), 3–4) to believe that pleasure gives personal development when, in fact, due to the disordered form of its consumption, it does not resolve a) and b), but it damages the body and disgust the body over time, making her look for a new more aggressive trigger, and 5) Emotional whirlwind: handling remorse, guilt, self-justification, despair, shame and promises based on a and b but also being inconsistent in finding the solution to the problem and therefore inconsistent in a coherence between beliefs and acting.

4   Answer Set Programming Solution Proposal

Student Model. Having a user model is fundamental in this kind of personalized systems as we have learned and adjusted to our particular case from the presented in [2]. The model is presented in our architecture for the particular

Table 1. Student model generated by E-friend based on the preferences and needs of the student.

Student model[a]	
Alias	Ale
Gender	Female
Sleep	Important
'Finding element'	High interest
Flow	Not interested
Mindfulness	Medium Interest
Level MFNS	Second week
Preferred MFNS exercise	Love and compassion
Cognitive therapy	Low interest
Hobby	Movies
FLAG status	Green
Concrete emotional status	Improving

Activities to support

1. Sleep proposed routines (listening to ocean wawes)
2. Casual conversation about movies
3. exercises "Finding element"
4. Mindfulness information and exercises
5. Academic information and support (advices)

[a] Academic information and support is a fixed interaction that always must be present in every dialogue session)

instantiated Mental Health Domain for students well-being. Below it will be referred the User Agent as student. The system assumes a student model that is almost empty at the beginning but is updated by the interaction between the student and the system. This model is constructed based on the preferences and needs of the student. Recall that the major point (and almost the unique) is to help the student to know herself better. See Table 1 for a concrete fictive student Alejandra. It is proposed to consider emotional modelling to complement the user profile and adapt the system responses based on the emotional states of the user. This could be useful at the moment to estimate the possibility that the user deceits the system. It can be obtained emotional information of the user through surveys, like in the above works, and complete profile and improve the quality of the system. Once the information is gathered, it can be modelled both emotions and cognitive processes that generate them computationally using the OCC Model [15]. Conceptually our ASP program uses a complex theory that involves Student Profile State, Knowledge of Enriching Talk theories (Mindfulness, CBT, 'Flow states', etc.) that will solve the DCP presented in Sect. 3. **Remark.** DCP optimization builds and propose a student dialogue session script. The recom-

Table 2. Example of logical rules for E-friend Enriching Talks Theories in ASP.

Logic Rule Example of Enriching Talks Theories in ASP
Well-being

E-friend normally proposes a mindfulness exercise of breathing due to observed high long term anxiety unless exception happens.
`candidate(T) :- mindfulness(T), long_term_anxiety(high),`
`belongs_category(T,Y), mindfulness_breath(Y), Not exception_well_being(T)`

Hobbie

E-friend normally proposes a movie related to a gender of movies liked by the student that has not been watched yet unless exception happens.
`candidate(T) :- movie(T), movie_category(Y), movie_example(T,Y),`
`middle_may_like(Y), not movie_watched(T), not exception_hobbie(T)`

Diagnostic[a]

E-friend diagnoses a status of positive stress for the student due to observations of student tackling academic university workload and green global emotional status.
`diagnostic(postive_stress) :- university_workload(light,difficult),`
`completed_academic_assignments(success),student_perception(positive_stress)`
`global_emotional_status(green)`

Academic

E-friend normally proposes academic information specialized in university interships due observed green global emotional status unless academic exception happens.
`candidate(T) :-`
`academic_info(T),belongs_category(T,university_interships),`
`global_emotional_status(green), not exception_academic(T)`

Casual chat dialogue

E-friend normally proposes a casual chat dialogue of a new subject belonging a different category of skilled subjects talked during past sessions if her observed global emotional status is green unless exception happens.
`candidate(T) :- new_subject(T),belongs_category(T,Y), last_subject(W), not`
`belongs_category(W,Y), accomplished_skilled(W),`
`global_emotional_status(green), not exception_casual_chat(T)`

Empathy

E-friend proposes animated gif resource for generating motivation empathy due the diagnostic for the student is anxiety but her global emotional status is green unless exception happens
`candidate(T) :- belongs_category(T,gif), diagnostic(anxiety),`
`gif_motivation(T), global_emotional_status(green), not exception_empathy(T)`

Emotions

E-friend generates emotions associated to deceipt, the cognitive structure is represented as logic rules in order to identify when the student tries to deceipt the system or itself. For example, a student feels shame if he/she carries out an action considered cheating, regardless of success.
`shame_student(Action) :- action(Action), negate_action(Action,Negation),`
`happens_student(Action), idl(Negation)`

[a] a). Possible domain values are Depression, Anxiety, Positive Stress, Negative Stress
b). Possible domain values for `global_emotional_status` are `green_flag`, `yellow_flag`, `red_flag` determined by the tendency progress of the student though the past sessions

mendations are derived from the diagnosis of emotional type theory and treat on what activities and conversations to follow for achieving and maximizing a good emotional status. The logistic determined by logical rules will provide for a good emotional status exercises, for a regular emotional status supportive exercises and for bad emotional status coaching assistance though chat-bot dialogue.

Enriching Talks Theories in Answer Sets Programming (ASP). It has been defined for this project five logic programming theories under ASP semantics to model the student profile and construct the chat script proposal for each session. In Table 2 examples of logic rules within E-friend are shown.

Hobbies Theory. Suggest exercises and conversation recommendations encompassing the student likes. **Build Script Theory.** Assemble activities suggested to the student, describes rules for assembling the AI-tasks to build the final script dialogue, logistic and partial order of dependency between activities that can be developed by the student through the advance of dialogue sessions. **Emotional Well-being Theory.** It states description in logic of the OCC Model of emotion [15] that has an objective to achieve and maximize happiness of the student. It is considered, inferred, modeled and represented the knowledge of intentions, beliefs and desires of the student. To achieve this, we implement an adaptation to the OCC Model [15] and [24], using answer set programming(ASP), and encode the student conversations sessions in terms of this model. **Diagnosis of Emotional Type Theory**. Diagnose the emotional status of the student inferred from the student conversation with the chat-bot. It keep track of the emotional status of the student through past conversation sessions to make a better diagnose. The description in logic defines three cases for emotional status: good, regular and bad. It is considered and processed answers given by the student during conversation sessions, the self appreciation reported by the student during conversation sessions and the participation response to the proposed dialogue during conversation sessions. **Well-being Theory.** Suggest mild therapies AI-task interactions to compose a enriching talk dialogue session considering the feedback of student profile. **Academic Theory.** Suggest AI-task interactions with the aim to upgrade the scholar status of the student that can be considered to compose a dialogue session considering academic and emotional student profile. **Empathy Theory.** Suggest AI-task interactions with the aim of strengthening the empathy with E-friend but mainly help the student to achieve a healthy emotional status. **Causal Chat Theory.** Suggest a AI-task interactions of casual chat dialogue within the student dialogue session having the main purpose of retrieving from the student relevant information that is out from the scope retrieval of traditional specific domain theories. **Prescription Theory.** It states description in logic of rules to infer and make recommendations that will be considered for building the student session script, the recommendations are derived from the diagnosis of emotional type theory and treat on what activities and conversations to follow for achieving and maximizing a good emotional status. The logistic determined by logical rules will provide for a good emotional status exercises, for a regular emotional status supportive exercises and for bad emotional status coaching assistance though chat-bot dialogue. Logical rules are examples of E-friend Enriching Talks Theories present in the ETalks-KB. Updates and believe revision are also fundamental concepts required in our application. There are many well known proposed solutions based on ASP such as [19]. There is promising work related to *ethical* chatbots [6] that could allow E-friend to become more respectful to improve its ethical interaction with the student.

The following is an example of the interaction between the student and E-friend. First, it is provided the context of the Ale's history. Then, the analysis of the dialogue, shown in Table 3, from the DAM's point of view.

"It is well known that Ale is very cooperative and try all the well-being exercises that E-friend suggests her to do. E-friend asked him at the beginning of the semester how does Ale feels about his courses. Ale replied that he is comfortable with them as well as with his professors. However, Ale expresses her insecurity about her mathematics course. Ale always had problems with Math. E-friend asked her again the same question after two weeks of classes and Ale gives the same answer as before. However, she mention this time that the professor of mathematics is very helpful and patient with her. After two more weeks, Ale is about to have partial exams. One of those days at a session (just before the exam), she says that she has hope to pass the exam. However, she says she is slow at exams that is his main concern. Ale and E-friend chat soon after she took her exam. She said to E-friend that she has doubts about having passed the exam. The exam had 10 questions and she answered seven of them. She had time to check six of them and she is positive about them. The last one that she tried, she answered in a hurry and she is not sure about it. She needs to have seven correct answers to pass the exam. Hence, she is in the borderline. She also said that she does not care about the grade as long as she accredited the exam. Ale and E-friend chat again, when Ale got her results..."

Table 3. Dialogue between the student and E-friend

Dialogue
1. - **E-friend:** Tell me John, do you have the result of your math exam?
2. - **Ale:** Well, yes, I got the result yesterday.
3. - **E-friend:** How was it?
4. - **Ale:** I only got one wrong answer
5. - **E-friend:** That is very good. I know that you did a great effort. Congratulations!
6. - **Ale:** Thank you
7. - **E-friend:** Do you feel to share anything else to me?
8. - **Ale:** Tonight, I am going with some of my friends to celebrate the end of the partial exams and that we did well

Based on the last context, Ale answered seven questions, and is sure she has six correct of those seven. Following the dialogue, in line four in Table 3, E-friend suspects that Ale failed the exam. She answered seven questions and has one wrong. There is no way to get seven right. Ale did not explicitly tell E-friend if she passed or failed the exam. E-friend, through DAM module, suspects that Ale tries to persuade, even deceit, to E-friend to think she passed the exam, because there is only one wrong answer in the exam. Maybe she passed the exam or maybe not. If she did, her responses were ambiguous. If she failed, then Ale may feel ashamed of herself and people may think she is not very smart. In this case, DAM should identify the ambiguity and would generate the emotion of shame according to the Emotions set of rules presented in Table 2, where the action is "to fail the exam". E-friend will use the result provided by DAM and will decide inform the facilitator: it is possible that the student is deceiving the system or itself, and create the warning or the alert, depending of the traffic light type.

5   Conclusions and Future Work

One contribution of this work[3] is to propose an application for a Reasoning Logical Based Intelligent Agent System Chat-bot for Dialogue Composition named E-friend[4]. It is proposed within the Architecture the use of Logic Programming (LP) to provide reasoning skill to E-friend. Our main contribution in this work is the use of Knowledge Representation Reasoning with LP theories modelling the knowledge of the user (beliefs, intentions, expectations, emotions as an extended version of theory of the mind using the OCC Model of emotions) to reason, plan and to optimally solve the DC problem. Another contribution is the design of an independent component that complements the theory of the mind, within E-friend, [23] with emotions in the user model LP theories [15] and [24] to try to detect the user's deception to the system. This last component with the aim to help the user to avoid deception for achieving human development and mental health through cognitive compassionate skills. E-friend is instantiated in Well-being Mental Health domain for optimal well-being development of first year university students. As future work it can be designed detect deception module in E-friend using LP theory under Epistemic ASP to model deception pre-conditions presented in Sect. 3.1 [23]. Also it could be used Possibilistic ASP or Probabilistic ASP to model Aggregating parameters presented in Sect. 3.3 [23].

References

1. Baskar, J., Janols, R., Guerrero, E., Nieves, J.C., Lindgren, H.: A multipurpose goal model for personalised digital coaching. In: Montagna, S., Abreu, P.H., Giroux, S., Schumacher, M.I. (eds.) A2HC/AHEALTH -2017. LNCS (LNAI), vol. 10685, pp. 94–116. Springer, Cham (2017). https://doi.org/10.1007/978-3-319-70887-4_6

---

[3] We thank the support of Psychologist Andres Munguia Barcenas.
[4] TheE-friendapplicationisavailableinhttps://github.com/luis-angel-montiel-moreno/efriend.

2. Baskar, J., Lindgren, H., et al.: Cognitive architecture of an agent for human-agent dialogues. In: Corchado, J.M. (ed.) PAAMS 2014. CCIS, vol. 430, pp. 89–100. Springer, Cham (2014). https://doi.org/10.1007/978-3-319-07767-3_9

3. Bell, S., Wood, C., Sarkar, A.: Perceptions of chatbots in therapy. In: Extended Abstracts of the 2019 CHI Conference on Human Factors in Computing Systems, p. LBW1712 (2019)

4. Bendig, E., Erb, B., Schulze-Thuesing, L., Baumeister, H.: The next generation: chatbots in clinical psychology and psychotherapy to foster mental health-a scoping review. Verhaltenstherapie 1–13 (2019)

5. Diano, F., Ferrata, F., Calabretta, R.: The development of a mindfulness-based mobile application to learn emotional self-regulation. In: PSYCHOBIT (2019)

6. Dyoub, A., Costantini, S., Lisi, F.A.: Towards ethical machines via logic programming 306, 333–339 (2019)

7. Fuentes, M.: The broken trap: the problematic of Sexual Addiction. Ediciones del Verbo Encarnado (2015). https://books.google.com.mx/books?id=Su2zCgAAQBAJ

8. Galindo, J.A., Dupuy-Chessa, S., Céret, É.: Toward a UI adaptation approach driven by user emotions (2017)

9. Greenberg, A.E., Smeets, P., Zhurakhovska, L.: Lying, guilt, and shame. Technical report, Mimeo (2014)

10. Inkster, B., Sarda, S., Subramanian, V.: An empathy-driven, conversational artificial intelligence agent (Wysa) for digital mental well-being: real-world data evaluation mixed-methods study. JMIR mHealth uHealth 6(11), e12106 (2018)

11. Jacobs, T.L., et al.: Intensive meditation training, immune cell telomerase activity, and psychological mediators. Psychoneuroendocrinology 36(5), 664–681 (2011)

12. Jingar, M., Lindgren, H.: Tangible communication of emotions with a digital companion for managing stress: an exploratory co-design study. In: Proceedings of the 7th International Conference on Human-Agent Interaction, pp. 28–36 (2019)

13. Luksha, P., Cubista, J., Laszlo, A., Popovich, M., Ninenko, I.: Educational ecosystems for societal transformation (2017)

14. Mostafa, M., Crick, T., Calderon, A.C., Oatley, G.: Incorporating emotion and personality-based analysis in user-centered modelling. In: Bramer, M., Petridis, M. (eds.) Research and Development in Intelligent Systems XXXIII, pp. 383–389. Springer, Cham (2016). https://doi.org/10.1007/978-3-319-47175-4_29

15. Ortony, A., Clore, G.L., Collins, A.: The Cognitive Structure of Emotions. Cambridge University Press, Cambridge (1990)

16. Osorio, M., Zepeda, C., Carballido, J.L.: MyUBot: towards an artificial intelligence agent system chat-bot for well-being and mental health. In: Accepted in Artificial Intelligence for HEaLth, PersonaLized MedIcine aNd WEllbeing Workshop at ECAI 2020 (2020)

17. Osorio, M., Zepeda, C., Carballido, J.L.: Towards a virtual companion system to give support during confinement. In: CONTIE (2020)

18. Osorio, M., Zepeda, C., Castillo, H., Cervantes, P., Carballido, J.L.: My university e-partner. In: CONTIE, pp. 150–1503 (2019)

19. Osorio, M., Cuevas, V.: Updates in answer set programming: an approach based on basic structural properties. Theory Pract. Log. Program. 7(4), 451–479 (2007)

20. Poirson, E., Cunha, C.D.: A recommender approach based on customer emotions. Expert Syst. Appl. 122, 281–288 (2019)

21. Rachman, S.: Betrayal: a psychological analysis. Behav. Res. Ther. 48(4), 304–311 (2010)

22. Ribeiro, I.J., Pereira, R., et al.: Stress and quality of life among university students: a systematic literature review. Health Prof. Educ. **4**(2), 70–77 (2018)
23. Sarkadi, S., Panisson, A.R., Bordini, R.H., McBurney, P., Parsons, S., Chapman, M.: Modelling deception using theory of mind in multi-agent systems. AI Commun. **32**(4), 287–302 (2019)
24. Sarlej, M.: A lesson learned: using emotions to generate stories with morals. Ph.D. thesis, Computer Science & Engineering, University of New South Wales (2014)
25. Schaub, T., Woltran, S.: Answer set programming unleashed! KI **32**(2–3), 105–108 (2018). https://doi.org/10.1007/s13218-018-0550-z
26. Vrij, A.: Why professionals fail to catch liars and how they can improve. Legal Criminol. Psychol. **9**(2), 159–181 (2004)
27. Walton, D.: The place of dialogue theory in logic, computer science and communication studies. Synthese **123**(3), 327–346 (2000)
28. World Health Organization: World health organization. WHO (2020). https://www.who.int/.

Deception in Epistemic Causal Logic

Chiaki Sakama[✉]

Wakayama University, 930 Sakaedani, Wakayama 640-8510, Japan
sakama@wakayama-u.ac.jp

Abstract. *Deception* is an act whereby one person causes another person to have a false belief. This paper formulates deception using causal relations between a speaker's utterance and a hearer's belief states in *epistemic causal logic*. Four different types of deception are considered: *deception by lying*, *deception by bluffing*, *deception by truthful telling*, and *deception by omission*, depending on whether a speaker believes what he/she says or not, and whether a speaker makes an utterance or not. Next several situations are considered where an act of deceiving happens. *Intentional deception* is accompanied by a speaker's intent to deceive. *Indirect deception* happens when false information is carried over from person to person. *Self-deception* is an act of deceiving the self. The current study formally characterizes various aspects of deception that have been informally argued in philosophical literature.

Keywords: Deception · Epistemic causal logic · Lying

1 Introduction

Deception is a part of human nature and is a topic of interest in philosophy and elsewhere. Most philosophers agree that an act of deceiving implies a success of the act, while they disagree as to whether deceiving must be intentional or not [3,18]. Deceiving is different from *lying*, in fact, there is deception without lying [1,34]. There is no consensus as to stating conditions for describing someone as *self-deceived* [8]. In this way, deception has been subject to extensive studies on the one hand, but deception argued in philosophical literature is mostly conceptual, on the other hand.

Deception is also a topic of interest in computer science and AI. Recent development of machine learning involves various forms of deceptive activities on social media [6]. Historically, the question *"Can computers deceive humans?"* has been argued since Turing's imitation game [31]. Castelfranchi [4] argued the possibility of artificial agents that deceive humans in several ways, not only for malicious reasons but also for goodwill and in our interest. For instance, an intelligent personal assistant might deceive us to make a right decision. One could imagine a medical counseling system which does not always inform patients of the true state of affairs. Clark [7] develops a *lying machine* and provides empirical evidence that the machine reliably deceives ordinary humans. Isaac and Bridewell [16] argue that robots must possess a theory of mind in order to respond effectively to deceptive communication. Some studies show that robots can gain advantage over adversaries by deceptive behaviors [28,35]. Deception is also of

© Springer Nature Switzerland AG 2021
S. Sarkadi et al. (Eds.): DeceptECAI 2020/DeceptAI 2021, CCIS 1296, pp. 105–123, 2021.
https://doi.org/10.1007/978-3-030-91779-1_8

particular interest in a game-theoretical perspective [11,15], and is adopted as a strategy of intelligent agents in multiagent systems [27,29,36]. In spite of the broad interest in this topic, however, relatively little study has been devoted to developing a formal theory of deception. A formal account of deception helps us to better understand what is deception, and to design artificial agents that can detect deceptive acts in virtual societies. Deception is a perlocutionary act that produces an effect in the belief state of an addressee by communication. Formulation of deception then needs a logic that can express belief of agents, communication between agents and effects of communication. In this respect, a logical language that has causal relations as well as epistemic modality is useful for the purpose.

In this paper, we use the *causal logic* of [14] to represent causal relations between a deceiver's speech act and its effect on belief states of an addressee. We define formulas for representing utterance and belief of agents, and introduce a set of axioms in *epistemic causal logic*. Using the logic, we formulate four different types of deception, *deception by lying*, *deception by bluffing*, *deception by truthful telling*, and *deception by omission*, and distinguish them from *attempted deception* that may fail to deceive. We next discuss various aspects of deception such as *intended deception*, *indirect deception* and *self-deception*. We address formal properties of those different sorts of deception.

The rest of this paper is organized as follows. Section 2 introduces the logical framework used in this paper. Section 3 formulates different types of deception and investigates formal properties. Section 4 presents various aspects of deception. Section 5 addresses comparison with related studies. Section 6 concludes with remarks.

2   Epistemic Causal Logic

We first review the *causal logic* of [14] that is used in this paper. Let $\mathscr{L}$ be a language of propositional logic. An *atom* is a propositional variable p in $\mathscr{L}$. A *literal* is an atom p or its negation $\neg p$. *Formulas* (or *sentences*) in $\mathscr{L}$ are defined as follows: (i) an atom p is a formula. (ii) If φ and ψ are formulas, then $\neg\varphi$, $\varphi \wedge \psi$, $\varphi \vee \psi$, $\varphi \supset \psi$, and $\varphi \equiv \psi$ are all formulas. In particular, $\top$ and $\bot$ represent valid and contradictory formulas, respectively. We often use parentheses "()" in a formula as usual. Throughout the paper, Greek letters λ, φ, ψ represent formulas.

An *interpretation I* is a complete and consistent (finite) set of literals.[1] A literal ℓ is *true* in an interpretation I iff $\ell \in I$. The truth value of a formula φ in I is defined based on the usual truth tables of propositional connectives. An interpretation I *satisfies* a formula φ (written $I \models \varphi$) iff φ is true in I. Given formulas φ and ψ,

$$\varphi \Rightarrow \psi \tag{1}$$

is called a *causal rule*. φ is called a *cause* and ψ is called an *effect*. The rule (1) means that "ψ is caused if φ is true". In particular, the rule $(\top \Rightarrow \psi)$ is a *fact* representing that ψ is true, which is abbreviated as ψ.

A *(causal) theory* is a finite set of causal rules. A theory T is identified with the conjunction of all rules in T. Given a theory T and an interpretation I, define

$$T^I = \{ \psi \mid (\varphi \Rightarrow \psi) \in T \text{ for some } \varphi \text{ and } I \models \varphi \}.$$

---

[1] That is, $\ell \in I$ iff $\neg\ell \notin I$ for any literal ℓ appearing in a theory.

Then I is a *model* of T if I is the unique model of T^I. If every model of T satisfies a formula F, then we say that T *entails* F (written $T \models F$). A theory T is *consistent* if it has a model; otherwise, T is *inconsistent* (written $T \models \bot$).

Example 1. Suppose the theory

$$T = \{p \Rightarrow q, \quad p \Rightarrow p, \quad \neg p \Rightarrow \neg p\}.$$

In T there is no cause for $\neg q$, then $\neg q$ is false or q is true. Since every true formula is caused, it must be the case that q is caused. This leads to the conclusion that p is true. As a result, T has the single model $\{p, q\}$. In fact, by putting $I = \{p, q\}$, it becomes $T^I = \{p, q\}$ and I is the unique model of T^I.

Note that $\Rightarrow$ is not identical to material implication in classical logic. In Example 1 if $\Rightarrow$ is replaced by material implication as: $T' = \{p \supset q, \quad p \supset p, \quad \neg p \supset \neg p\}$ then $p \supset p$ and $\neg p \supset \neg p$ are tautologies and can be removed. As a result, $\{\neg p, q\}$ and $\{\neg p, \neg q\}$ are also models of T', but these are not models of T. In fact, $p \Rightarrow p$ and $\neg p \Rightarrow \neg p$ are not tautologies in a causal theory. Formally, if a causal theory T contains $\varphi \Rightarrow \psi$ then T entails $\varphi \supset \psi$ but not vice versa.

Actions and their effects are represented by a causal theory. In this paper we consider an action as an utterance by an agent. Suppose that an agent a utters a sentence φ to an agent b at time t. The situation is represented by the atom $U_{ab}^t \varphi$. A belief state of an agent is represented as a fluent. When an agent a believes (resp. disbelieves) a sentence φ at time t, it is represented by the literal $B_a^t \varphi$ (resp. $\neg B_a^t \varphi$). Beliefs are possibly nested, for instance, the atom $B_b^{t+1} B_a^t \varphi$ represents that an agent b believes at $t+1$ that an agent a believes φ at t. By contrast, factual sentences are considered persistent and written as φ without time. Note that we handle $B_a^t \varphi$ or $B_b^{t+1} B_a^t \varphi$ as an *atom* in a theory, so that B_a^t is not an operator in modal epistemic logic.[2] This enables us to define the semantics without introducing a Kripke structure and to introduce necessary axioms depending on the objective. For the current use, the following axioms of utterance and belief are introduced. Let φ and ψ be sentences. Given agents a, b and time t,

(axioms of utterance): $\quad U_{ab}^t \varphi \Rightarrow U_{ab}^t \varphi \quad$ and $\quad \neg U_{ab}^t \varphi \Rightarrow \neg U_{ab}^t \varphi$.

(axioms of belief): $\quad B_a^t \varphi \Rightarrow B_a^t \varphi \quad$ and $\quad \neg B_a^t \varphi \Rightarrow \neg B_a^t \varphi$.

$\qquad\qquad\qquad B_a^t \varphi \equiv B_a^t \psi \ $ if $\ \varphi \equiv \psi$.

$\qquad\qquad\qquad B_a^t (\varphi \wedge \psi) \equiv B_a^t \varphi \wedge B_a^t \psi$.

(axioms of inertia): $\quad B_a^t \varphi \wedge B_a^{t+1} \varphi \Rightarrow B_a^{t+1} \varphi \quad$ and $\quad \neg B_a^t \varphi \wedge \neg B_a^{t+1} \varphi \Rightarrow \neg B_a^{t+1} \varphi$.

(axiom of truth): $\quad B_a^t \top \ $ for any t.

(axiom of rationality): $\quad \neg B_a^t \bot \ $ for any t if an agent a is *rational*.

(axiom of credibility): $\quad U_{ab}^t \varphi \Rightarrow B_b^{t+1} \varphi \ $ if an agent b is *credulous*.

(axiom of reflection): $\quad U_{ab}^t \varphi \Rightarrow B_b^{t+1} B_a^t \varphi \ $ if an agent b is *reflective*.

The axioms of utterance represent that an utterance or non-utterance has a cause of this. The axioms of belief represent similar effects. The axioms of inertia represent that an agent retains beliefs unless there is a reason to abandon it. The axiom of rationality is assumed for agents having consistent beliefs. The axiom of credibility represents

---

[2] $B_a^t \varphi$ is considered an atom such as "$b\_a\_t\_\varphi$".

that if a speaker utters a sentence then a hearer believes it. The axiom of reflection represents that if a speaker utters a sentence then a hearer believes that the speaker believes the sentence. The first four axioms are always assumed, while the last three axioms are conditionally assumed. Note that the axiom of rationality is identified with $B_a^t\varphi \supset \neg B_a^t\neg\varphi$ as:

$$\neg B_a^t\bot \equiv \neg B_a^t(\varphi \wedge \neg\varphi) \text{ (axioms of belief)}$$
$$\equiv \neg(B_a^t\varphi \wedge B_a^t\neg\varphi) \text{ (axioms of belief)}$$
$$\equiv \neg B_a^t\varphi \vee \neg B_a^t\neg\varphi \text{ (De Morgan's law)}$$

A causal logic with these axioms is called the *epistemic causal logic*.

3   Deception in Epistemic Causal Logic

3.1   Deception by Lying

Deception is different from lying. Carson [3] says:

> "unlike 'lying' the word 'deception' connotes success. An act must actually mislead someone (cause someone to have false beliefs) if it is to count as a case of deception. Many lies are not believed and do not succeed in deceiving anyone" [3, p. 55].

He then illustrates the relationship between lying, deception, and attempted deception as in Fig. 1.

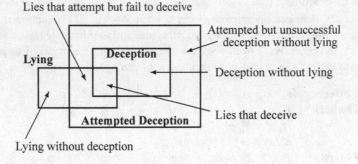

Fig. 1. Lying, deception and attempted deception [3]

Our primary interest in this section is to formulate "lies that deceive".[3] In this paper, we consider communication between two agents. Let a be an agent who utters a sentence (called a *speaker*), and b an agent who is an addressee (called a *hearer*). We first define the act of lying.

---

[3] Carson considers bluffing a type of lying and views deception by bluffing as lies that deceive. In this paper, we distinguish lying and bluffing, and view deception by bluffing as deception without lying.

Definition 1 (lying). Let a and b be two agents and φ a sentence. Then *lying* is defined as

$$\text{LIE}^t_{ab}(\varphi) \overset{def}{=} B^t_a \neg\varphi \wedge U^t_{ab}\varphi \tag{2}$$

We say that a *lies* to b at t on the sentence φ.

By (2) a lies to b if a utters a believed-false sentence φ to b. Here we consider lying as a statement of a sentence, while it does not necessarily imply oral communication but it could be any type of communication using sentences. Note that a believes φ but the actual falsity of φ is not required in (2). Thus, if a speaker utters a believed-false sentence φ that is in fact true, then it is still lying. In this paper it does not matter whether lying involves *intention* to deceive.[4] Deception by lying is then defined as follows.

Definition 2 (deception by lying). Let a and b be two agents and φ a sentence. Then *deception by lying* (DBL) is defined as

$$\text{DBL}^{t+1}_{ab}(\varphi) \overset{def}{=} \neg\varphi \wedge (\text{LIE}^t_{ab}(\varphi) \Rightarrow B^{t+1}_b\varphi). \tag{3}$$

We say that a *deceives by lying* to b at $t+1$ on the sentence φ.

By (3) deception by lying is such that a lies to b at t on a false sentence φ, which causes b's believing φ at the next time step $t+1$. In contrast to lying, the actual falsity of φ is required. $\text{DBL}^{t+1}_{ab}(\varphi)$ is often written as $\text{DBL}_{ab}(\varphi)$ if time is unimportant in the context.

Example 2. Suppose a salesperson who lies that an investment is worth buying. The situation is represented by (3) with $a =$ salesperson, $b =$ customer, and $\varphi =$ "an investment is worth buying" that is actually false. DBL then results in the customer's believing φ.

Note that (3) does not address whether a hearer believes φ *before* the act of lying. DBL happens whenever a hearer believes a false sentence φ as a result of lying by a speaker.

Example 3. Consider a theory

$$T = \text{LIE}^t_{ab}(\varphi) \wedge \text{DBL}^{t+1}_{ab}(\varphi).$$

Then T has two models:[5]

$$M_1 = \{\neg\varphi,\ B^t_a\neg\varphi,\ U^t_{ab}\varphi,\ B^{t+1}_a\neg\varphi,\ B^t_b\varphi,\ B^{t+1}_b\varphi\},$$
$$M_2 = \{\neg\varphi,\ B^t_a\neg\varphi,\ U^t_{ab}\varphi,\ B^{t+1}_a\neg\varphi,\ \neg B^t_b\varphi,\ B^{t+1}_b\varphi\}.$$

In both M_1 and M_2, a's belief in $\neg\varphi$ does not change from t to $t+1$ by the axioms of inertia. On the other hand, there are two different states of b's believing φ at t. M_1 represents that $\text{DBL}^{t+1}_{ab}(\varphi)$ contributes causally toward b's continuing the false belief in φ. By contrast, M_2 represents that $\text{DBL}^{t+1}_{ab}(\varphi)$ contributes causally toward b's acquiring the false belief in φ. Since $B^{t+1}_b\varphi$ is true in each model, it holds that

$$T \models B^{t+1}_b\varphi.$$

---

[4] We later consider intention in deceiving.

[5] Here, we omit $B^t_x\top$ and $B^{t+1}_x\top$ where $x = a, b$.

The situation of M_1 corresponds to *positive deception simpliciter* and M_2 corresponds to *positive deception secundum quid* in [5].

$\mathrm{DBL}_{ab}(\varphi)$ requires that φ is actually false. So if a speaker a utters a believed-false statement φ which is in fact true, then the speaker lies but DBL does not happen. The situation is formally stated as $\varphi \wedge \mathrm{DBL}_{ab}^{t+1}(\varphi) \models \bot$.

Example 4. A student, Bob, who believes that there will be no exam in tomorrow's math-class, tells his friend Mike that there will be an exam in tomorrow's math-class. Mike, who was absent from the math-class last week, believes Bob's information. The next day, it turns out that there is an exam in the class. In this case, Bob lies to Mike but Bob does not deceive Mike (and Mike does not believe that Bob lies to him).

Lying on a false sentence succeeds to deceive if a hearer is credulous.

Proposition 1. *Let a and b be two agents and φ a sentence. If b is credulous, then*

$$\neg\varphi \wedge \mathrm{LIE}_{ab}^{t}(\varphi) \models B_b^{t+1}\varphi.$$

Proof. Suppose an interpretation I such that $I \models \neg\varphi \wedge \mathrm{LIE}_{ab}^{t}(\varphi)$. Since b is credulous, $I \models U_{ab}^{t}\varphi$ implies $I \models B_b^{t+1}\varphi$ by the axiom of credibility. □

DBL on the valid sentence always fails. By contrast, DBL on the contradictory sentence fails if a hearer is rational.

Proposition 2. *Let a and b be two agents.*

- $\mathrm{DBL}_{ab}^{t+1}(\top) \models \bot$.
- $\mathrm{LIE}_{ab}^{t}(\bot) \wedge \mathrm{DBL}_{ab}^{t+1}(\bot) \models \bot$ *if b is rational.*

Proof. $\mathrm{DBL}_{ab}^{t+1}(\top) \equiv \bot$ by definition. $\mathrm{LIE}_{ab}^{t}(\bot) \wedge \mathrm{DBL}_{ab}^{t+1}(\bot)$ implies $B_b^{t+1}\bot$. If b is rational, this is impossible by the axiom of rationality. □

Suppose that a speaker a lies to b on the sentence φ but a hearer b already believes the contrary. If b is rational, then DBL on φ fails.

Proposition 3. *Let a and b be two agents and φ a sentence. If b is rational, then*

$$B_b^t\neg\varphi \wedge \mathrm{LIE}_{ab}^{t}(\varphi) \wedge \mathrm{DBL}_{ab}^{t+1}(\varphi) \models \bot.$$

Proof. $B_b^t\neg\varphi$ implies $B_b^{t+1}\neg\varphi$ by the axioms of inertia, and $B_b^{t+1}\neg\varphi$ implies $\neg B_b^{t+1}\varphi$ by the axiom of rationality. On the other hand, $\mathrm{LIE}_{ab}^{t}(\varphi) \wedge \mathrm{DBL}_{ab}^{t+1}(\varphi)$ implies $B_b^{t+1}\varphi$. Hence, $B_b^{t+1}\varphi \wedge \neg B_b^{t+1}\varphi \equiv \bot$. □

If a rational hearer is credulous, on the other hand, the hearer *revises* his/her belief and lying succeeds to deceive even if the hearer believes the contrary.

Proposition 4. *Let a and b be two agents and φ a sentence. If b is credulous and rational, then*

$$\neg\varphi \wedge B_b^t\neg\varphi \wedge \mathrm{LIE}_{ab}^{t}(\varphi) \models B_b^{t+1}\varphi.$$

Proof. For an interpretation $I \models \neg\varphi \land B_b^t \neg\varphi \land \mathsf{LIE}_{ab}^t(\varphi)$, $I \models U_{ab}^t\varphi$ implies $I \models B_b^{t+1}\varphi$ by the axiom of credibility, thereby $I \models \neg B_b^{t+1}\neg\varphi$ by the axiom of rationality. In this case, the axioms of inertia are not applied, and $I \models B_b^t\neg\varphi$ does not imply $I \models B_b^{t+1}\neg\varphi$. Then the result holds by Proposition 1. □

Suppose that a hearer is rational and reflective, and believes that a speaker is also rational. In this case, the hearer does not believe that a speaker is lying.

Proposition 5. *Let a and b be two agents and φ a sentence. If b is rational and reflective, and believes that a speaker a is rational, then*

$$\mathsf{LIE}_{ab}^t(\varphi) \land B_b^{t+1}(\mathsf{LIE}_{ab}^t(\varphi)) \models \bot.$$

Proof. $B_b^{t+1}(\mathsf{LIE}_{ab}^t(\varphi)) = B_b^{t+1}(B_a^t\neg\varphi \land U_{ab}^t\varphi)$ implies $B_b^{t+1}B_a^t\neg\varphi$ (axioms of belief). As b believes that a is rational, then $B_b^{t+1}(B_a^t\neg\varphi \supset \neg B_a^t\varphi)$ and $B_b^{t+1}B_a^t\neg\varphi$ imply $B_b^{t+1}\neg B_a^t\varphi$ (axioms of belief). Since b is reflective, $U_{ab}^t\varphi$ in $\mathsf{LIE}_{ab}^t(\varphi)$ implies $B_b^{t+1}B_a^t\varphi$ (axiom of reflection). Hence, $B_b^{t+1}\neg B_a^t\varphi \land B_b^{t+1}B_a^t\varphi \equiv B_b^{t+1}\bot$ (axioms of belief). This is impossible, since b is rational. □

Proposition 5 implies that if a rational and reflective hearer believes that a rational speaker is lying, there is no chance of DBL to succeed. Propositions 2, 3 and 5 characterize different situations where "lies that attempt but fail to deceive". In other words, they provide necessary conditions for DBL to succeed. If a rational hearer is not credulous, it is necessary that he/she does not believe to the contrary. If a rational hearer is reflective, it is necessary that he/she does not believe that a rational speaker is lying. Note that if an agent a successfully deceives another agent b by a lie φ, there is no guarantee that a can also deceive b using a stronger lie $\varphi \land \lambda$. A simple case is shown by putting $\lambda = \neg\varphi$, then $\mathsf{LIE}_{ab}^t(\varphi \land \neg\varphi) \land \mathsf{DBL}_{ab}^{t+1}(\varphi \land \neg\varphi)$ fails if b is rational.

3.2 Deception by Bluffing

We next provide an instance of "deception without lying" in Fig. 1. When a speaker utters a sentence φ while he/she is uncertain about the truth of φ, we call it *bluffing*.

Definition 3 (bluffing). Let a and b be two agents and φ a sentence. Then *bluffing* is defined as

$$\mathsf{BLUF}_{ab}^t(\varphi) \overset{def}{=} \neg B_a^t\varphi \land \neg B_a^t\neg\varphi \land U_{ab}^t\varphi \qquad (4)$$

We say that *a bluffs b* at *t* on the sentence φ.

By (4) a *bluffing agent a* believes neither φ nor $\neg\varphi$ when it utters φ. In case of lying (2), a speaker disbelieves φ but believes $\neg\varphi$. In bluffing a speaker also disbelieves $\neg\varphi$. The situation is also called *bullshit* in [13, 22, 24]. Deception by bluffing is then defined as follows.

Definition 4 (deception by bluffing). Let a and b be two agents and φ a sentence. Then *deception by bluffing* (DBB) is defined as

$$\mathsf{DBB}_{ab}^{t+1}(\varphi) \overset{def}{=} \neg\varphi \land (\mathsf{BLUF}_{ab}^t(\varphi) \Rightarrow B_b^{t+1}\varphi). \qquad (5)$$

We say that *a deceives b* by bluffing at $t+1$ on the sentence φ.

$\mathrm{DBB}^{t+1}_{ab}(\varphi)$ is often written as $\mathrm{DBB}_{ab}(\varphi)$ if time is unimportant in the context.

Example 5. Bob, who does not know whether there will be an exam in tomorrow's math-class, tells his friend Mike that there will be no exam in tomorrow's math-class. Mike believes Bob's information. The next day, it turns out that there is an exam in the class. In this case, Bob deceives Mike by bluffing.

Like DBL, bluffing on a false sentence succeeds to deceive if a hearer is credulous.

Proposition 6. *Let a and b be two agents and φ a sentence. If b is credulous, then*

$$\neg\varphi \wedge \mathrm{BLUF}^t_{ab}(\varphi) \models B^{t+1}_b\varphi.$$

Proof. Suppose an interpretation I such that $I \models \neg\varphi \wedge \mathrm{BLUF}^t_{ab}(\varphi)$. Since b is credulous, $I \models U^t_{ab}\varphi$ implies $I \models B^{t+1}_b\varphi$ by the axiom of credibility. $\square$

Both $\mathrm{DBB}_{ab}(\top)$ and $\mathrm{DBB}_{ab}(\bot)$ are inconsistent.

Proposition 7. *Let a and b be two agents. Then,*

$$\mathrm{DBB}^{t+1}_{ab}(\top) \vee \mathrm{DBB}^{t+1}_{ab}(\bot) \models \bot$$

Proof. Both $\mathrm{BLUF}^t_{ab}(\top)$ and $\mathrm{BLUF}^t_{ab}(\bot)$ imply $\neg B^t_a\top$ which violates the axiom of truth. The cause of (5) cannot be true, then $\mathrm{DBB}^{t+1}_{ab}(\top) \vee \mathrm{DBB}^{t+1}_{ab}(\bot)$ has no model. $\square$

$\mathrm{DBB}_{ab}(\varphi)$ fails if a rational hearer believes $\neg\varphi$ at t.

Proposition 8. *Let a and b be two agents and φ a sentence. If b is rational, then*

$$B^t_b\neg\varphi \wedge \mathrm{BLUF}^t_{ab}(\varphi) \wedge \mathrm{DBB}^{t+1}_{ab}(\varphi) \models \bot.$$

Proof. $B^t_b\neg\varphi$ implies $B^{t+1}_b\neg\varphi$ (axioms of inertia), and $B^{t+1}_b\neg\varphi$ implies $\neg B^{t+1}_b\varphi$ (axiom of rationality). $\mathrm{BLUF}^t_{ab}(\varphi) \wedge \mathrm{DBB}^{t+1}_{ab}(\varphi)$ implies $B^{t+1}_b\varphi$. Hence, $B^{t+1}_b\varphi \wedge \neg B^{t+1}_b\varphi$. $\square$

If a rational hearer is credulous, bluffing succeeds to deceive even if the hearer believes the contrary.

Proposition 9. *Let a and b be two agents and φ a sentence. If b is credulous and rational, then*

$$\neg\varphi \wedge B^t_b\neg\varphi \wedge \mathrm{BLUF}^t_{ab}(\varphi) \models B^{t+1}_b\varphi.$$

Proof. For an interpretation $I \models \neg\varphi \wedge B^t_b\neg\varphi \wedge \mathrm{BLUF}^t_{ab}(\varphi)$, $I \models U^t_{ab}\varphi$ implies $I \models B^{t+1}_b\varphi$ by the axiom of credibility, thereby $I \models \neg B^{t+1}_b\neg\varphi$ by the axiom of rationality. In this case, the axioms of inertia are not applied, and $I \models B^t_b\neg\varphi$ does not imply $I \models B^{t+1}_b\neg\varphi$. Then the result holds by Proposition 6. $\square$

If a hearer is rational and reflective, he/she does not believe that a speaker is bluffing.

Proposition 10. *Let a and b be two agents and φ a sentence. If b is rational and reflective, then*

$$\mathrm{BLUF}^t_{ab}(\varphi) \wedge B^{t+1}_b(\mathrm{BLUF}^t_{ab}(\varphi)) \models \bot.$$

Proof. $B_b^{t+1}(\text{BLUF}_{ab}^t(\varphi))$ implies $B_b^{t+1}(\neg B_a^t\varphi \wedge \neg B_a^t\neg\varphi)$, thereby $B_b^{t+1}\neg B_a^t\varphi$ (axioms of belief). As b is reflective, $U_{ab}^t\varphi$ in $\text{BLUF}_{ab}^t(\varphi)$ implies $B_b^{t+1}B_a^t\varphi$ (axiom of reflection). Hence, $B_b^{t+1}\neg B_a^t\varphi \wedge B_b^{t+1}B_a^t\varphi \equiv B_b^{t+1}\bot$ (axioms of belief). This is impossible, since b is rational. $\qquad\square$

Recall that attempted DBL fails if a rational and reflective hearer believes that a *rational* speaker is lying (Proposition 5). By contrast, attempted DBB fails if a rational and reflective hearer believes that a speaker is bluffing (Proposition 10). Note that in the latter case, it is not required that a hearer believes that a speaker is rational. The difference comes from $B_b^{t+1}(\text{LIE}_{ab}^t(\varphi))$ and $B_b^{t+1}(\text{BLUF}_{ab}^t(\varphi))$. $B_b^{t+1}(\text{LIE}_{ab}^t(\varphi))$ implies $B_b^{t+1}B_a^t\neg\varphi$, while $B_b^{t+1}(\text{BLUF}_{ab}^t(\varphi))$ implies $B_b^{t+1}\neg B_a^t\varphi$. To have $B_b^{t+1}\neg B_a^t\varphi$ in the former case, it is required that b believes that a is rational. This observation implies the next results.

Proposition 11. *Let a and b be two agents and φ a sentence. If b is rational and reflective, then*

- $\text{LIE}_{ab}^t(\varphi) \wedge B_b^{t+1}(\text{BLUF}_{ab}^t(\varphi)) \models \bot$.
- $\text{BLUF}_{ab}^t(\varphi) \wedge B_b^{t+1}(\text{LIE}_{ab}^t(\varphi)) \models \bot$ *if b believes that a is rational.*

By Propositions 10 and 11, attempted DBB fails if a rational and reflective hearer believes that (i) a speaker is bluffing, or (ii) a rational speaker is lying.

3.3 Deception by Truthful Telling

Truthful telling is the opposite of lying—a speaker utters a believed-true sentence.

Definition 5 (truthful telling). Let a and b be two agents and φ a sentence. Then *truthful telling* is defined as

$$\text{TRT}_{ab}^t(\varphi) \stackrel{def}{=} B_a^t\varphi \wedge U_{ab}^t\varphi \tag{6}$$

We say that *a truthfully tells b at t on the sentence φ*.

The actual truth of φ is not the matter in (6). One may deceive others by honestly telling what he/she believes to be true.

Example 6. Bob, who believes that there will be no exam in tomorrow's math-class, tells his friend Mike that there will be no exam in tomorrow's math-class. Mike believes Bob's information. The next day, it turns out that there is an exam in the class. In this case, Bob deceives Mike by truthful telling.

The above example illustrates another instance of "deception without lying". We call this type "deception by truthful telling" that is formally defined as follows.

Definition 6 (deception by truthful telling). Let a and b be two agents and φ a sentence. Then *deception by truthful telling* (DBT) is defined as

$$\text{DBT}_{ab}^{t+1}(\varphi) \stackrel{def}{=} \neg\varphi \wedge (\text{TRT}_{ab}^t(\varphi) \Rightarrow B_b^{t+1}\varphi). \tag{7}$$

In (7) a's truthful utterance of φ makes a hearer b believe a false sentence φ. DBT is less malicious than DBL or DBB because a speaker truthfully tells a (misbelieved) fact. $\mathsf{DBT}_{ab}^{t+1}(\varphi)$ is often written as $\mathsf{DBT}_{ab}(\varphi)$ if time is unimportant in the context. By definition, DBL, DBB and DBT are mutually exclusive. Like DBL and DBB, truthful telling on a false sentence succeeds to deceive if a hearer is credulous.

Proposition 12. *Let a and b be two agents and φ a sentence. If b is credulous, then*

$$\neg\varphi \wedge \mathsf{TRT}_{ab}^{t}(\varphi) \models B_b^{t+1}\varphi.$$

Proof. Suppose an interpretation I such that $I \models \neg\varphi \wedge \mathsf{TRT}_{ab}^{t}(\varphi)$. Since b is credulous, $I \models U_{ab}^{t}\varphi$ implies $I \models B_b^{t+1}\varphi$ by the axiom of credibility. $\square$

Proposition 13. *Let a and b be two agents. Then,*

$$\mathsf{DBT}_{ab}^{t+1}(\top) \models \bot.$$

Proof. When $\varphi \equiv \top$, (7) becomes $\bot$. $\square$

By contrast, $\mathsf{DBT}_{ab}^{t+1}(\bot)$ may succeed if both a speaker and a hearer are irrational.

Proposition 14. *Let a and b be two agents. If both a and b are irrational, then*

$$\mathsf{TRT}_{ab}^{t}(\bot) \wedge \mathsf{DBT}_{ab}^{t+1}(\bot) \models B_a^{t+1}\bot \wedge B_b^{t+1}\bot.$$

Proof. The result holds by definition and the axioms of inertia. $\square$

Proposition 14 characterizes a situation that an irrational speaker believes a false sentence, and he/she truthfully tells a hearer who is also irrational. As a result, the hearer believes the false sentence. As an example, a mathematician a claims that he/she finds a proof of squaring the circle, which is known to be impossible today. A hearer b, who is not well-informed in mathematics, believes it. This is a case of deception by truthful telling of $\mathsf{DBT}_{ab}(\bot)$. $\mathsf{DBT}_{ab}^{t+1}(\varphi)$ fails if a rational hearer believes $\neg\varphi$ at t.

Proposition 15. *Let a and b be two agents and φ a sentence. If b is rational, then*

$$B_b^{t}\neg\varphi \wedge \mathsf{TRT}_{ab}^{t}(\varphi) \wedge \mathsf{DBT}_{ab}^{t+1}(\varphi) \models \bot.$$

Proof. $B_b^{t}\neg\varphi$ implies $B_b^{t+1}\neg\varphi$ (axioms of inertia), and $B_b^{t+1}\neg\varphi$ implies $\neg B_b^{t+1}\varphi$ (axiom of rationality). $\mathsf{TRT}_{ab}^{t}(\varphi) \wedge \mathsf{DBT}_{ab}^{t+1}(\varphi)$ implies $B_b^{t+1}\varphi$. Hence, $B_b^{t+1}\varphi \wedge \neg B_b^{t+1}\varphi$. $\square$

If a rational hearer is credulous, truthful telling succeeds to deceive even if the hearer believes the contrary.

Proposition 16. *Let a and b be two agents and φ a sentence. If b is credulous and rational, then*

$$\neg\varphi \wedge B_b^{t}\neg\varphi \wedge \mathsf{TRT}_{ab}^{t}(\varphi) \models B_b^{t+1}\varphi.$$

Proof. For an interpretation $I \models \neg\varphi \wedge B_b^{t}\neg\varphi \wedge \mathsf{TRT}_{ab}^{t}(\varphi)$, $I \models U_{ab}^{t}\varphi$ implies $I \models B_b^{t+1}\varphi$ by the axiom of credibility, thereby $I \models \neg B_b^{t+1}\neg\varphi$ by the axiom of rationality. In this case, the axioms of inertia are not applied, and $I \models B_b^{t}\neg\varphi$ does not imply $I \models B_b^{t+1}\neg\varphi$. Then the result holds by Proposition 12. $\square$

DBT will not happen if a rational and reflective hearer believes that a (rational) speaker is lying/bluffing.

Proposition 17. *Let a and b be two agents and φ a sentence. Suppose that a hearer b is rational and reflective.*

- $\mathsf{TRT}^t_{ab}(\varphi) \wedge B^{t+1}_b(\mathsf{LIE}^t_{ab}(\varphi)) \models \bot$ *if b believes that a is rational.*
- $\mathsf{TRT}^t_{ab}(\varphi) \wedge B^{t+1}_b(\mathsf{BLUF}^t_{ab}(\varphi)) \models \bot.$

Proof. $U^t_{ab}\varphi$ in $\mathsf{TRT}^t_{ab}(\varphi)$ implies $B^{t+1}_b B^t_a \varphi$ by the axiom of reflection. $B^{t+1}_b(\mathsf{LIE}^t_{ab}(\varphi))$ implies $B^{t+1}_b B^t_a \neg\varphi$, and b's believing a's rationality implies $B^{t+1}_b \neg B^t_a \varphi$. Then, $B^{t+1}_b B^t_a \varphi \wedge B^{t+1}_b \neg B^t_a \varphi \equiv B^{t+1}_b \bot$ (axioms of belief). Also, $B^{t+1}_b(\mathsf{BLUF}^t_{ab}(\varphi))$ implies $B^{t+1}_b \neg B^t_a \varphi$. Then, $B^{t+1}_b B^t_a \varphi \wedge B^{t+1}_b \neg B^t_a \varphi \equiv B^{t+1}_b \bot$. This is impossible, since b is rational. □

3.4 Deception by Omission

Sometimes deception is done by *withholding information*. For instance, suppose a person who is selling a used car that has some problem in its engine. If he/she sells the car without informing a customer of the problem, it is deception by withholding information [3]. It is also called *deception by omission*, which is contrasted with *deception by commission* that involves an act of providing information [5].

Definition 7 (withholding information). Let a and b be two agents and φ a sentence. Then *withholding information* (WI) is defined as

$$\mathsf{WI}^t_{ab}(\varphi) \overset{def}{=} B^t_a \varphi \wedge \neg U^t_{ab}\varphi. \tag{8}$$

Deception by omission is then defined as follows.

Definition 8 (deception by omission). Let a and b be two agents and φ a sentence. Then *deception by omission* (DBO) is defined as

$$\mathsf{DBO}^{t+1}_{ab}(\varphi) \overset{def}{=} \varphi \wedge (\mathsf{WI}^t_{ab}(\varphi) \Rightarrow \neg B^{t+1}_b \varphi). \tag{9}$$

By (9) deception by omission happens when a speaker believes a true fact while provides no information of it. As a result, a hearer disbelieves the fact. $\mathsf{DBO}^{t+1}_{ab}(\varphi)$ is often written as $\mathsf{DBO}_{ab}(\varphi)$ if time is unimportant in the context.

Proposition 18. *Let a and b be two agents.*

- $\mathsf{DBO}^{t+1}_{ab}(\bot) \models \bot.$
- $\mathsf{WI}^t_{ab}(\top) \wedge \mathsf{DBO}^{t+1}_{ab}(\top) \models \bot.$

Proof. By definition, $\mathsf{DBO}^{t+1}_{ab}(\bot)$ has no model. When $\varphi \equiv \top$, the effect of (9) is $\neg B^{t+1}_b \top$. However, $\neg B^{t+1}_b \top$ does not happen by the axiom of truth. □

$\mathsf{DBO}^{t+1}_{ab}(\varphi)$ fails if a hearer is a rational agent who believes φ at t.

Proposition 19. *Let a and b be two agents and φ a sentence. If b is rational, then*

$$B_b^t \varphi \wedge WI_{ab}^t(\varphi) \wedge DBO_{ab}^{t+1}(\varphi) \models \perp.$$

Proof. $B_b^t \varphi$ implies $B_b^{t+1} \varphi$ by the axioms of inertia, while $WI_{ab}^t(\varphi) \wedge DBO_{ab}^{t+1}(\varphi)$ implies $\neg B_b^{t+1} \varphi$. Hence, $B_b^{t+1} \varphi \wedge \neg B_b^{t+1} \varphi$, and the result holds.   □

One may argue that it would not be appropriate to regard (9) as deception. It happens that a person *a* does not tell his/her belief φ to another person *b*, and even if it results in *b*'s ignorance of the true sentence φ it is not called deception. Deception by omission is usually accompanied with an intention of concealing. Then we argue deception accompanied with an intention in the next section.

4   Various Aspects of Deception

4.1   Intentional Deception

Deception is often distinguished between *intentional deception* and *unintentional* one [5].[6] DBL, DBB, DBT and DBO in Sect. 3 represent unintentional deception, that is, a speaker does not necessarily intend to deceive a hearer. In $DBL_{ab}(\varphi)$, a speaker *a* lies a believed-false sentence φ to a hearer *b*, while the speaker may not believe that lying will result in the hearer's believing the false sentence φ. For instance, when a speaker says something manifestly false as a joke, he/she does not expect a hearer to believe it. In $DBT_{ab}(\varphi)$, a speaker tells his/her belief to a hearer, so he/she would not expect it to result in deceiving. To formulate a speaker's intention to deceive, four types of deception are respectively modified as follows.

Definition 9 (intentional deception). Let *a* and *b* be two agents and φ, ψ sentences. Then, *intentional deception by lying* (I-DBL), *intentional deception by bluffing* (I-DBB), *intentional deception by truthful telling* (I-DBT), and *intentional deception by omission* (I-DBO) are respectively defined as follows.

$$I\text{-}DBL_{ab}^{t+1}(\varphi) \overset{def}{=} \neg\varphi \wedge (LIE_{ab}^t(\varphi) \wedge B_a^t B_b^{t+1} \varphi \Rightarrow B_b^{t+1} \varphi)$$

$$I\text{-}DBB_{ab}^{t+1}(\varphi) \overset{def}{=} \neg\varphi \wedge (BLUF_{ab}^t(\varphi) \wedge B_a^t B_b^{t+1} \varphi \Rightarrow B_b^{t+1} \varphi)$$

$$I\text{-}DBT_{ab}^{t+1}(\varphi, \psi) \overset{def}{=} \neg\psi \wedge (TRT_{ab}^t(\varphi) \wedge B_a^t(B_b^{t+1}\varphi \supset B_b^{t+1}\psi) \wedge B_a^t \neg\psi \Rightarrow B_b^{t+1}\psi)$$

$$I\text{-}DBO_{ab}^{t+1}(\varphi) \overset{def}{=} \varphi \wedge (WI_{ab}^t(\varphi) \wedge B_a^t \neg B_b^t \varphi \Rightarrow \neg B_b^{t+1}\varphi)$$

As before, $I\text{-}DBL_{ab}^{t+1}(\varphi)$ (resp. $I\text{-}DBB_{ab}^{t+1}(\varphi)$, $I\text{-}DBT_{ab}^{t+1}(\varphi, \psi)$, and $I\text{-}DBO_{ab}^{t+1}(\varphi)$) is often written as $I\text{-}DBL_{ab}(\varphi)$ (resp. $I\text{-}DBB_{ab}(\varphi)$, $I\text{-}DBT_{ab}(\varphi, \psi)$, and $I\text{-}DBO_{ab}(\varphi)$) if time is unimportant in the context.

---

[6] The meaning of the term "intentional deception" is different from "attempted deception" in Fig. 1. Intentional deception is a type of deception that involves the success of deceiving, while this is not always the case in attempted deception.

In I-DBL and I-DBB, the additional formula $B_a^t B_b^{t+1} \varphi$ in the cause says that a speaker a believes that a hearer b will believe the false sentence φ in the next time step. With this belief a utters φ to b at t, which we consider that a has an intention to deceive b. In I-DBT, on the other hand, a speaker a truthfully tells φ while a believes that a hearer b's believing φ leads to b's believing another sentence ψ in the next time step. Moreover, a believes the falsity of ψ and it is in fact false, which causes b's believing ψ. We call it intentional deception by truthful-telling because a expects that b's believing a believed-false sentence. In I-DBO, a speaker a withholds φ while believing b's ignorance of φ, which causes b's disbelieving φ (or prevents b from believing φ) in the next time step. In this case, we consider that a has an intention to conceal φ from b and call it intentional deception by omission.

Note that we do not introduce an additional predicate such as I_a to represent intention. Instead, we represent intention of a speaker by encoding a fact that a speaker recognizes the effect of his/her deceptive act on the hearer. Since intentional deception introduces additional causes to unintentional one, formal properties addressed in Sect. 3 hold for intentional deception as well (except DBT). When the distinction between intentional and unintentional DBL (resp. DBB, DBT, or DBO) is unimportant, we write as (I-)DBL (resp. (I-)DBB, (I-)DBT or (I-)DBO).

For a rational speaker DBT can be intentional only if a hearer comes to believe a false sentence that is *different* from the sentence of utterance.

Proposition 20. *Let a and b be two agents and φ a sentence. If a is rational, then*

$$\text{I-DBT}_{ab}(\varphi, \varphi) \models \bot.$$

Proof. $\text{TRT}_{ab}^t(\varphi)$ involves $B_a \varphi$ while I-DBT$_{ab}(\varphi, \varphi)$ contains $B_a \neg \varphi$ in its cause. Then $B_a \varphi \wedge B_a \neg \varphi \equiv B_a \bot$, which violates the axiom of rationality.   □

Compared to others, I-DBT generally requires advanced techniques for a speaker because a deceiver is requested to select a sentence to be uttered that is different from the false fact which the deceiver wants a hearer to believe. The situation captures some feature of deception that "the deceiver takes a more circuitous route to his success, where lying is an easier and more certain way to mislead" [1, p. 440]. According to studies in psychology, children lie by four years or earlier, mainly for avoiding punishment [10]. Very young children do not have advanced techniques of deception, then most deception by them is of the type (I-)DBL$_{ab}(\varphi)$ or (I-)DBB$_{ab}(\varphi)$ or (I-)DBO$_{ab}(\varphi)$ that is the most simple form of deception.

4.2 Indirect Deception

Suppose that an agent a lies to another agent b on a false sentence φ. Then b, who believes φ, truthfully tells φ to another agent c, which results in c's believing the false sentence φ. In this case, is a deceiving c as well as b?

Example 7. John, who visits a clinic for a medical check-up, is diagnosed as having a serious cancer. A doctor does not want to discourage him and lies to John that he is normal. John has no symptom giving him no reason to believe his cancer, and he told his wife that the result of a medical test is normal. In this scenario, a doctor intentionally deceives John by lying and John unintentionally deceives his wife by truthful telling.

The situation of Example 7 is represented in our formulation as: $\text{I-DBL}_{ab}^{t+1}(\varphi) \wedge \text{DBT}_{bc}^{t+2}(\varphi)$ where $a =$ doctor, $b =$ John, $c =$ wife, and $\varphi =$ normal. In this case, we consider that a doctor indirectly deceives John's wife. Generally, acts of deceiving produce indirect deception as follows.

Definition 10 (indirect deception). Let a, b and c be three agents and φ, ψ sentences. Then *indirect deception by lying* (IN-DBL), *indirect deception by bluffing* (IN-DBB), *indirect deception by truthful telling* (IN-DBT), and *indirect deception by omission* (IN-DBO) are defined as follows:

$$\text{IN-DBL}_{ac}(\varphi) \stackrel{def}{=} (\text{I-})\text{DBL}_{ab}^{t+1}(\varphi) \wedge \text{DBT}_{bc}^{t+2}(\varphi).$$

$$\text{IN-DBB}_{ac}(\varphi) \stackrel{def}{=} (\text{I-})\text{DBB}_{ab}^{t+1}(\varphi) \wedge \text{DBT}_{bc}^{t+2}(\varphi).$$

$$\text{IN-DBT}_{ac}(\varphi) \stackrel{def}{=} \text{DBT}_{ab}^{t+1}(\varphi) \wedge \text{DBT}_{bc}^{t+2}(\varphi).$$

$$\text{IN-DBO}_{ac}(\varphi) \stackrel{def}{=} (\text{I-})\text{DBO}_{ab}^{t+1}(\varphi) \wedge \neg U_{bc}^{t+1}\varphi \Rightarrow \neg B_c^{t+2}\varphi.$$

$$\text{IN-I-DBT}_{ac}(\varphi, \psi) \stackrel{def}{=} \text{I-DBT}_{ab}^{t+1}(\varphi, \psi) \wedge \text{DBT}_{bc}^{t+2}(\psi).$$

In $\text{IN-DBL}_{ac}(\varphi)$, a's lying on a sentence φ results in b's believing a false sentence φ, and then b's truthful telling on φ results in c's believing φ. $\text{IN-DBB}_{ac}(\varphi)$ and $\text{IN-DBT}_{ac}(\varphi)$ represent similar situations. In $\text{IN-DBO}_{ac}(\varphi)$, a's withholding φ results in b's disbelieving a true sentence φ. Then b does not inform c of φ, which results in c's disbelieving φ. $\text{IN-I-DBT}_{ac}(\varphi, \psi)$ represents indirect DBT that accompanies intention. By definition, indirect deception IN-DBL, IN-DBB, IN-DBT and IN-I-DBT succeed iff both a's deceiving b and b's deceiving c succeed. In contrast, IN-DBO succeeds if a's deceiving b succeeds.

In each definition, an agent a may have intention to deceive b, while an agent b does not have intention to deceive c. If an agent b also has intention to deceive c, then b is actively involved in the deceptive act. As a result, a is less responsible for c's being deceived, and we do not call it indirect deception. Note also that in each definition, an agent b makes a truthful statement (or no statement in case of IN-DBO). If this is not the case, suppose that

$$(\text{I-})\text{DBL}_{ab}^{t+1}(\varphi) \wedge \text{DBL}_{bc}^{t+2}(\neg\varphi).$$

$(\text{I-})\text{DBL}_{ab}^{t+1}(\varphi)$ causes $B_b^{t+1}\varphi$, then b lies to c on the contrary $\neg\varphi$. In this case, $(\text{I-})\text{DBL}_{ab}^{t+1}(\varphi)$ requires $\neg\varphi$ in the precondition, while $\text{DBL}_{bc}^{t+2}(\neg\varphi)$ requires φ, which is impossible.

Generally, indirect deception could be chained like

$$(\text{I-})\text{DBL}_{ab}^{t+1}(\varphi) \wedge \text{DBT}_{bc}^{t+2}(\varphi) \wedge \text{DBT}_{cd}^{t+3}(\varphi) \wedge \cdots$$

Such a situation happens when retweeting fake information on social media.

4.3   Self-deception

Self-deception is an act of deceiving the self. Due to its paradoxical nature, self-deception has been controversial in philosophy and psychology [8,9,19,30]. It is said that self-deception involves a person holding contradictory beliefs $B_a\bot$, or believing and disbelieving the same sentence at the same time $B_a\varphi \wedge \neg B_a\varphi$. In each case, it violates the classical principle of consistency that rational agents are assumed to follow.[7] In this section, we characterize self-deception in our formulation.

Definition 11 (self-deception). Let a be an agent and φ, ψ sentences. Then, $(\text{I-})\text{DBL}_{aa}(\varphi)$, $(\text{I-})\text{DBB}_{aa}(\varphi)$, $\text{DBT}_{aa}(\varphi)$, $\text{I-DBT}_{aa}(\varphi, \psi)$, and $(\text{I-})\text{DBO}_{aa}(\varphi)$ are called *self-deception*.

As such, a speaker and a hearer are identical in self-deception. Consequently, conflict may arise between belief as a speaker and belief as a hearer.

Proposition 21. *Let a be an agent and φ a sentence. Then,*

$$\text{LIE}_{aa}^{t}(\varphi) \wedge \text{DBL}_{aa}^{t+1}(\varphi) \models B_a^{t+1} \bot.$$

Proof. By definition, $\text{LIE}_{aa}^{t}(\varphi)$ implies $B_a^t \neg\varphi$ which implies $B_a^{t+1}\neg\varphi$ by the axioms of inertia. On the other hand, $\text{DBL}_{aa}^{t+1}(\varphi)$ implies $B_a^{t+1}\varphi$. Hence, $B_a^{t+1}\neg\varphi \wedge B_a^{t+1}\varphi \equiv B_a^{t+1}\bot$. $\square$

Proposition 21 shows that $\text{DBL}_{aa}^{t+1}(\varphi)$ involves a mental state of an agent who has contradictory belief wrt a false fact φ. This is possible only when the agent is irrational.[8] On the other hand, if a rational agent is credulous, self-deception does not involve contradictory belief.

Proposition 22. *Let a be an agent and φ a sentence. If a is credulous and rational, then*

$$\text{LIE}_{aa}^{t}(\varphi) \wedge \text{DBL}_{aa}^{t+1}(\varphi) \not\models B_a^{t+1} \bot.$$

Proof. If a is credulous, $U_{aa}^t\varphi$ implies $B_a^{t+1}\varphi$ by the axiom of credibility. As a is rational, $B_a^{t+1}\varphi$ implies $\neg B_a^{t+1}\neg\varphi$ by the axiom of rationality. Then the axioms of inertia do not produce $B_a^{t+1}\neg\varphi$ from $B_a^t\neg\varphi$. Hence, $B_a^{t+1}\bot$ is not entailed. $\square$

Proposition 22 shows that a credulous agent revises its belief from $B_a^t\neg\varphi$ to $B_a^{t+1}\varphi$. As a result, contradictory belief is not produced. Propositions 21 and 22 are directly extended to $\text{I-DBL}_{aa}^{t+1}(\varphi)$. Next, suppose that an agent self-deceives by bluffing.

$$\text{BLUF}_{aa}^{t}(\varphi) \wedge \text{DBB}_{aa}^{t+1}(\varphi) \models \neg B_a^t\varphi \wedge B_a^{t+1}\varphi.$$

Thus, $\text{BLUF}_{aa}^{t}(\varphi) \wedge \text{DBB}_{aa}^{t+1}(\varphi)$ implies $B_a^{t+1}\varphi$ then the axioms of inertia do not imply $\neg B_a^{t+1}\varphi$ from $\neg B_a^t\varphi$. So a does not have contradictory belief as a result of $\text{DBB}_{aa}(\varphi)$. In case of self-deception by omission, it holds that

$$\text{WI}_{aa}^{t}(\varphi) \wedge \text{DBO}_{aa}^{t+1}(\varphi) \models B_a^t\varphi \wedge \neg B_a^{t+1}\varphi.$$

An agent a believes a true sentence φ at t while he/she does not refer to it. Then a does not believe it in the next time step. The situation represents that a person, who believes something true but does not refer to it, will *forget* it. It is interesting to observe that the

---

[7] "In short, self-deception involves an inner conflict, perhaps the existence of contradiction" [9, p. 588].

[8] Jones [17] characterizes a group of "self-deception positions" consistently using KD as the logic of belief.

effects of $DBB_{aa}(\varphi)$ and $DBO_{aa}(\varphi)$ are symmetric. In case of $DBB_{aa}(\varphi)$, a disbelieves φ at t but believes it at $t+1$; in case of $DBO_{aa}(\varphi)$, on the other hand, a believes φ at t but disbelieves it at $t+1$.

$DBT_{aa}(\varphi)$ does not involve inconsistency by definition, while inconsistency arises if it is accompanied by intention. This is because $I\text{-}DBT_{aa}^{t+1}(\varphi, \psi)$ has $B_a^t \neg \psi$ in its cause and $B_a^{t+1} \psi$ in its effect. Since $B_a^t \neg \psi$ implies $B_a^{t+1} \neg \psi$ by the axioms of inertia, a will have the contradictory belief $B_a^{t+1} \bot$. In contrast, $I\text{-}DBB_{aa}(\varphi)$ and $I\text{-}DBO_{aa}(\varphi)$ do not involve inconsistency.

When self-deception implies $B_a^{t+1} \bot$, a rational agent cannot deceive oneself. On the other hand, contradiction does not arise if the axioms of inertia are not assumed. McLaughlin [20] argues that one can intentionally deceive oneself by losing relevant disbelief by the time one is to be taken in by the deceitful act. The following scenario is a modification of the "appointment example" of [20, p. 31].[9]

Example 8. There is a meeting three months ahead, say, on March 31. Mary is a member of the meeting but she is unwilling to attend it. She then deliberately recorded the wrong date, say, April 1st, for the meeting in her online calendar. Mary is very busy and has completely forgotten the actual date of the meeting. On April 1st, her online assistant informs her of the meeting, and she realizes that she missed the meeting.

Indirect self-deception is represented by putting $a = c$ in Definition 10. The situation of Example 8 is then represented by IN-DBL as

$$IN\text{-}DBL_{aa}(\varphi) = I\text{-}DBL_{ab}^{t+1}(\varphi) \wedge DBT_{ba}^{t+2}(\varphi)$$

where $a = $ Mary, $b = $ online assistant, and $\varphi = $ "Meeting on April 1st". It holds that

$$LIE_{ab}^t(\varphi) \wedge B_a^t B_b^{t+1} \varphi \wedge I\text{-}DBL_{ab}^{t+1}(\varphi) \wedge TRT_{ba}^{t+1}(\varphi) \wedge DBT_{ba}^{t+2}(\varphi) \models B_a^{t+2} \neg \varphi \wedge B_a^{t+2} \varphi.$$

In the absence of the axioms of inertia, however, $B_a^{t+2} \neg \varphi$ is not entailed, so $IN\text{-}DBL_{aa}(\varphi)$ succeeds. As observed in this subsection, *self-deception does not always involve contradictory belief.* One can deceive the self using (I-)DBB, (I-)DBO or DBT. Moreover, if one does not retain his/her own belief over time, one can deceive himself/herself by IN-DBL without introducing contradictory belief. To the best of our knowledge, this is a new finding that has not yet been formally reported in the literature.

5   Related Work

There are some studies attempting to formulate deception using modal logic. Firozabadi *et al.* [12] formulate deception using a modal logic of action. According to their definition, an action of an agent is considered deceptive if he/she either does not have a belief about the truth value of some proposition but makes another agent believe that the proposition is true or false, or he/she believes that the proposition is true/false but makes another agent believe the opposite. These two cases are formally represented as: $\neg B_a \varphi \wedge E_a B_b \varphi$ or $B_a \neg \varphi \wedge E_a B_b \varphi$ where $E_a \psi$ means "an agent a brings about that ψ". Their formulation represents the result of deceptive action but does not represent which

---

[9] McLaughlin calls it "self-induced deception".

type of (speech) acts bring about false belief on a hearer. O'Neill [21] formulates deception using a modal logic of intentional communication. According to his definition, deception happens when a intends b to believe something that a believes to be false, and b believes it. The situation is formally represented as: $Dec_{ab}\,\varphi := I_a B_b \varphi \wedge B_a \neg \varphi \wedge B_b \varphi$. Attempted deception is defined by removing the conjunct $B_b \varphi$ in $Dec_{ab}\,\varphi$. $Dec_{ab}\,\varphi$ does not represent that b comes to have a false belief φ as a result of an action by a. Thus, a deceives b when b believes φ without any action of a. The problem comes from the fact that their logic has no mechanism of representing an action and its effect. Baltag and Smets [2] introduce a logic of conditional doxastic actions. $Lie_a(\varphi)$ represents an action in which an agent a publicly lies that she knows φ while in fact she does not know it. $True_a(\varphi)$ represents an action in which a makes a public truthful announcement that she knows φ. They have preconditions $\neg K_a \varphi$ and $K_a \varphi$, respectively. If a hearer already knows that φ is false, the action $Lie_a(\varphi)$ does not succeed. Hence, it does not allow a hearer's belief revision. The precondition $\neg K_a \varphi$ of $Lie_a(\varphi)$ represents the ignorance of φ which is not considered lying but bluffing in this paper. They argue deception by lying but do not distinguish it from deception without lying.

Jones [17] analyzes self-deception in the form of the Montaigne-family (e.g. $\neg B_a \varphi \wedge B_a B_a \varphi$) and concludes that self-deception cannot be represented in the logic of belief KD45 in a consistent manner. da Costa and French [8] formulates the inconsistent aspects of self-deception using *paraconsistent doxastic logic*. Those studies, as well as most philosophical studies, view self-deception as a state of mind having contradictory or inconsistent belief and argue how to resolve it. In contrast, we capture self-deception as an instance of deception in which a speaker and a hearer are identical. It is formulated not as a static belief state of an agent but as an effect of a cause in the belief state. In this setting we show that self-deception does not always involve contradiction.

Van Ditmarsch *et al.* [32,33] study dynamic aspects of lying and bluffing using dynamic epistemic logic. It provides logics for different types of agents and investigates how the belief of an agent is affected by (un)truthful announcements. In their study, truthful announcements are not used for misleading hearers. Sarkadi *et al.* [22,27] model deceptive agents using a BDI-like architecture and realize it in an agent-oriented programming language. The proposed model employs a *theory of mind* to analyze deceptive interactions among agents. The language has rich vocabularies to represent mental states of agents as well as reasoning mechanisms such as default reasoning and backward induction. The goal of their study is building a computational model for deceptive agents and implementing it in multi-agent environments.

Sakama *et al.* [24] formulate deception in which a speaker makes a truthful statement expecting that a hearer will misuse it to draw a wrong conclusion. It is similar to intentional deception by truthful telling in this paper, while it does not represent the *effect* of a deceptive act on a hearer's side. In this sense, deception formulated in [24] corresponds to attempted deception in this paper. Sakama and Caminada [25] provide a logical account of different categories of deception that were given by [5]. They use a modal logic of action and belief developed by [23], which is different from our current formulation. Moreover, the study does not distinguish deception by lying and deception without lying, as done in this paper. Sakama *et al.* [26] study logical account of lies, bullshit, and withholding information, while their use in deception is not formally handled.

6   Concluding Remarks

This paper introduced a formal account of deception using an epistemic causal logic that can express both an act of deceiving and its effect on hearers' belief. We formulated different types of deception and argued their semantic properties. The current study focuses on the declarative aspect of deception. From the computational perspective, a causal rule of the form: $\ell_1 \wedge \cdots \wedge \ell_n \Rightarrow \ell_0$, where ℓ_i is a literal, is translated into a logic programming rule: $\ell_0 \leftarrow not\ \overline{\ell_1}, \ldots, not\ \overline{\ell_n}$ under the answer set semantics, where not is negation as failure and $\overline{\ell_i}$ is the literal complementary to ℓ_i [14]. Since the causal theory used in this paper consists of rules of this form, deception introduced in this paper could be implemented using logic programming.

The framework introduced in this paper is simple and has room for further extension. There is a situation in which a speaker simulates a conclusion that a hearer is likely to reach based on information the speaker provides and inference the hearer could execute. For instance, intentional deception by lying I-DBL$_{ab}^{t+1}(\varphi)$ in Sect. 4.1 is extended to $\neg\psi \wedge (\text{LIE}_{ab}^{t}(\varphi) \wedge B_a^t B_b^t(\varphi \supset \psi) \wedge B_a^t \neg\psi \Rightarrow B_b^{t+1}\psi)$, where a speaker a simulates modus ponens executed by a hearer b and lying on φ brings about hearer's believing the false fact ψ. As such, the current framework is extended to handle more complicated cases by taking *a theory of mind* into consideration. Those extensions are left for future study.

References

1. Adler, J.E.: Lying, deceiving, or falsely implicating. J. Philos. **94**, 435–452 (1997)
2. Baltag, A., Smets, S.: The logic of conditional doxastic actions. In: Apt, K.R., van Rooij, R. (eds.) New Perspectives on Games and Interaction. Texts in Logic and Games, vol. 4, pp. 9–31. Amsterdam University Press (2008)
3. Carson, T.L.: Lying and Deception: Theory and Practice. Oxford University Press, Oxford (2010)
4. Castelfranchi, C.: Artificial liars: why computers will (necessarily) deceive us and each other? Ethics Inf. Technol. **2**, 113–119 (2000)
5. Chisholm, R.M., Feehan, T.D.: The intent to deceive. J. Philos. **74**, 143–159 (1977)
6. Chiluwa, I.E., Samoilenko, S.A. (eds.).: Handbook of Research on Deception, Fake News, and Misinformation Online. Information Science Reference/IGI Global (2019). https://doi.org/10.4018/978-1-5225-8535-0
7. Clark, M.: Mendacity and deception: uses and abuses of common ground. In: AAAI Fall Symposium, FS-11-02. AAAI Press (2011)
8. da Costa, N.C.A., French, S.: Belief, contradiction and the logic of self-deception. Am. Philos. Q. **27**, 179–197 (1990)
9. Demos, R.: Lying to oneself. J. Philos. **57**, 588–595 (1960)
10. Ekman, P.: Why Kids Lie: How Parents Can Encourage Truthfulness. Scribner (1989)
11. Ettinger, D., Jehiel, P.: A theory of deception. Am. Econ. J.: Microecon. **2**, 1–20 (2010)
12. Firozabadi, B.S., Tan, Y.H., Lee, R.M.: Formal definitions of fraud. In: McNamara, P., Prakken, H. (eds.) Norms, Logics and Information Systems: New Studies in Deontic Logic and Computer Science, pp. 275–288. IOS Press (1999)
13. Frankfurt, H.G.: On Bullshit. Princeton University Press, Princeton (2005)
14. Giunchiglia, E., Lee, J., Lifschitz, V., McCain, N., Turner, H.: Nonmonotonic causal theories. Artif. Intell. **153**, 49–104 (2004)

15. Hespanha, J.P., Ateskan, Y.S., Kizilocak, H.: Deception in non-cooperative games with partial information. In: Proceedings of 2nd DARPA-JFACC Symposium on Advances in Enterprise Control (2000)

16. Isaac, A., Bridewell, W.: White lies on silver tongues: why robots need to deceive (and how). In: Robot Ethics 2.0: From Autonomous Cars to Artificial Intelligence, Chap. 11. Oxford University Press (2017)

17. Jones, A.J.I.: On the logic of self-deception. South Am. J. Log. **1**, 387–400 (2015)

18. Mahon, J.E.: A definition of deceiving. J. Appl. Philos. **21**, 181–194 (2007)

19. McLaughlin, B.P., Rorty, A.O. (eds.): Perspectives on Self-Deception. University of California Press (1988)

20. McLaughlin, B.P.: Exploring the possibility of self-deception in belief. In: [19], pp. 29–62 (1988)

21. O'Neill, B.: A formal system for understanding lies and deceit. In: Jerusalem Conference on Biblical Economics (2003)

22. Panisson, A.R., Sarkadi, S., Mcburney, P., Parsons, S., Bordini, R.H.: Lies, bullshit, and deception in agent-oriented programming languages. In: Proceedings of 20th International Trust Workshop, pp. 50–61 (2018)

23. Pörn, I.: On the nature of social order. In Fenstad, J.E., et al. (eds.) Logic, Methodology, and Philosophy of Science, VIII. Elsevier (1989)

24. Sakama, C., Caminada, M., Herzig, A.: A logical account of lying. In: Janhunen, T., Niemelä, I. (eds.) JELIA 2010. LNCS (LNAI), vol. 6341, pp. 286–299. Springer, Heidelberg (2010). https://doi.org/10.1007/978-3-642-15675-5_25

25. Sakama, C., Caminada, M.: The many faces of deception. Thirty Years of Nonmonotonic Reasoning (NonMon@30), Lexington, KY, USA (2010)

26. Sakama, C., Caminada, M., Herzig, A.: A formal account of dishonesty. Log. J. IGPL **23**, 259–294 (2015)

27. Sarkadi, S., Panisson, A.R., Bordini, R.H., Mcburney, P., Parsons, S., Chapman, M.: Modelling deception using theory of mind in multi-agent systems. AI Commun. **32**(3), 1–16 (2019)

28. Shim, J., Arkin, R.C.: Biologically-inspired deceptive behavior for a robot. In: Ziemke, T., Balkenius, C., Hallam, J. (eds.) SAB 2012. LNCS (LNAI), vol. 7426, pp. 401–411. Springer, Heidelberg (2012). https://doi.org/10.1007/978-3-642-33093-3_40

29. Staab, E., Caminada, M.: On the profitability of incompetence. In: Bosse, T., Geller, A., Jonker, C.M. (eds.) MABS 2010. LNCS (LNAI), vol. 6532, pp. 76–92. Springer, Heidelberg (2011). https://doi.org/10.1007/978-3-642-18345-4_6

30. Trivers, R.: The Folly of Fools: The Logic of Deceit and Self-Deception in Human Life. Basic Books (2011)

31. Turing, A.M.: Computing machinery and intelligence. Mind **59**, 433–460 (1950)

32. van Ditmarsch, H., van Eijck, J., Sietsma, F., Wang, Y.: On the logic of lying. In: van Eijck, J., Verbrugge, R. (eds.) Games, Actions and Social Software. LNCS, vol. 7010, pp. 41–72. Springer, Heidelberg (2012). https://doi.org/10.1007/978-3-642-29326-9_4

33. van Ditmarsch, H.: Dynamics of lying. Synthese **191**, 745–777 (2014)

34. Vincent, J.M., Castelfranchi, C.: On the art of deception: how to lie while saying the truth. In: Parret, H., Sbisa, M., Verschueren, J. (eds.) Possibilities and Limitations of Pragmatics, pp. 749–777. J. Benjamins (1981)

35. Wagner, A.R., Arkin, R.C.: Acting deceptively: providing robots with the capacity for deception. J. Soc. Robot. **3**, 5–26 (2011)

36. Zlotkin, G., Rosenschein, J. S.: Incomplete information and deception in multi-agent negotiation. In: Proceedings of 12th IJCAI, pp. 225–231. Morgan Kaufmann (1991)

Influencing Choices by Changing Beliefs: A Logical Theory of Influence, Persuasion, and Deception

Grégory Bonnet[1]([⊠]), Christopher Leturc[2], Emiliano Lorini[3], and Giovanni Sartor[4,5]

[1] Normandie University, UNICAEN, ENSICAEN, CNRS, GREYC, Caen Cedex, France
gregory.bonnet@unicaen.fr
[2] Institut Henri Fayol, Mines Saint-Étienne, Saint-Étienne, France
[3] CNRS-IRIT, Toulouse University, Toulouse, France
[4] EUI-Florence, Fiesole, Italy
[5] University of Bologna, Bologna, Italy

Abstract. We model persuasion, viewed as a deliberate action through which an agent (persuader) changes the beliefs of another agent's (persuadee). This notion of persuasion paves the way to express the idea of persuasive influence, namely inducing a change in the choices of the persuadee by changing her beliefs. It allows in turns to express different aspects of deception. To this end, we propose a logical framework that enables expressing actions and capabilities of agents, their mental states (desires, knowledge and beliefs), a variety of agency operators as well as the connection between mental states and choices. Those notions, once combined, enable us to capture, the notion of influence, persuasion and deception, as well as their relation.

Keywords: Agency models · Causality reasoning · Knowledge reasoning

1 Introduction

In many contexts, agents need the cooperation of others, to achieve their goals. To this end, they may influence others, namely execute actions leading others to perform further actions. Influence may result from impeding or enabling certain actions by others (removing or adding choices), but also from changing the mental states of others (removing or adding beliefs). In the first case we speak of *regimentation*, while in the second we speak of *persuasion*. In this paper, we focus on persuasion, *i.e.* on the deliberate action through which agents (persuaders) changes the beliefs of other agents (persuadees).

Persuasion in the human-machine interaction raises serious ethical and legal issues, as more and more often automated systems engage in attempts at influencing human choices through persuasive messages. Such persuasive activities may be determined by interests that are not aligned with the interests of their addressees, but are rather determined by the economic or political goals of the senders (or their principals). Automated persuaders may also be *deceivers*, *e.g.* agents which present fake information or anyway induce the persuadees into actions the latter will regret (bad economic, personal

© Springer Nature Switzerland AG 2021
S. Sarkadi et al. (Eds.): DeceptECAI 2020/DeceptAI 2021, CCIS 1296, pp. 124–141, 2021.
https://doi.org/10.1007/978-3-030-91779-1_9

or political choices). To adequately respond to this challenge, it is important to have a clear conceptual framework, that enables us to capture the different ways in which influence, persuasion and deception can be deployed, so that adequate responses to each of such ways can be developed, through human or also computational interventions. Let us precise that, as we are mainly interested in artificial agents (automated persuaders), we will consider in this article rational agents. The anthropomorphic expression (persuader, persuadee, mental state) are just shortcuts that we use for convenience.

In the AI field, persuasion and related notions have been approached from different perspectives. Following seminal work on argumentation [28], persuasion has been modelled through structured argumentation [19], abstract argumentation [6,7], probabilistic argumentation [13], possibilistic belief revision [9], abstract argumentation combined with dynamic epistemic logic [20]. Some logical approaches have addressed notions related to persuasion, such as social influence [16,24], manipulation (influence on choices) [15], lying and deception [23,27], or changing other agents' degrees of beliefs [8]. The original contribution of this work consists in providing a logical account of the way in which a persuader by changing the beliefs of the persuadee, influences the action of the latter. We aim indeed to provide a formal theory of the micro-foundations of deception, persuasion and influence, i.e., an account of the cognitive attitudes and agentive aspects that are involved in the persuasion and influence, and elucidate their relationship. For this purpose we provide a rich framework that expresses actions and capabilities of agents and their mental states (desires, knowledge and beliefs) as well as the connection between mental states and choices. In order to keep the framework simple while being expressive, we focus on a qualitative framework (such as Boolean games [26]) where agents' preferences are not presented by continuous utility functions but rather by a qualitative three-valued scale desirable/undesirable/neutral. Then We express two notions of rationality (an optimistic and a pessimistic one), several agency operators (such as the so-called 'Chellas' STIT [12], the deliberative and the rational STIT operators [16]) and different ways to influence agents' choices through belief change.

Relative to this rich background addressing partial aspects of persuasion processes, our model will be useful for better understanding and modelling the dynamics of social influence, especially those between artificial and human agents. It will also be relevant from a regulatory perspective, since it allows to pinpoint those instance in which online interactions, in virtue of their logical structure, can be viewed as detrimental to trustful and productive interaction, and thus call for normative limitations. It can also be relevant in the special cases where persuasion and deception can be of interest in social relationship to protect somebody [2]. Our contribution has the advantage of providing a comprehensive model which captures the whole persuasive process including the mental states of the persuader, his persuading action, the modified mental states of persuadee and her resulting action. The model also captures the connection between influence, regimentation and persuasion, and enables to link persuasion with game theory. This article is organized as follow. Firstly, in Sect. 1 we introduce a running example. Then we define in Sect. 2 our logical framework and, in Sect. 3, we show how this framework can express notions of optimistic and pessimistic rationality, and a variety of agency operators. We then combine those notions in Sect. 4 to express deception, persuasion, regimentation and influence, and their relationships. Finally, we apply our framework to the running example.

Running Example. John is feeling back pain, and consequently he is consulting websites that offer medical advice as well as the opportunity to purchase drugs. A message from a bot promises, for a fair price, a drug which is said to be an excellent remedy that would eliminate all pain, and can be used for any length of time without producing any dependency. This message persuades John to buy the drug and he starts taking it. However the bot has deceived John because the bot knows that the drug creates addiction, with serious health consequences. John's wife Ann, comes to know that such pills are dangerous. She then removes all pills from the closet. As a consequence John does not take the drug. This example shows two patterns of influence. The first is successful and misleading persuasion (deception) by the website, *i.e.*, successful influencing by providing false information. The second stage consists in Ann successfully influencing John through regimentation, i.e., by removing a choice option.

2   Logical Framework

In this section, we present a modal logic language which supports reasoning about (i) actions and capabilities of agents and coalitions, (ii) agents' epistemic states and desires as well as their connection with agents' choices. We first present its syntax and its semantic interpretation (Sects. 2.1 and 2.2). Then, in Sect. 2.3, we provide a sound and complete axiomatization of its set of validities.

2.1   Syntax

Assume a countable set of atomic propositions $Atm = \{p, q, \ldots\}$, a finite set of agents $Agt = \{1, \ldots, n\}$, a finite set of atomic action names $Act = \{a, b, \ldots\}$. The set Act includes the (in)action skip, *i.e.*, the action of doing nothing. We define $Prop$ to be the set of propositional formulas, that is, the set of all Boolean combinations of atomic propositions. The set of non-empty sets of agents, also called *coalitions*, is defined by $2^{Agt*} = 2^{Agt} \setminus \{\emptyset\}$. Elements of 2^{Agt*} are noted $H, J, \ldots$ A coalition H's joint action is defined to be a function $\delta_H : H \longrightarrow Act$. Coalition H's set of joint actions is noted $JAct_H$. Its elements are noted $\delta_H, \delta'_H, \ldots$ For notational convenience, we simply write $JAct$ instead of $JAct_{Agt}$ to denote the grand coalition's set of joint actions. Its elements are noted $\delta, \delta', \ldots$ Moreover, we write Act_i instead of $JAct_{\{i\}}$ to denote agent i's set of individual actions. Its elements are noted $a_i, b_i, \ldots$ We define $JAct^*$ to be the set of all finite sequences of joint actions from $JAct$. Elements of $JAct^*$ are noted $\epsilon, \epsilon', \ldots$ The empty sequence of joint actions is denoted by *nil*. Infinite sequences of joint actions are called *histories*. The set of all histories is noted $Hist$ and its elements are noted $h, h', \ldots$ Elements of $JAct^* \cup Hist$ are noted $\tau, \tau', \ldots$ For every $\tau_1, \tau_2 \in JAct^* \cup Hist$, we write $\tau_1 \sqsubseteq \tau_2$ to mean that either $\tau_1 = \tau_2$ or τ_1 is an initial subsequence of τ_2, *i.e.*, there is $\tau_3 \in JAct^* \cup Hist$ such that $\tau_2 = \tau_1; \tau_3$. The language $\mathcal{L}$ is defined by the following grammar:

$$\epsilon ::= \delta \mid \epsilon;\epsilon$$
$$\varphi ::= p \mid occ(\epsilon) \mid plaus_i \mid good_i \mid bad_i \mid neutral_i \mid \neg\varphi \mid \varphi_1 \wedge \varphi_2 \mid [\![\delta]\!]\varphi \mid \Box\varphi \mid K_i\varphi$$

where p ranges over Atm, i ranges over Agt, δ ranges over $JAct$ and ϵ ranges over $JAct^*$. The other Boolean constructions $\top$, $\bot$, $\vee$, $\rightarrow$ and $\leftrightarrow$ are defined from p, $\neg$ and $\wedge$ in the standard way. We note $\mathcal{L}^-$ the fragment of $\mathcal{L}$ without operators $[\![\delta]\!]$ defined by the following grammar:

$$\varphi ::= p \mid occ(\epsilon) \mid plaus_i \mid good_i \mid neutral_i \mid bad_i \mid \neg\varphi \mid \varphi_1 \wedge \varphi_2 \mid \Box\varphi \mid K_i\varphi$$

$\mathcal{L}$ has special atomic formulas of four different kinds. The atomic formulas $occ(\epsilon)$ represent information about occurrences of joint action sequences. The formula $occ(\epsilon)$ has to be read "the joint action sequence ϵ is going to occur".

The following abbreviations capture interesting action-related concepts. For every $H \in 2^{Agt*}$, joint action sequence $\epsilon \in JAct^*$ and joint action $\delta_H \in JAct_H$ we define:

$$choose(\epsilon,\delta_H) \overset{\text{def}}{=} \bigvee_{\substack{\delta \in JAct: \\ \forall i \in H, \delta_H(i)=\delta(i)}} occ(\epsilon;\delta)$$

$$can(\epsilon,\delta_H) \overset{\text{def}}{=} \Diamond choose(\epsilon,\delta_H)$$

$choose(\epsilon,\delta_H)$ has to be read "the joint action sequence ϵ is going to occur and will be followed by coalition H's joint action δ_H". For convenience, when $\epsilon = nil$, we write $choose(\delta_H)$ instead of $choose(nil,\delta_H)$. Formula $can(\epsilon,\delta_H)$ has to be read "coalition H can choose the joint action δ_H at the end of the joint action sequence ϵ".

The atomic formula $plaus_i$ is used to identify the histories in agent i's information set that she considers plausible. It has to be read "the current history is considered plausible by agent i". The other atomic formulas $good_i$, bad_i and $neutral_i$ are used to rank the histories that an agent envisages at a given world according to their value for the agent (*i.e.*, how much a given history promotes the satisfaction of the agent's desires). They are read, respectively, "the current history is good/bad/neutral for agent i". Let us notice it is an agent-centric point-of-view. Each $good_i$, bad_i and $neutral_i$ atoms are defined only from agent i's perspective.

$\mathcal{L}$ has three kinds of modal operators: $[\![\delta]\!]$, $\Box$ and K_i. $\Box$ is the so-called historical necessity operator. The formula $\Box\varphi$ has to be read "φ is true in all histories passing through the current moment". We define $\Diamond$ to be the dual of $\Box$, *i.e.*, $\Diamond\varphi \overset{\text{def}}{=} \neg\Box\neg\varphi$ where $\Diamond\varphi$ has to be read "φ is true in at least one history passing through the current moment". $[\![\delta]\!]$ is a dynamic operator describing the fact that if the joint action δ is performed then it will lead to a state in which a given state of affairs holds. In particular, $[\![\delta]\!]\varphi$ has to be read "if the joint action δ is performed, then φ will be true after its execution". Finally, K_i is a modal operator characterizing the concept of *ex ante* (or *choice-independent*) knowledge [4,16,22]. The formula $K_i\psi$ has to be read "agent i knows that φ is true independently from her current choice" or "agent i thinks that φ is true for any choice she could have made". The dual of the operator K_i is denoted by $\hat{K}_i$, *i.e.*, $\hat{K}_i\varphi \overset{\text{def}}{=} \neg K_i\neg\varphi$. *Ex ante* knowledge is distinguished from *ex post* knowledge. *Ex ante* knowledge characterizes an agent's knowledge assuming that no decision has yet been made by him, whereas *ex post* knowledge characterizes an agent's knowledge assuming that the agent has made his decision about which action to take, but might still be uncertain about the decisions of others. The concept of *ex post* knowledge is expressed by the following operator K_i^{post}:

$$K_i^{post}\varphi \stackrel{\text{def}}{=} \bigwedge_{a_i \in Act_i} (\text{choose}(a_i) \to K_i(\text{choose}(a_i) \to \varphi))$$

where $K_i^{post}\varphi$ has to be read "agent i knows that φ is true, given her actual choice". From the special atomic formula plaus_i and the epistemic operator K_i, we define a belief operator:

$$B_i\varphi \stackrel{\text{def}}{=} K_i(\text{plaus}_i \to \varphi)$$

The formula $B_i\varphi$ has to be read "agent i believes that φ". According to this definition, an agent believes that φ if and only if φ is true at all states in the agent's information set at which φ is true. The dual of the operator B_i is denoted by $\widehat{B}_i$, *i.e.*, $\widehat{B}_i\varphi \stackrel{\text{def}}{=} \neg B_i \neg \varphi$.

Similarly to Situation Calculus [21], we describe actions in terms of their positive and negative effect preconditions. In particular, we introduce two functions γ^+ and γ^- with domain $Agt \times Act \times Atm$ and codomain $\mathcal{L}^-$. The formula $\gamma^+(i, a, p)$ describes the *positive effect preconditions* of action a performed by agent i with respect to p, whereas $\gamma^-(i, a, p)$ describes the *negative effect preconditions* of action a performed by agent i with respect to p. Formula $\gamma^+(i, a, p)$ represents the conditions under which agent i will make p *true* by performing action a, if no other agent interferes with i's action; while $\gamma^-(i, a, p)$ represents the conditions under which i will make p *false* by performing a, if no other agent interferes with i's action. We assume that "making p true" means changing the truth value of p from false to true, whereas "making p false" means changing the truth value of p from true to false. The reason why an action's effect preconditions range over $\mathcal{L}^-$ and not over $\mathcal{L}$ is that they should be independent from the effects of the action described by dynamic formulas of type $[\![\delta]\!]\varphi$.

Example 1. Let us consider the story given in Sect. 1, and use it to illustrate the γ^+ and γ^- functions. We shall use the following vocabulary:

$$Agt = \{Ann, John, Bot\},$$
$$Act = \{take, suggest, hide, skip\},$$
$$Atm = \{has_{John,drug}, ingested_{John,drug}, addicted_{John}, pain_{John}\}$$

The actions' effect preconditions can be defined as:

$$\gamma^+(Bot, suggest, p) = p \text{ for all } p \in Atm,$$
$$\gamma^-(Bot, suggest, p) = \neg p \text{ for all } p \in Atm,$$
$$\gamma^+(John, take, ingested_{John,drug}) = has_{John,drug},$$
$$\gamma^+(i, a, ingested_{John,drug}) = \bot$$

Moreover, if $a \neq take$ or $i \neq John$, we have:

$$\gamma^-(i, a, ingested_{John,drug}) = \neg\text{choose}(take_{John})$$

Finally, for all $a \in Act$ and $i \in Agt$, we have:

$$\gamma^+(i, a, has_{John,drug}) = has_{John,drug} \wedge \neg\mathsf{choose}(hide_{Ann})$$

$$\gamma^-(Ann, hide, has_{John,drug}) = \top$$

The effect preconditions specify that the speech act of suggestion has no effect on material facts. Ingesting the drug presupposes possession of it, while not ingesting it presupposes not having taken it. Finally, John will still have the drug unless Ann hides it, while John will not have the drug if Ann hides it.

2.2 Semantics

The semantics for the language $\mathcal{L}$ is a possible world semantics with accessibility relations associated with each modal operator, with a function designating the history starting in a given world, a plausibility function and a trichotomous utility function relative to histories.

Definition 1. *A model is a tuple* $M = \langle W, \mathcal{H}, \equiv, (\mathcal{E}_i)_{i \in Agt}, \mathcal{P}, \mathcal{U}, \mathcal{V} \rangle$ *where: (i)* W *is a non-empty set of worlds, (ii)* $\mathcal{H} : W \longrightarrow Hist$ *is a history function, (iii)* $\equiv$ *and every* $\mathcal{E}_i$ *are equivalence relations on* W, *(iv)* $\mathcal{P} : W \times Agt \longrightarrow \{0, 1\}$ *is a plausibility function, (v)* $\mathcal{U} : W \times Agt \longrightarrow \{0, 1, -1\}$ *is a utility function, and (vi)* $\mathcal{V} : W \longrightarrow 2^{Atm}$ *is a valuation function.*

For each binary relation $\mathcal{R} \in \{\equiv, \mathcal{E}_1, \dots, \mathcal{E}_n\}$, we set $\mathcal{R}(w) = \{v \in W : w\mathcal{R}v\}$. As usual $p \in \mathcal{V}(w)$ means that proposition p is true at world w. $\equiv$-equivalence classes are called *moments*. If w and v belong to the same moment (*i.e.*, $w \equiv v$), then the history starting in w (*i.e.*, $\mathcal{H}(w)$) and the history starting in v (*i.e.*, $\mathcal{H}(v)$) are said to be alternative histories (*viz.*, histories starting at the same moment). The concept of moment is the one used in STIT logic [5, 12] and, more generally, in the Ockhamist theory of time [25,29]. For every world $w \in W$, $\mathcal{H}(w)$ identifies the history starting in w. For notational convenience, for all $\epsilon \in JAct^*$, $i \in Agt$, $a \in Act$ and $w \in W$, we write $\epsilon; a \sqsubseteq_i \mathcal{H}(w)$ to mean that there is $\delta \in JAct$ such that $\delta(i) = a$ and $\epsilon; \delta \sqsubseteq \mathcal{H}(w)$.

We define the actual choice function $\mathcal{C}_{act} : W \times Agt \longrightarrow Act$: for every $w \in W$, $i \in Agt$ and $a \in Act$, we have $\mathcal{C}_{act}(w, i) = a$ iff there exists $\delta \in JAct$ such that $\delta(i) = a$ and $\delta \sqsubseteq \mathcal{H}(w)$. Furthermore, we define the available choice function $\mathcal{C}_{avail} : W \times Agt \longrightarrow 2^{Act}$: for every $w \in W$, $i \in Agt$ and $a \in Act$, we have $a \in \mathcal{C}_{avail}(w, i)$ iff there exists $\delta \in JAct$ and $v \equiv (w)$ such that $\delta(i) = a$ and $\delta \sqsubseteq \mathcal{H}(v)$.

The equivalence relations $\mathcal{E}_i$ are used to interpret the epistemic operators K_i. The set $\mathcal{E}_i(w)$ is the agent i's *information set* at world w: the set of worlds that agent i envisages at w or, shortly, agent i's set of epistemic alternatives at w. As $\mathcal{E}_i$ is an equivalence relation, if $w\mathcal{E}_i v$ then agent i has the same information set at w and v. The function $\mathcal{P}$ specifies the possibility value of a history for an agent. In particular, $\mathcal{P}(w, i) = 1$ (resp. $\mathcal{P}(w, i) = 0$) means that the history starting in w is considered plausible (resp. not plausible) by agent i. We define agent i's belief set at world w, denoted by $\mathcal{B}_i(w)$, as the set of worlds in i's information set at w that i considers plausible: $\mathcal{B}_i(w) = \mathcal{E}_i(w) \cap \{v \in W : \mathcal{P}(v, i) = 1\}$.

Consequently, the complementary set $\mathcal{E}_i(w) \setminus \mathcal{B}_i(w)$ is the set of worlds that agent i envisages at w but that she does not consider plausible. Since $\mathcal{E}_i$ is an equivalence relation, the following properties for belief hold. Note that $\mathcal{B}_i \subseteq \mathcal{E}_i$ and if $w\mathcal{E}_i v$ then $\mathcal{B}_i(w) = \mathcal{B}_i(v)$, where $\mathcal{B}_i = \{(w,v) \in W \times W : v \in \mathcal{B}_i(w)\}$. Moreover, $\mathcal{B}_i$ is transitive and Euclidean. These properties correspond to the combination of belief and knowledge studied in [14].

The function $\mathcal{U}$ assigns the utility value $\mathcal{U}(w,i)$ of the history starting in w for agent i. In particular, $\mathcal{U}(w,i) = 1$, $\mathcal{U}(w,i) = -1$ and $\mathcal{U}(w,i) = 0$, mean respectively that the history starting in w is good/bad/neutral for agent i. A history is good for an agent if the agent obtains what she likes and avoids what she dislikes along it. It is bad for the agent if the agent does not avoid what she dislikes and does not obtain what she likes along it. Finally, it is neutral for the agent if either the agent does not obtain what she likes and avoids what she dislikes along it, or the agent obtains what she likes and does not avoid what she dislikes along it. Our simplified account of utility presupposes that every agent is identified with a single appetitive desire (*i.e.*, what the agent likes) and a single aversive desire (*i.e.*, what the agent dislikes).

We impose the following three constraints on models. For all $w, v \in W$, $\delta \in JAct$, $\epsilon \in JAct^*$, $i \in Agt$ and $a \in Act$:

(C1) if for all $i \in Agt$ there is $u_i \in \equiv(w)$ such that $\epsilon;\delta(i) \sqsubseteq_i \mathcal{H}(w)$, then there is $u \in\equiv(w)$ such that $\epsilon;\delta \sqsubseteq \mathcal{H}(u)$;

(C2) if there is $v \in\equiv(w)$ such that $\epsilon;a \sqsubseteq_i \mathcal{H}(v)$ then, for every $u \in \mathcal{E}_i(w)$, there is $z \in\equiv(u)$ such that $\epsilon;a \sqsubseteq_i \mathcal{H}(z)$;

(C3) if there is $v \in\equiv(w)$ such that $\epsilon;a \sqsubseteq_i \mathcal{H}(v)$, then there is $u \in \mathcal{E}_i(w)$ such that $\epsilon;a \sqsubseteq_i \mathcal{H}(u)$;

(C4) if $w \equiv v$ then $\mathcal{E}_i(w) = \mathcal{E}_i(v)$;

(C5) $\mathcal{B}_i(w) \neq \emptyset$.

According to the Constraint **C1**, if every individual action in a joint action δ can be chosen at the end of the joint action sequence ϵ, then the individual actions in δ can be chosen simultaneously at the end of ϵ. The Constraint **C1** is a variant of the assumption of *independence of agents* of STIT logic. More intuitively, this means that agents can never be deprived of choices due to the choices made by other agents. The Constraint **C2** is a basic assumption about agents' knowledge over their abilities: if an agent i can choose action a at the end of the joint action sequence ϵ, then he knows this. In other words, an agent has perfect knowledge about the actions he can choose at the end of a joint sequence. The Constraint **C3** characterizes the basic property of *ex ante* knowledge: if an agent i can choose action a at the end of joint action sequence ϵ, then there is a history that the agent considers possible in which he chooses action a at the end of the joint action sequence ϵ. In other words, for every action that an agent can choose, there is a history that the agent considers possible in which he chooses this action. According to Constraint **C4**, an agent's knowledge is moment-determinate, *i.e.*, it does not depend on the specific history at which it is evaluated. This assumption is justified by the fact that the only thing which can vary at a given moment are the agents' choices, but not the agents' ex ante epistemic states. Finally, Constraint **C5** is a normality requirement for beliefs: there should be at least a world in an agent's information set that the agent considers possible. $\mathcal{L}$-formulas are interpreted relative to a model $M = (W, \mathcal{H}, \equiv, (\mathcal{E}_i)_{i \in Agt}, \mathcal{P}, \mathcal{U}, \mathcal{V})$ and a world w in W as follows. (We omit boolean cases as they are standard.)

$$M, w \models \text{occ}(\epsilon) \iff \epsilon \sqsubseteq \mathcal{H}(w)$$
$$M, w \models \text{plaus}_i \iff \mathcal{P}(w, i) = 1$$
$$M, w \models \text{good}_i \iff \mathcal{U}(w, i) = 1$$
$$M, w \models \text{bad}_i \iff \mathcal{U}(w, i) = -1$$
$$M, w \models \text{neutral}_i \iff \mathcal{U}(w, i) = 0$$
$$M, w \models [\![\delta]\!]\varphi \iff \text{if } M, w \models \text{occ}(\delta) \text{ then } M^\delta, w \models \varphi$$
$$M, w \models \Box\varphi \iff \forall v \in W : \text{if } w \equiv v \text{ then } M, v \models \varphi$$
$$M, w \models \text{K}_i\varphi \iff \forall v \in W : \text{if } w\mathcal{E}_i v \text{ then } M, v \models \varphi$$

where model M^δ is defined according to Definition 2 below. Note that the belief operator B_i we defined in Sect. 2.1 as an abbreviation has the following interpretation: $M, w \models \text{B}_i\varphi$ if and only if $\forall v \in W : \text{if } w\mathcal{B}_i v \text{ then } M, v \models \varphi$.

Definition 2 (Update via joint action). *Let* $M = (W, \mathcal{H}, \equiv, (\mathcal{E}_i)_{i \in Agt}, \mathcal{P}, \mathcal{U}, \mathcal{V})$ *be a model. The update of* M *by joint action* δ *is the tuple:*

$$M^\delta = (W^\delta, \mathcal{H}^\delta, \equiv^\delta, (\mathcal{E}_i^\delta)_{i \in Agt}, \mathcal{P}^\delta, \mathcal{U}^\delta, \mathcal{V}^\delta)$$

where:

$$
\begin{aligned}
W^\delta &= \{w \in W : M, w \models \text{occ}(\delta)\} \\
\mathcal{H}^\delta(w) &= h \text{ if } \mathcal{H}(w) = \delta'; h \text{ for some } \delta' \in JAct \\
\equiv^\delta &= \equiv \cap (W^\delta \times W^\delta) \\
\mathcal{E}_i^\delta &= \mathcal{E}_i \cap (W^\delta \times W^\delta) \\
\mathcal{P}^\delta(w, i) &= \mathcal{P}(w, i) \text{ if } \mathcal{B}_i(w) \cap W^\delta \neq \emptyset \\
\mathcal{P}^\delta(w, i) &= 1 \text{ otherwise} \\
\mathcal{U}^\delta(w, i) &= \mathcal{U}(w, i)
\end{aligned}
$$

$$
\begin{aligned}
\mathcal{V}^\delta(w) = \Big(&\mathcal{V}(w) \setminus \{p : (\exists a \in Act, i \in Agt : \\
&\delta(i) = a \text{ and } M, w \models \gamma^-(i, a, p)) \text{ and} \\
&(\nexists b \in Act, j \in Agt : \delta(j) = b \text{ and} \\
&M, w \models \gamma^+(j, b, p))\}\Big) \cup \\
&\{p : (\exists a \in Act, i \in Agt : \delta(i) = a \text{ and} \\
&M, w \models \gamma^+(i, a, p)) \text{ and} \\
&(\nexists b \in Act, j \in Agt : \delta(j) = b \text{ and} \\
&M, w \models \gamma^-(j, b, p))\}
\end{aligned}
$$

The performance of a joint action δ modifies the physical facts via the positive effect preconditions and the negative effect preconditions, defined above (see the definition of $\mathcal{V}^\delta$). In particular, if there is an action in the joint action δ whose positive effect preconditions with respect to p hold and there is no other action in the joint action δ whose negative effect preconditions with respect to p hold, then p will be true after the occurrence of δ; if there is an action in the joint action δ whose negative effect preconditions with respect to p hold and there is no other action in the joint action δ whose positive effect preconditions with respect to p hold, then p will be false after the occurrence of δ. Besides, the occurrence of the joint action δ makes the current history advance one step forward (see the definition of $\mathcal{H}^\delta$). As to the equivalence relations $\equiv$ and $\mathcal{E}_i$ for historical necessity and *ex ante* knowledge, they are restricted to the set of worlds in which the joint action δ occurs (see the definitions of $\equiv^\delta$ and $\mathcal{E}_i^\delta$). The joint action δ does not modify the agents' utilities over histories (see the definitions of $\mathcal{U}^\delta$). Finally, as for the update of the epistemic plausibility function $\mathcal{P}$, two cases are possible. If the update removes all plausible worlds from the agent's information set, then the plausibility function is reinitialized and all worlds in the agent's information set become plausible. This is a form of drastic revision which guarantees preservation of Constraint **C5**. Otherwise, nothing changes and the agent keeps the same beliefs as before the update. As stated by the following proposition, the update via a joint action preserves the constraints on models.

Proposition 1. *If M is a model then M^δ is a model too.*

Notions of validity and satisfiability for formulas in $\mathcal{L}$ relative to models is defined in the usual way. The fact that a formula φ is valid is noted $\models \varphi$.

2.3   Axiomatization

We call **EVAL** (*Epistemic Volitional Action Logic*) the extension of propositional logic by the principles in Figs. 1, 2 and 3 and the following rule of replacement of equivalents:

$$\frac{\varphi_1 \leftrightarrow \varphi_2}{\psi \leftrightarrow \psi[\varphi_1/\varphi_2]} \tag{RE}$$

They consist in (i) a theory for the special atomic formulas, (ii) S5-principles for the epistemic and historical necessity operators, and (iii) reduction axioms which allow to eliminate all the dynamic operators $[\![\delta]\!]$ from formulas.

As the next theorem indicates, they provide an axiomatics.

Theorem 1. *The logic **EVAL** is sound and complete for the class of models of Definition 1.*

Regarding complexity, we believe that checking satisfiability of formulas in the fragment $\mathcal{L}^-$ can be polynomially reduced to satisfiability checking for star-free PDL with converse of atomic programs that, by adapting the technique in [10], can be proved to be in PSPACE. Given the polysize satisfiability preserving reduction from $\mathcal{L}$-formulas to $\mathcal{L}^-$-formulas based on the reduction axioms of Proposition 3, this guarantees that checking satisfiability of formulas in $\mathcal{L}$ is also in PSPACE. As for PSPACE-hardness, it follows from the fact that **EVAL** is a conservative extension of multi-agent epistemic logic $S5^n$, whose satisfiability problem is known to be PSPACE-hard [11]. Future work will be devoted to prove this conjecture. Nevertheless, it is of interest to have a decidable logic to deal with artificial agents.

$$\mathsf{occ}(\epsilon) \to \bigvee_{\delta \in JAct} \mathsf{occ}(\epsilon;\delta) \qquad \textbf{(OneJAct)}$$

$$\mathsf{occ}(nil) \qquad \textbf{(EmptySeq)}$$

$$\mathsf{occ}(\epsilon;\delta) \to \neg\mathsf{occ}(\epsilon;\delta') \text{ if } \delta \neq \delta' \qquad \textbf{(UniqueJAct)}$$

$$\mathsf{occ}(\epsilon) \to \mathsf{occ}(\epsilon') \text{ if } \epsilon' \sqsubseteq \epsilon \qquad \textbf{(SubSeqJAct)}$$

$$\mathsf{good}_i \vee \mathsf{neutral}_i \vee \mathsf{bad}_i \qquad \textbf{(ComplUtil)}$$

$$x_i \to \neg y_i \text{ if } x, y \in \{\mathsf{good}, \mathsf{neutral}, \mathsf{bad}\} \text{ and } x \neq y \qquad \textbf{(UniqueUtil)}$$

$$\Big(\bigwedge_{i \in Agt} \Diamond\mathsf{choose}(\epsilon,a_i) \Big) \to \Diamond\mathsf{choose}(\epsilon,\delta_{Agt}) \qquad \textbf{(IndepAgt)}$$

$$\mathsf{can}(\epsilon,a_i) \to \mathsf{K}_i\mathsf{can}(\epsilon,a_i) \qquad \textbf{(KnowCan)}$$

$$\mathsf{can}(\epsilon,a_i) \to \widehat{\mathsf{K}}_i\mathsf{choose}(\epsilon,a_i) \qquad \textbf{(ExAnteKnow)}$$

$$\mathsf{K}_i\varphi \to \Box\mathsf{K}_i\varphi \qquad \textbf{(MomDetKnow)}$$

$$\widehat{\mathsf{K}}_i\mathsf{plaus}_i \qquad \textbf{(NormBel)}$$

Fig. 1. Theory for the atomic formulas

$$(\blacksquare\varphi \wedge \blacksquare(\varphi \to \psi)) \to \blacksquare\psi \ (K_\blacksquare) \qquad \blacksquare\varphi \to \varphi \ (\mathbf{T_\blacksquare})$$
$$\blacksquare\varphi \to \blacksquare\blacksquare\varphi \quad (4_\blacksquare) \qquad \neg\blacksquare\varphi \to \blacksquare\neg\blacksquare\varphi \ (5_\blacksquare)$$
$$\frac{\varphi}{\blacksquare\varphi} \quad (\mathbf{Nec_\blacksquare})$$

Fig. 2. S5-system for knowledge and historical necessity with $\blacksquare \in \{\Box\} \cup \{K_1\} \cup \ldots \cup \{K_n\}$

3 Agency and Rationality Types

We now represent agency operators and two opposite rationality types, namely, the optimistic (or risk seeking) agent Rat_i^{opt} and the pessimistic (or risk averse) agent Rat_i^{pess}:

$$\mathsf{Rat}_i^{opt} \stackrel{\text{def}}{=} \bigvee_{a_i \in Act_i} \Big(\mathsf{choose}(a_i) \wedge \bigwedge_{\substack{b_i \in Act_i: \\ b_i \neq a_i}} (\mathsf{can}(b_i) \to ((\widehat{\mathsf{B}}_i(\mathsf{neutral}_i \wedge \mathsf{choose}(b_i)) \to$$

$$\widehat{\mathsf{B}}_i((\mathsf{neutral}_i \vee \mathsf{good}_i) \wedge \mathsf{choose}(a_i))) \wedge$$

$$(\widehat{\mathsf{B}}_i(\mathsf{good}_i \wedge \mathsf{choose}(b_i)) \to \widehat{\mathsf{B}}_i(\mathsf{good}_i \wedge \mathsf{choose}(a_i)))))\Big)$$

$$\mathsf{Rat}_i^{pess} \stackrel{\text{def}}{=} \bigvee_{a_i \in Act_i} \Big(\mathsf{choose}(a_i) \wedge \bigwedge_{\substack{b_i \in Act_i: \\ b_i \neq a_i}} (\mathsf{can}(b_i) \to ((\widehat{\mathsf{B}}_i(\mathsf{neutral}_i \wedge \mathsf{choose}(a_i)) \to$$

$$\widehat{\mathsf{B}}_i((\mathsf{neutral}_i \vee \mathsf{bad}_i) \wedge \mathsf{choose}(b_i))) \wedge$$

$$(\widehat{\mathsf{B}}_i(\mathsf{bad}_i \wedge \mathsf{choose}(a_i)) \to \widehat{\mathsf{B}}_i(\mathsf{bad}_i \wedge \mathsf{choose}(b_i)))))\Big)$$

As Proposition 2 highlights, a rationally optimistic agent makes a certain choice from her set of available choices, if she believes that its best possible outcome is at least as good as the best possible outcome of the other available choices. A rationally

$$[\delta]\neg\varphi \quad\leftrightarrow (occ(\delta) \to \neg[\delta]\varphi)$$

$$[\delta](\varphi \wedge \psi) \leftrightarrow ([\delta]\varphi \wedge [\delta]\psi)$$

$$[\delta]p \quad\quad\leftrightarrow (occ(\delta) \to ((\bigvee_{i\in Agt} \gamma^+(i,\delta(i),p)\wedge$$
$$\bigwedge_{j\in Agt:j\neq i} \neg\gamma^-(j,\delta(j),p))\vee$$
$$(p \wedge \bigwedge_{i\in Agt} \neg\gamma^-(i,\delta(i),p))\vee$$
$$(p \wedge \bigvee_{i\in Agt} \gamma^+(i,\delta(i),p))))$$

$$[\delta]occ(\epsilon) \leftrightarrow (occ(\delta) \to occ(\delta;\epsilon))$$

$$[\delta]plaus_i \leftrightarrow \Big(occ(\delta) \to (B_i\neg occ(\delta)\vee$$
$$(\hat{B}_i occ(\delta) \wedge plaus_i))\Big)$$

$$[\delta]good_i \leftrightarrow (occ(\delta) \to good_i)$$

$$[\delta]neutral_i \leftrightarrow (occ(\delta) \to neutral_i)$$

$$[\delta]bad_i \leftrightarrow (occ(\delta) \to bad_i)$$

$$[\delta]\Box\varphi \leftrightarrow (occ(\delta) \to \Box(occ(\delta) \to [\delta]\varphi))$$

$$[\delta]K_i\varphi \leftrightarrow (occ(\delta) \to K_i(occ(\delta) \to [\delta]\varphi))$$

Fig. 3. Reduction axioms for the dynamic operators

pessimistic agent makes a certain choice, if she believes that its worse possible outcome is at least as good as the worse possible outcome of the other available choices.

Proposition 2. *Let* $M = (W, \mathcal{H}, \equiv, (\mathcal{E}_i)_{i\in Agt}, \mathcal{P}, \mathcal{U}, \mathcal{V})$ *be a model and let* $w \in W$. *Then,* $M, w \models Rat_i^\star$ *iff:*

$$\mathcal{C}_{act}(w,i) \in \arg\max_{b\in\mathcal{C}_{avail}(w,i)} \max_{\substack{v\in\mathcal{B}_i(w):\\ \mathcal{C}_{act}(v,i)=b}} \mathcal{U}(v,i) \text{ if } \star = opt$$

$$\mathcal{C}_{act}(w,i) \in \arg\max_{b\in\mathcal{C}_{avail}(w,i)} \min_{\substack{v\in\mathcal{B}_i(w):\\ \mathcal{C}_{act}(v,i)=b}} \mathcal{U}(v,i), \text{ if } \star = pess$$

In the language $\mathcal{L}$, we can express a variety of agency operators from STIT theory [5,12]. Indeed, EVAL can be seen as a variant of STIT with explicit actions: while in STIT an action is identified with the result brought about by a coalition (*i.e.*, in STIT one can only express that a given coalition H sees to it that φ), in EVAL an action is identified both with the result brought about by the coalition and with the means used by the coalition to bring about the result. For instance, the so-called 'Chellas' operator $[H\text{:cstit}]$ of STIT is definable in our language as follows:

$$[H\text{:cstit}]\varphi \stackrel{def}{=} \bigvee_{\delta_H\in JAct_H} \Big(\text{choose}(\delta_H) \wedge \bigwedge_{\substack{\delta'\in JAct:\\ \forall i\in H, \delta_H(i)=\delta'(i)}} \Box(\text{choose}(\delta') \to \varphi)\Big)$$

This means that the coalition H sees to it that φ if and only if, the agents in H choose some joint action δ_H such that, no matter what the agents outside H choose, if the agents in H choose δ_H then φ will be true. The 'deliberative' STIT operator is also definable:

$$[H\text{:dstit}]\varphi \stackrel{def}{=} [H\text{:cstit}]\varphi \wedge \neg\Box\varphi.$$

Deliberative STIT adds the negative condition $\neg\Box\varphi$ to Chellas STIT. It captures the fact that for a coalition H to see to it that φ, φ should not be inevitable (according to deliberative STIT, action is not compatible with necessity). Having formalized rationality types, we can define two rational STIT operators, $[H{:}\mathrm{rstit}]^{opt}$ and $[H{:}\mathrm{rstit}]^{pess}$:

$$[H{:}\mathrm{rstit}]^{\star}\varphi \stackrel{\mathrm{def}}{=} \bigwedge_{i \in H} \mathrm{Rat}_i^{\star} \rightarrow [H{:}\mathrm{cstit}]\varphi$$

with $\star \in \{opt, pess\}$. Formula $[H{:}\mathrm{rstit}]^{opt}\varphi$ (resp. $[H{:}\mathrm{rstit}]^{pess}\varphi$) has to be read "coalition H sees to it that that φ in an optimistic (resp. pessimistic) rational way". The latter means that if all agents in H are optimistically (resp. pessimistically) rational, then they see to it that φ. Note that we could also define deliberative STIT counterparts of the previous (Chellas STIT-based) rational STIT operators, in which operator $[H{:}\mathrm{cstit}]$ is replaced by operator $[H{:}\mathrm{dstit}]$. Our language also integrates a temporal dimension allowing us to express the LTL operator 'next': $X\varphi \stackrel{\mathrm{def}}{=} \bigvee_{\delta \in JAct} \langle\!\langle \delta \rangle\!\rangle \varphi$.

4   Influence, Persuasion and Deception

In this section, we define influence, persuasion, and deception. We also highlight the relationship between influence and persuasion, namely when an agent is persuaded to do an action a, it means that she may have acted differently but found rational to do a. Firstly, let us define influence. Influencing consists in an agent i (the influencer) intentionally seeing to it that another agent j (the influence) rationally sees to it that a proposition φ. As we have two kinds of rationality types, we can define two kinds of influence with $\star \in \{opt, pess\}$.

$$\mathsf{Influences}^{\star}(i, j, \varphi) \stackrel{\mathrm{def}}{=} \mathsf{K}_i^{post}[\{i\}{:}\mathrm{dstit}]X[\{j\}{:}\mathrm{rstit}]^{\star}\varphi$$

Let us now define persuasion as the intentional action of changing another agent's mental state [17, 18]. Persuasion consists in an agent i (the persuader) knowingly seeing to it that another agent j (the persuadee) believes that a certain fact φ is true.

$$\mathsf{Persuades}(i, j, \varphi) \stackrel{\mathrm{def}}{=} \mathsf{K}_i^{post}[\{i\}{:}\mathrm{dstit}]X\mathsf{B}_j\varphi$$

As the persuader knowingly sees to it that the persuadee will have a given belief, this definition expresses two different kinds of persuasion. One agent i may persuade another agent j either acquire a new belief that she does not have or to maintain a belief that she already has. Interestingly, a relationship between persuasion and influence can be deduced. An agent i influences an agent j to make a given choice a if i persuades j that choosing a is good for j and that all other choices are not good while knowing that j will be optimistically rational and can possibly choose a.

Proposition 3. *Let $i, j \in Agt$ and $a_j, b_j \in Act_j$. Then,*

$$\models (\mathsf{Persuades}(i, j, \widehat{\mathsf{B}}_j(\mathrm{choose}(a_j) \wedge \mathrm{good}_j) \wedge \bigwedge_{b \neq a}(\mathrm{choose}(b_j) \rightarrow \neg\mathrm{good}_j))$$

$$\wedge \mathsf{K}_i X(\mathrm{Rat}_j^{opt} \wedge \Diamond\mathrm{choose}(a_j))) \rightarrow \mathsf{Influences}^{opt}(i, j, \mathrm{choose}(a_j))$$

Firstly, by using $(\mathsf{K}_i\varphi \rightarrow \mathsf{K}_i\Box\varphi)$, $(\Diamond\varphi \wedge \Box\varphi \rightarrow \Diamond(\varphi \wedge \psi))$, $(\mathsf{B}_j\varphi \rightarrow \widehat{\mathsf{B}}_j\varphi)$, $(X\varphi \wedge X\psi \rightarrow X(\varphi \wedge \psi))$ and previous definition of persuasion, we easily prove that (Persuades

$(i, j, \text{choose}(a_j) \rightarrow \text{good}_j \wedge \bigwedge_{b \neq a} (\text{choose}(b_j) \rightarrow \neg\text{good}_j)) \wedge K_i \, X \, (\text{Rat}_j^{opt} \wedge \Diamond$
$\text{choose}(a_j))) \rightarrow K_i \, [\{i\}:\text{dstit}] \, X \, (\text{Rat}_j^{opt} \wedge \Diamond \, \text{choose}(a_j) \wedge \widehat{B}_j \, (\text{choose}(a_j) \rightarrow \text{good}_j$
$\wedge \bigwedge_{b \neq a} (\text{choose}(b_j) \rightarrow \neg\text{good}_j)))))$. Secondly, since $(K_i \, [\{i\}:\text{dstit}] \, X \, (\text{Rat}_j^{opt} \wedge \Diamond$
$\text{choose}(a_j) \wedge \widehat{B}_j \, (\text{choose}(a_j) \rightarrow \text{good}_j \wedge \bigwedge_{b \neq a} (\text{choose}(b_j) \rightarrow \neg \, \text{good}_j))) \rightarrow K_i$
$[\{i\}:\text{dstit}] \, X \, (\text{Rat}_j^{opt} \rightarrow [\{j\}:\text{cstit}] \, \text{choose}(a_j)))$, – intuitively this tautology means that since the only one good action for agent j is a_j and since all other actions are either bad$_j$ or neutral$_j$ (because of $\neg\text{good}_j$), necessarily the only optimistic rational choice for j is to choose a_j –, and since we have the following equivalence : $(K_i \, [\{i\}:\text{dstit}] \, X$ $(\text{Rat}_j^{opt} \rightarrow [\{j\}:\text{cstit}] \, \text{choose}(a_j)) \equiv \text{Influences}^{opt} \, (i, j, \text{choose}(a_j)))$ we then immediately prove by modus ponens the theorem.

The previous validity shows how an optimistically rational agent can be influenced through persuasion. Similar theorems can be proved for pessimistically rational agents but are omitted due to space constraints. The idea in this case is simply to persuade agent j that action a has no bad consequence while all other actions have it. Thank to persuasion we can now define deception. Deception consists in persuasion of a proposition φ under the assumption that the persuader believes that φ is false. For instance, consider the student that tells the professor that he could not study for family commitments (when he had no such commitments).

$$\text{Deceives}(i, j, \varphi) \stackrel{\text{def}}{=} \text{Persuades}(i, j, \varphi) \wedge B_i X \neg\varphi$$

Let us notice that we only capture successful deception, and we do not explicitly model deception by truthfully telling. Indeed, truthfully telling is simply captured by persuasion, as we do not make assumption on the persuader's intention (an agent can simply persuade another one in a malevolent intention, which capture truthfully telling deception). Smooth-talking is weaker than deceiving, since it only requires that the persuader is uncertain whether φ is true or false. Consider the journalist spreading the news that Obama was a muslim, without having any clue on the matter. Formally, it is equivalent to what Sakama *et al.* called "bullshitting" [23].

$$\text{PersuadesBySmoothTalking}(i, j, \varphi) \stackrel{\text{def}}{=} \text{Persuades}(i, j, \varphi) \wedge \neg K_i^{post} X \neg\varphi \wedge \neg K_i^{post} \neg X \neg\varphi$$

Let us notice we use *ex post* knowledge in this definition as we want to represent to complete uncertainty about φ. We do not want the persuader being able to belief φ being either true or false. We can also distinguish three types of belief deception, a benevolent, a malevolent and a reckless form. In the malevolent form, the persuader i deceives the persuadee j into believing a proposition φ, given that i believes that believing φ will have bad consequences for j. An agent z will accomplish an action if z believes that the action has good consequences (and no bad ones). Consider for instance the case of the charlatan offering a miraculous cure for boldness. Or consider the website ensuring gamblers that they are going with certainty to gain a lot of money.

$$\text{MalevolentDeception}(i, j, \varphi) \stackrel{\text{def}}{=} \text{Deceives}(i, j, \varphi) \wedge B_i X(B_j\varphi \rightarrow \text{bad}_j)$$

A benevolent deception consists for the deceiver to transmit a false proposition, believing that believing that proposition is good for the deceived. Consider for instance the atheist philosopher, who persuades the credulous citizens that if they act morally, they are going to heaven, in order to induce them to behave well.

$$\text{BenevolentDeception}(i, j, \varphi) \stackrel{\text{def}}{=} \text{Deceives}(i, j, \varphi) \wedge B_i X(B_j\varphi \rightarrow \text{good}_j)$$

The last form is reckless deception. It consists for the deceiver to transmit a false proposition, while not knowing whether that proposition is good or bad for the deceived. Consider for instance the case of Boris Johnson, who did not know (or did not care) whether Brexit would be good or bad for Britain, but induced people to believe that Brexit would provide money for the NHS, a belief that would lead them to vote for Brexit. He did not know whether this belief (which led to Brexit) would be good or bad for them.

$$\text{RecklessDeception}(i, j, \varphi) \overset{\text{def}}{=} \text{Deceives}(i, j, \varphi) \wedge$$
$$\neg K_i^{post} X(B_j \varphi \to good_j) \wedge \neg K_i^{post} X(B_j \varphi \to bad_j)$$

Application to the Running Example. Let us consider the actions' effect preconditions in Example 1, given the following hypotheses on agents' knowledge: (1, 2) the bot knows that its suggestion will persuade john that taking the pill will remove his pain and he will not get addicted, (3) the bot and Ann know that John will also believe that this is good for him, (4) the bot knowingly makes the suggestion and it knows if it makes the suggestion, John will be aware of it, (5) the Bot knows that John has the drug, that Ann does not hide the drug and that John can choose to not take the drug, (6) Ann will knowingly hide the drug, (7) Ann knows that John will possibly have the drug and can choose to take it, (8) the Bot knows that John will be optimistically rational. Finally, (9) the bot knows that ingesting the drug will create addiction, and being addicted is bad.

$$\varphi_1 \overset{\text{def}}{=} K_{Bot} \Box B_{John}(choose(suggest_{Bot}) \to X(\neg pain_{John} \leftrightarrow choose(take_{John})))$$

$$\varphi_2 \overset{\text{def}}{=} K_{Bot} \Box B_{John}(choose(suggest_{Bot}) \to X(choose(take_{John}) \to \neg addicted_{John}))$$

$$\varphi_3 \overset{\text{def}}{=} K_{Bot} \Box B_{John} X(good_{John} \leftrightarrow (\neg addicted_{John} \wedge \neg pain_{John})) \wedge$$
$$K_{Ann} \Box B_{John} X(good_{John} \leftrightarrow (\neg addicted_{John} \wedge \neg pain_{John}))$$

$$\varphi_4 \overset{\text{def}}{=} K_{Bot}(choose(suggest_{Bot}) \wedge (choose(suggest_{Bot}) \to K_{John}(choose(suggest_{Bot}))))$$

$$\varphi_5 \overset{\text{def}}{=} K_{Bot}(\Box(has_{John,drug}) \wedge \neg choose(hide_{Ann}) \wedge \Diamond \neg choose(take_{John}))$$

$$\varphi_6 \overset{\text{def}}{=} X K_{Ann} choose(hide_{Ann})$$

$$\varphi_7 \overset{\text{def}}{=} K_{Ann} X \Diamond(choose(take_{John}) \wedge has_{John,drug})$$

$$\varphi_8 \overset{\text{def}}{=} K_{Bot} \Box X Rat_{John}^{opt}$$

$$\varphi_9 \overset{\text{def}}{=} K_{Bot} \Box X((ingested_{John,drug} \to addicted_{John}) \wedge (addicted_{John} \leftrightarrow bad_{John}))$$

From premises $\varphi_1, \ldots, \varphi_8$, we can then deduce Proposition 4 which means that, in a first step, the Bot influences John to ingest the drug by persuasion, *i.e.* suggesting him that his unique good option is to take the drug. In the next step, Ann influences John to not ingest the drug by removing the choice to take the drug. With φ_9, we can also deduce Proposition 5 which means that the bot malevolently deceives John about the fact that ingesting the drug will not make him addict.

Proposition 4.

$$\models (\varphi_1 \wedge \varphi_2 \wedge \varphi_3 \wedge \varphi_4 \wedge \varphi_5 \wedge \varphi_6 \wedge \varphi_7 \wedge \varphi_8) \rightarrow (\text{Influences}^{opt}(Bot, John,$$

$$\text{X} ingested_{John,drug}) \wedge \text{X Influences}^{opt}(Ann, John, \text{X}\neg ingested_{John,drug}))$$

Firstly, we can prove that the bot knows that John knows it suggests him to take drug by applying axiom K on K_{Bot} *i.e.*: $\varphi_4 \rightarrow K_{Bot}K_{John}$choose($suggest_{Bot}$) We also consider the following theorem, that can be easily proved, $\forall a \in Act, \forall i, j \in Agt$: $(B_j(\text{choose}(a_i) \rightarrow \text{X}\varphi) \wedge K_j \text{choose}(a_i)) \rightarrow [\{i\}:\text{cstit}]\text{XB}_j\varphi$. The proof relies on the fact that knowledge implies beliefs and $B_j\text{X}\varphi' \rightarrow \text{XB}_j\varphi'$. By generalization with $\square$ and since $K_j$choose(a_i) $\rightarrow$ choose(a_i), we immediately prove the STIT and so the theorem. This theorem means that if one agent j believes that an action made by another agent i will imply a consequence and j knows i does this action, then the agent i sees to it that it will imply the agent j believes this consequence to be true. The theorem allows us to prove that if the bot suggests John to take the drug then, the bot knows John will believe taking the drug implies something good for him *i.e.* **the bot persuades John of it**. Starting from the assumptions, we prove this by substitution, augmentation, generalization (with K_{Bot}) and normal properties of modalities K, B and X, the following theorem. Note that the robot has an *ex-post* knowledge of the consequences of its action of suggesting. We have:

$$(\varphi_1 \wedge \varphi_2 \wedge \varphi_3 \wedge \varphi_4) \rightarrow$$

$$K_{Bot}^{post}\Big(\big((B_{John}(\text{choose}(suggest_{Bot}) \rightarrow \text{X}((\neg pain_{John} \leftrightarrow \text{choose}(take_{John}))$$

$$\wedge (\text{choose}(take_{John}) \rightarrow \neg addicted_{John}))) \wedge K_{John}\text{choose}(choose_{Bot}))$$

$$\rightarrow [Bot:\text{cstit}]\text{XB}_{John}(\text{choose}(take_{John}) \rightarrow good_{John}))\Big)$$

By contraposition on φ_3, we prove that it is not good for John to be addicted or having pain and allows us to prove that John believes that the only good option for him is to take the drug:

$$(\varphi_1 \wedge \varphi_2 \wedge \varphi_3) \rightarrow K_{Bot}\square B_{John}((addicted_{John} \rightarrow \neg\text{choose}(take_{John}))$$

$$\wedge (pain_{John} \rightarrow \neg\text{choose}(take_{John})) \wedge (\neg\text{choose}(take_{John}) \equiv \text{choose}(skip_{John})))$$

$$\rightarrow K_{Bot}\square B_{John}(\neg\text{choose}(take_{John}) \equiv \neg good_{John})$$

Since John is assumed to be rationally optimistic with the hypothesis φ_8 and as the unique good option for John is to take the drug, then John takes the drug *i.e.* we have the following validity:

$$(\text{choose}(take_{John}) \rightarrow good_{John}) \wedge \text{Rat}_{John}^{opt} \wedge$$

$$\bigwedge_{b \neq take} (\text{choose}(b_{John}) \rightarrow \neg good_{John}) \rightarrow \text{choose}(take_{John})$$

As John is rationally optimistic, he rationally sees to it that he ingests drugs. Finally, let us notice that since John takes the drug, then John is also able to take the drug due to the theorem choose($take_{John}$) $\rightarrow \Diamond$choose($take_{John}$). Furthermore, John can either do the action skip or $take_{drug}$. By generalization, all agents know:

$$(\Diamond\text{choose}(take_{John}) \wedge \bigvee_{b \neq take} \Diamond\text{choose}(b_{John})) \rightarrow \Diamond\neg\text{choose}(take_{John})$$

Furthermore since the preconditions for taking drugs is to have drugs in regard to the frame, $i.e.$ $\gamma^{+}(John, take, ingested_{John,drug}) = has_{John,drug}$, and having drugs implies that Ann does not hide drugs $i.e.$ $\forall a \in Act$ and $i \in Agt$ $\gamma^{+}(i, a, has_{John,drug}) = has_{John,drug} \wedge \neg\text{choose}(hide_{Ann})$ and we have these preconditions by φ_5, we deduce that John is able to take drugs or skipping. Then, as $\gamma^{-}(i, a, ingested_{John,drug}) = \neg\text{choose}(take_{John})$, $i.e.$ not taking the drugs would imply $\neg\text{X}ingested_{John,drug}$, we have that it is not necessary for John to take drugs, with the previous validity. Thus, by applying axioms in Fig. 3, we deduce the negative part of deliberative STIT operator, $i.e.$ the bot deliberately sees to it that John is going to ingest drugs:

$$(\varphi_1 \wedge \varphi_2 \wedge \varphi_3 \wedge \varphi_4 \wedge \varphi_5 \wedge \varphi_8) \rightarrow \text{K}_{Bot}^{post}([Bot:\text{dstit}]\text{X}(\text{Rat}_{John}^{opt} \rightarrow \text{X}ingested_{John,drug}))$$

Consequently:

$$(\varphi_1 \wedge \varphi_2 \wedge \varphi_3 \wedge \varphi_4 \wedge \varphi_5 \wedge \varphi_8) \rightarrow \text{Influences}^{opt}(Bot, John, \text{X}ingested_{John,drug})$$

For the second part of the implication, let us notice that since Ann hides drugs, John has only one possible action which is to skip. It is necessarily a rationally pessimistic choice but also an optimistic one, because of the following theorem:

$$\Diamond\text{choose}(skip_{John}) \wedge \neg\Diamond\neg\text{choose}(skip_{John}) \rightarrow \text{Rat}_{John}^{opt} \wedge \text{Rat}_{John}^{pess}$$

With the same method and with hypothesis φ_6 and φ_7 we can prove the second part:

$$(\varphi_1 \wedge \varphi_2 \wedge \varphi_3 \wedge \varphi_4 \wedge \varphi_5 \wedge \varphi_6 \wedge \varphi_7 \wedge \varphi_8) \rightarrow$$
$$(\text{XInfluences}^{opt}(Ann, John, \text{X}\neg ingested_{John,drug}))$$

Proposition 5.

$$\models (\varphi_1 \wedge \varphi_2 \wedge \varphi_3 \wedge \varphi_4 \wedge \varphi_5 \wedge \varphi_8 \wedge \varphi_9) \rightarrow$$
$$(\text{MalevolentDeception}(Bot, John, ingested_{John,drug} \wedge \neg addicted_{John,drug}))$$

We can prove it as previously. By adding hypothesis φ_9, we also prove a malevolent deception from the bot since it persuades John that he will not be addicted if he takes drugs while the bot knows the contrary, and being addicted is bad for John.

5   Conclusion

We have modelled influence on choices through belief change. To the end, we have introduced a logical framework covering capabilities, choices and mental states, and have expressed, through the combination of these notion, rationality and agency operators. We have also expressed formally the way in which persuasion leads to influence, $i.e.$ the way in which by modifying the beliefs of agents, the latter can be induced to act accordingly. This has enabled us to distinguish two ways in which agents can be influenced: (a), through persuasion, $i.e.$ by changing their beliefs, or (b) though regimentation, $i.e.$ by changing the options that are available to them. Moreover, it allows us to express different kind of deception, such as malevolent and benevolent deception. In the future, we would like to extend the framework towards a quantitative model in order to represent graded beliefs [8]. Other perspectives are to reformulate our framework into a concurrent game structure [3] to deal with a richer notion of time, and to incorporate emotions as in the OCC model [1] to express richer notions of rationality.

References

1. Adam, C., Gaudou, B., Herzig, A., Longin, D.: OCC's emotions: a formalization in a BDI logic. In: Euzenat, J., Domingue, J. (eds.) AIMSA 2006. LNCS (LNAI), vol. 4183, pp. 24–32. Springer, Heidelberg (2006). https://doi.org/10.1007/11861461_5
2. Alistair, M.C., Isaac, W.B.: White lies on silver tongues: why robots need to deceive (and how). In: Robot Ethics 2.0: From Autonomous Cars to Artificial Intelligence, pp. 157–172. Oxford Scholarship Online (2017)
3. Alur, R., Henziger, T.A., Kupferman, O.: Alternating-time temporal logic. J. ACM **49**(5), 672–713 (2002)
4. Aumann, R., Dreze, J.: Rational expectations in games. Am. Econ. Rev. **98**(1), 72–86 (2008)
5. Belnap, N., Perloff, M., Xu, M.: Facing the Future: Agents and Choices in Our Indeterminist World. Oxford University Press, Oxford (2001)
6. Bench-Capon, T.J.M.: Persuasion in practical argument using value-based argumentation frameworks. J. Log. Comput. **13**(3), 429–448 (2003)
7. Bonzon, E., Maudet, N.: On the outcomes of multiparty persuasion. In: McBurney, P., Parsons, S., Rahwan, I. (eds.) ArgMAS 2011. LNCS (LNAI), vol. 7543, pp. 86–101. Springer, Heidelberg (2012). https://doi.org/10.1007/978-3-642-33152-7_6
8. Budzyńska, K., Kacprzak, M.: A logic for reasoning about persuasion. Fund. Inform. **85**, 1–15 (2008)
9. Da Costa Pereira, C., Tettamanzi, A., Villata, S.: Changing one's mind: erase or rewind? Possibilistic belief revision with fuzzy argumentation based on trust. In: 22nd IJCAI, pp. 164–171 (2011)
10. Giacomo, G.D.: Eliminating "converse" from converse PDL. J. Logic Lang. Inf. **5**(2), 193–208 (1996)
11. Halpern, J.Y., Moses, Y.: A guide to completeness and complexity for modal logics of knowledge and belief. Artif. Intell. **54**(2), 319–379 (1992)
12. Horty, J.: Agency and Deontic Logic. Oxford University Press, Oxford (2001)
13. Hunter, A.: Modelling the persuadee in asymmetric argumentation dialogues for persuasion. In: 24th IJCAI, pp. 3055–3061 (2015)
14. Kraus, S., Lehmann, D.: Knowledge, belief and time. Theor. Comput. Sci. **58**, 155–174 (1988)
15. Leturc, C., Bonnet, G.: A deliberate BIAT logic for modeling manipulations. In: 20th AAMAS, pp. 699–707 (2020)
16. Lorini, E., Sartor, G.: A STIT logic analysis of social influence. In: 13th AAMAS, pp. 885–892 (2014)
17. O'Keffe, D.J.: Persuasion: Theory and Research, 3rd edn. Sage Publications, Thousand Oaks (2015)
18. Poggi, I.: The goals of persuasion. Pragmat. Cogn. **13**(2), 297–335 (2005)
19. Prakken, H.: Formal systems for persuasion dialogue. Knowl. Eng. Rev. **21**(2), 163–188 (2006)
20. Proietti, C., Yuste-Ginel, A.: Persuasive argumentation and epistemic attitudes. In: Soares Barbosa, L., Baltag, A. (eds.) DALI 2019. LNCS, vol. 12005, pp. 104–123. Springer, Cham (2020). https://doi.org/10.1007/978-3-030-38808-9_7
21. Reiter, R.: Knowledge in Action: Logical Foundations for Specifying and Implementing Dynamical Systems. MIT Press, Cambridge (2001)
22. Roy, O.: Epistemic logic and the foundations of decision and game theory. J. Indian Council Philos. Res. **27**(2), 283–314 (2010)
23. Sakama, C., Caminada, M., Herzig, A.: A formal account of dishonesty. Logic J. IGPL **23**(2), 259–294 (2015)

24. Santos, F., Carmo, J.: Indirect action, influence and responsibility. In: Brown, M.A., Carmo, J. (eds.) Deontic Logic, Agency and Normative Systems. WC, pp. 194–215. Springer, London (1996). https://doi.org/10.1007/978-1-4471-1488-8_11

25. Thomason, R.H.: Combinations of tense and modality. In: Gabbay, D., Guenthner, F. (eds.) Handbook of Philosophical Logic, pp. 135–165. Springer, Dordrecht (1984). https://doi.org/10.1007/978-94-009-6259-0_3

26. Van Benthem, J., Girard, P., Roy, O.: Dependencies between players in Boolean games. Int. J. Approximate Reasoning **50**(6), 899–914 (2009)

27. van Ditmarsch, H., van Eijck, J., Sietsma, F., Wang, Y.: On the logic of lying. In: van Eijck, J., Verbrugge, R. (eds.) Games, Actions and Social Software. LNCS, vol. 7010, pp. 41–72. Springer, Heidelberg (2012). https://doi.org/10.1007/978-3-642-29326-9_4

28. Walton, D., Krabbe, E.C.W.: Commitment in Dialogue: Basic Concepts of Interpersonal Reasoning. SUNY Series in Logic and Language, State University of New York Press (1995)

29. Zanardo, A.: Branching-time logic with quantification over branches: the point of view of modal logic. J. Symb. Log. **61**(1), 143–166 (1996)

Machine Learning Approches

Towards a Framework for Challenging ML-Based Decisions

Clément Henin[1,2]([envelope]) [iD] and Daniel Le Métayer[1]

[1] Univ Lyon, Inria, INSA Lyon, CITI, Villeurbanne, France
{clement.henin,daniel.le-metayer}@inria.fr
[2] École des Ponts ParisTech, Champs-sur-Marne, France

Abstract. The goal of the work presented in this paper is to provide techniques to challenge the results of an algorithmic decision system relying on machine learning. We highlight the differences between explanations and justifications and outline a framework to generate evidence to support or to dismiss challenges. We also present the results of a preliminary study to assess users' perception of the different types of challenges proposed here and their benefits to detect incorrect results.

Keywords: Challenge · Justification · Machine learning · Training · Dataset · Evidence

1 Introduction

When Machine Learning (ML) is used in a decision process, which is increasingly common, a key issue is the trust that can be placed in the system. Trusting an ML system in this context cannot be taken for granted, especially if the decision can have a significant impact on the affected people. Indeed, it is well-known that these systems can go wrong for many reasons, intentional or not. The goal of the work presented in this paper is to provide techniques to challenge the results of an Algorithmic Decision System (hereinafter "ADS") relying on ML and to reply to these challenges. We assume that the code of the ADS is not available or accessible; therefore, we have to follow a "black box" analysis approach. A first idea to achieve this goal would be to resort to post-hoc explanations. Explainable AI has become a very active research area in recent years and many explanation methods have been published in the literature. However, explanations fall short of our objective for different reasons. The first and most fundamental reason is that their goal is to ensure that the results of the system can be understood by humans, not that they are necessarily correct, or "good". Understanding is obviously a precondition for trust but it is not sufficient, as discussed below. In order to address this issue, we focus on *justifications* rather than explanations here. The word "justification" has been used in the XAI literature, but very often without any precise characterization and sometimes as a synonym of "explanation". In this paper, we propose a precise definition of justifications and highlight the differences between explanations and justifications in Sect. 2.

© Springer Nature Switzerland AG 2021
S. Sarkadi et al. (Eds.): DeceptECAI 2020/DeceptAI 2021, CCIS 1296, pp. 145–156, 2021.
https://doi.org/10.1007/978-3-030-91779-1_10

Then, we outline our interactive framework based on challenges and justifications in Sect. 3. The results of a preliminary study to assess users' perception of the different types of justifications proposed here and their benefits to detect incorrect results are sketched in Sect. 4. We discuss related work in Sect. 5 and conclude with avenues for further research in Sect. 6.

2   Challenges and Justifications

As suggested in the introduction, we believe that a clear distinction should be made between explanations and justifications. Many definitions have been proposed for these terms which are also used interchangeably by some authors. In this paper, we propose the following characterizations, which are consistent with [15]:

- The goal of an explanation is to make it possible for a human being (designer, user, affected person, etc.) to understand (a result or the whole system). In contrast, the goal of a justification is to make it possible for a human being to challenge (a result or the whole system) or to enhance his trust in the system (or a particular result). Even if they often support each other, the two goals are different: a user can understand the logic leading to the production of a particular result without agreeing on the fact that this result is correct or good; vice versa, he may want to challenge a result (being convinced that it is incorrect or bad) without understanding the logic behind the algorithm.
- Explanations are descriptive and intrinsic in the sense that they only depend on the system itself[1]. In contrast, justifications are normative and extrinsinc in the sense that they depend on a reference (or a norm) according to which the correctness or quality of the results can be assessed. Indeed, in order to claim that a result is correct or good, it is necessary to refer to an independent definition of what a correct or good result is.

Considering that our goal in this paper is to help human beings to challenge the results of an ADS or to enhance their trust in these results, we focus on justifications here. Technically speaking, to design a system allowing users to challenge a decision based on an ADS, we first need to define precisely the types of challenges that the user can express and the ways for the system to address these challenges, that is to say to produce justifications. Different forms of challenges and justifications are conceivable. For example, justifications can refer to explicit norms such as "the gender attribute must not have any impact on the results" or to implicit norms expressed through datasets of previous decisions. In this paper, we focus on ADS relying on machine learning and justifications expressed with respect to the learning dataset. This dataset is therefore considered as the reference for correct or "good" decisions, which implies that much

---

[1] This is also the case for "causal explanations": even though the notion of cause is very complex and it is used with a variety of different meanings in the literature, causal explanations are generally based on relations between ADS inputs and outputs, without reference to any external norm [2].

attention must be paid to reviewing it and ensuring that it is indeed representative of the requirements for the ADS. If it is not the case, for instance if the dataset is biased against a minority group, then justifications may be useful to highlight the bias. For example, if a justification relies on a racial bias and it turns out to be technically valid (i.e. supported by the learning dataset), then the affected person can challenge the system itself and bring the case to court. In this regard, we should stress the fact that such a justification system should be seen as a support tool for individuals and human decision makers rather than an automatic tool to establish the legitimacy of a challenge or a justification. In practice, the dataset is used by the system to generate (1) evidence to support the challenge or (2) evidence to the contrary (to support a justification for the decision) or (3) both types of evidence (when the dataset is not conclusive).

The precise definitions of challenges and justifications and the generation of evidence to support them are presented in the next section.

3 Outline of the Framework

In this paper, we focus on dynamic or interactive justifications, that is to say justifications that are produced as a reply to a given challenge, leading to an interactive challenge and justification process. The intuition is that interactive justifications are more likely to address the concerns of the challenger. This is also in line with the current trend towards interactive explanations. In the case of an ADS based on machine learning, justifying a decision amounts to convince the user that the decision is consistent with the training samples.

We present the two types of challenges considered here in Sect. 3.1 and justifications in Sect. 3.2. Then we sketch the algorithm used to produce evidence to support a challenge or a justification in Sect. 3.3. The outcomes of the process are described in Sect. 3.4. For the sake of simplicity, we assume that the decision, which is taken by a machine learning algorithm D, is binary[2] with output 1 associated with a positive decision (e.g. credit request accepted) and output 0 associated with a negative decision (e.g. credit request rejected). A challenge is used by the "plaintiff" to reverse a decision (i.e. to obtain a positive decision) while a justification is produced by the "defendant" to support a decision.

3.1 Challenges

In order to illustrate the different types of challenges considered here, let us take as an example of plaintiff a student whose application to a university has been rejected. A possible way to challenge the decision would be for the student to argue that his or her application should have been accepted because he or she has an average grade of 16 in mathematics and 15 in geography. The implicit rule used by the student, which we call an *absolute claim*, is: "any application with an average grade equal to (or greater than) 16 in mathematics and 15 in

---

[2] The framework can be easily extended to non-binary decisions.

geography should be accepted". It is worth noting that the claim used by the student does not need to involve all grades. For example, if the student has an average grade of 7 in English, it is not in his or her interest to put forward this grade in a claim.

The general definition of this type of claim is provided by Eq. 1:

$$\forall x \in \Delta, \ C(x) \implies D(x) = 1 \tag{1}$$

where Δ is the set of input data (e.g. average grade records for the university application example), C is the condition and D the decision. For absolute claims, we assume that condition C takes the form of a conjunction of properties of the attributes of its argument. In the above example, we have $C(x) = x.maths \geq 16 \wedge x.geo \geq 15$.

Another way to challenge the decision would be for the student to compare his or her application with the application of another student who has been accepted. For example, the student having better average grades than this other student in mathematics and in geography could argue that he or she should therefore be accepted also. In this case, the implicit rule used by the student, which we call a *relative claim*, is: "if student S_1 has better average grades than student S_2 in mathematics and in geography and S_2's application is accepted, then S_1's application should also be accepted".

The general definition of this type of claim is provided by Eq. 2.

$$\forall x \in \Delta, \exists y \in \Delta, \ D(y) = 1 \wedge C(x,y) \implies D(x) = 1 \tag{2}$$

In the above example, we have $C(x,y) = x.maths \geq y.maths \wedge x.geo \geq y.geo$.

3.2   Justifications

The notation introduced in the previous section makes it possible to express challenges based on claims but we have not discussed the validity of these claims so far. For example, it is possible to define nonsensical claims such as: "any application with an average grade less than 10 in mathematics should be accepted". The next step is therefore to provide ways to process a claim and to build a reply. To this respect, it is worth pointing out that the reference for the assessment of a claim is the training dataset of the ADS. In other words, we consider a statistical setting rather than a logical framework here. Let us assume, for example, that in the training dataset of the ADS, 70% of the 600 applicants with grades above 16 in mathematics and above 15 in geography were accepted. At first sight, the challenge of the student would seem legitimate. However, a more precise analysis may show that none of the 125 applications having grades above 16 in mathematics, above 15 in geography, but less than 8 in English were accepted. This justification may reflect the fact that a minimum grade in English is necessary to enter this university. Generally speaking, a justification is a refinement of the claim of the challenge providing evidence that the decision for the case under consideration is justified by the training dataset. By refinement, we mean the conjunction of the claim with further conditions on the attributes of the case under consideration ($x.english \leq 8$ in the above example). In this example, the refinement of the claim is provided by Eq. 3 with $C(x) = x.maths \geq 16 \wedge x.geo \geq 15 \wedge x.english \leq 8$.

$$\forall x \in \Delta, \ C(x) \implies D(x) = 0 \tag{3}$$

As discussed above, both challenges and justifications rely on claims that should be supported by evidence extracted from the training data set. In the next section, we show how this evidence can be generated and how the resulting claims can be assessed.

3.3 Generation of Evidence

In the example discussed in the previous section, the evidence for the justification seems convincing because its coverage (the size of the group) is not too low (125) and the ratio (0%) leaves little room for doubt. The two main outstanding issues at this stage are the following: first, how to generate such evidence and then, how to assess and compare them? The goal of a justification system is to exploit the training dataset to generate the strongest evidence to support or to dismiss a claim. Since bigger groups tend to have a ratio closer to the population average, there is usually a tension between high ratio and high coverage objectives. Finding an acceptable compromise between these two objectives is the biggest challenge to generate strong evidence. Before getting into more technical details about the generation algorithm, it is important to note that the system can be used to generate both evidence to support a challenge (hence in favour of the plaintiff) and evidence to support a justification (hence in favour of the defendant). This is all more important given that the plaintiff may not have access to the training dataset or have the required expertise to produce on his first try the best challenge.

Technically speaking, a justification is a refinement of the initial challenge, that is to say the conjunction of the property defining the challenge and additional conditions on attributes. Therefore, the generation of evidence amounts to a rule mining problem: the goal is to find the set of rules achieving the best compromise between the ratio and coverage objectives. To avoid exponential complexity in the number of rules, we use a greedy algorithm adding at each step the best rule according to a heuristic selection process. More precisely, the algorithm enumerates all possible rules and selects the candidate leading to the best ratio/coverage compromise. To this aim, we use the p-value of a T-test to select the rule that defines the subset of the training data which is the most significantly different from the subset of the preceding iteration. Only evidence with a p-value below a certain threshold is considered as valid. If no rule meeting this requirement can be found, then the algorithm returns en empty result. More details and the pseudo-code can be found in B.

3.4   Possible Outcomes

When the evidence supporting the challenge is weak and strong evidence can be provided to support a justification, the outcome of the process described in the previous section should be that the challenge is not valid. Vice versa, when evidence can be generated to support a challenge but the claim cannot be refined to generate a justification, the outcome should be that the challenge is valid. However, there are situations in which reasonable evidence can be produced to support both a challenge and a justification of the decision. The next issue to address is therefore the assessment of the strength of evidence data and the comparison between different types of evidence. The first rule is that if Evidence E_1 has a higher coverage and higher ratio[3] than Evidence E_2, then E_1 is stronger than E_2. However, the outcome is less obvious when E_1 has higher coverage than E_2 but E_2 has higher ratio. Different heuristics can be used to deal with this kind of cases. For example, a threshold can be defined to filter out evidence with a too small coverage, which should be considered as non-significant.

In some situations, the outcome of the process can be non-conclusive, meaning that reasonable evidence is available to support both the challenge and the justification. This type of conclusion should not be seen as a failure of the system as such decisions are likely to be close to a decision boundary of the ADS and may thus be open to discussion. In any case, it should be emphasized that the outcomes of a justification system should always be seen as suggestions to a human agent in charge of taking the final decision (i.e. validating the challenge or the justification).

4   User Study

In order to evaluate the efficiency of the techniques proposed here to detect unjustified decisions and the intuitive nature of our framework, we conducted a user study using an online platform. Considering that the design of the framework is still in progress, this study should be seen as a preparatory step for a more ambitious user validation of the final version. The experimental protocol was the following: decisions were presented to the users, some of these decisions were produced by the ADS, while others had purposely been modified in such a way that they were not supported by the training data. Users were asked to find which decisions were unjustified in different contexts corresponding to the possibility to issue a given type of challenge and to receive a justification in return.

The analysis of the empirical data consisted of a comparison of the proportions of successfully identified unjustified decisions for users benefitting from one of our approaches (absolute claims and relative claims) or not (considering three baseline scenarios). We also collected the levels of confidence declared by the users on a 5-Likert scale. Although the relative claims and justifications defined

---

[3] Ratio of decisions equal to 1 for challenge claims and ratio of decisions equal to 0 for justification claims.

by Eq. 2 performed better than all baseline scenarios, the differences are not significant (see the results in Appendix A). Thus the evaluation does not provide strong evidence of the benefit of this type of help to detect unjustified decisions. Several reasons may explain these non-conclusive results. First, the sample size is rather small (16 people). Second, the interface should be more self-explanatory, both about the approach and about the use case. Indeed, most users did not have any expertise in the justice sector (to which the decision system was related) and some of them explicitly complained about the fact that they did not understand very well the impact of the different features on the decision. Last but not least, more effort should be made to improve the case study to put users in a situation that would reflect as closely as possible a real decision challenging situation. Therefore, although the experiment is not conclusive, it provides good insights on the way to improve it to assess the final version of the system. Further details on the study can be found in Appendix A.

5   Related Works

In the field of explainable AI, the distinction between explanations and justifications is sometimes blurred. However, a series of works [5–7,15,18,19] refer to justifications as ways of ensuring that a decision is good (in contrast to understanding a decision), which is in line with the approach followed in this paper. However, the need to refer to an extrinsic norm is usually not mentioned explicitly. In addition, previous work does not involve the notion of challenge and the generation of interactive justifications. In other papers [13], justifications are seen as ways to make understandable the inner operations of a complex system (in a white-box setting). The normative nature of justifications was mentioned in the field of intelligent systems [11]: "an intelligent system exhibits justified agency if it follows society's norms and explains its activities in those terms". However, these norms are not characterized precisely, in particular the role of the training data is not mentioned. On this matter, [12] qualifies explanations as "unjustified" when there are not supported by training data. Therefore, justifiability applies to explanations in this context rather than to the decisions themselves. From a different perspective, [8], introduces several justifications in machine learning that aim at justifying an ADS as a whole rather than individual decisions. To the best of our knowledge, none of these contributions introduce a precise definition of justification of a decision based on a machine learning algorithm, or define a practical framework to challenge and to justify decisions.

The interest for more interactions with humans when conceiving and using ML takes several forms [1]. The need to conceive explanations as an interactive process has been argued by several authors [16,17]. The "human-in-the-loop" approach leverages on human feedback during the training process to obtain more accurate classifiers [10]. A lot of work has also been done on argumentation and dialog games [3,4,14] but the focus in these areas is generally the logical structure of the framework to express and to relate arguments or the protocol to exchange arguments. In contrast, we take an empirical approach to assess challenges and justifications here and we consider a very basic protocol (challenge-justification sequences). Closer to our work, [9] relies on "debates" between two competing algorithms exchanging arguments and counterarguments to convince a human user that their classification is correct. However, the goal of this work is to "align an agent's actions with the values and preferences of humans" which is seen as a "training-time problem". Our objective in this paper was different but an interesting avenue for further research could be the application of our approach to design or to improve an ADS.

6   Conclusion

The need to provide ways to challenge the results of an ADS is often highlighted but, to our best knowledge, no dedicated framework has been proposed so far. In this paper we have presented a work in progress whose ultimate goal is precisely to address this need. As mentioned earlier, challenges and justifications can take many different forms. In this paper, we have focused on ADS relying on machine learning and justifications expressed with respect to the learning dataset. In practice, justifications can also refer to explicit norms (e.g. legal or ethical norms) expressed by logical rules. Furthermore, norms may be mandatory or relative. An example of relative norm could be "minimize payment defaults" in a bank credit ADS. Similarly, different types of justifications can be generated depending on the available data (learning data set, ground truth data, historical ADS data, etc.). However, beyond these differences, a common "challenge and justification" framework can be defined to accomodate different types of situations and provide more control to human beings on ADS. The work outlined in this paper is a first step towards this framework, which is currently under construction.

A   User Study: Methods and Results

The user study was conducted using an online platform[4]. We trained a K-nearest neighbors classifier on the Propublica COMPAS[5] database to predict the like-lihood of recidivism. To keep the task simple, 6 features only were used. Deci-sions are sampled from the training data. We modified the model classification of half of them to create unjustified cases. Five types of assistance were ran-domly assigned: *absolute* claim, *relative* claim, counterfactual, k-neighbours and no assistance. The first two are derived directly from the framework, while the last three are part of the control group. Each user performed 10 tasks, 2 tasks per assistance type. In addition, users were asked to give their levels of confi-dence on a 5-Likert scale and an optional comment. We collected 160 completed tasks from 16 people (32 per assistance type) over 10 days of experiment. Users were mostly researchers and PhD students in the field of applied mathematics and computer science. No significant differences (p-value $> .05$) was found in

---

[4] https://ml-advocate.inrialpes.fr/ (in French).

[5] https://github.com/propublica/compas-analysis.

the average number of correct answers between the different assistance types neither in the declarative confidence levels, although relative claims had best average values (see all result in Table 1).

Table 1. Results of the user study. Relative claims performed better than all other assistance although difference is not significant. There is no significant difference in Likert declarative confidences.

Assistance type	N tasks	Mean	95% conf. interval	Likert mean
Absolute claim	32	53%	(35%, 71%)	3.5
Relative claim	32	63%	(45%, 80%)	3.3
Counterfactual	32	56%	(38%, 74%)	3.4
K-neighbours	32	56%	(38%, 74%)	3.3
∅	32	56%	(38%, 74%)	3.3

B   Rule Search Algorithm

The objective of the rule search algorithm is to find the set of rules that defines the subset of the training data for which the average decision is the most significantly distinct (lowest p-value) from the average decision of the training subset defined by the claim. The set of rules is found with a greedy algorithm. At each step, the rule performing best according to an heuristic is selected until one of the two stopping criteria is met. At each step, the algorithm works as follow (see Algorithm 1):

1. select all training data satisfying the rules of the claim and the rule set.
2. Enumeration of all possible rules. For all values appearing in the selected data, and for all operators ($\geq$, $\leq$, = for numerical value or = for categorical values) create a rule candidate.
3. select only candidate rules that the file of interest, that is the subject of the challenge, satisfies,
4. select Pareto optimal rules with respect to the coverage and ratio. High coverage and low ratio are used to search for evidence to support justifications and high coverage and high ratio are to search for evidence to support challenges (see Algorithm 2),
5. then select the rule with the lowest p-value.

The search continues until one of the two stopping criteria is met:

- ratio of the resulting rule is sufficiently low (to support justifications) or sufficiently high (to support challenges). See line 5–6 of Algorithm 1. In this case, the algorithm returns the current rule set.
- the difference of means after addition of the best rule candidate is not significant (p-value > .2 in the current implementation). See line 9–16 of Algorithm 1. In this case, the algorithm returns nothing.

Input: FileOfInterest, claim, trainingData, pvalThreshold
Result: Best significant set of rules, if any

1 initialization
2 $ruleSet \leftarrow \emptyset$
3 $d \leftarrow \{x \in trainingData, claim(x)\}$
4 $ratio \leftarrow size(\{x \in d, D(x) = 1\})/size(d)$
5 $threshold \leftarrow ratio/2$
      `/*` $threshold \leftarrow (1 + ratio)/2$ `for supporting justifications`   `*/`
6 **while** $ratio > threshold$ **do**
          `/* Or` $ratio < threshold$ `if is used to find an evidence to support`
              `the challenge`   `*/`
7      $paretoFront \leftarrow$ **ParetoOptimalRules**$(d, FileOfInterest)$
8   Select RuleBest with lowest p-value from paretoFront
9      $d_{RuleBest} \leftarrow \{x \in d, RuleBest(x)\}$
10     $pValBest \leftarrow T\text{-}test(\{D(x), x \in d_{RuleBest}\}, \{D(x), x \in d \setminus d_{RuleBest}\})$
11   **if** $pvalue < pvalThreshold$ **then**
12   Append $rule$ to $ruleSet$
13         $d \leftarrow \{x \in d, RuleBest(x)\}$
14         $ratio \leftarrow size(\{x \in d, D(x) = 1\})/size(d)$
15   **else**
16   Exit While and return nothing
17   **end**
18 **end**
19 **return** $RuleSet$

Algorithm 1: Rule Search Algorithm

1 **Function ParetoOptimalRules**$(TrainingSubset, FileOfInterest)$:
2      $pareto \leftarrow \emptyset$
3   **for** $candidate$ **in** all possible rules that $FileOfInterest$ satisfies **do**
4          $d_{candidate} \leftarrow \{x \in TrainingSubset, candidate(x)\}$
5          $cover \leftarrow size(d_{candidate})$
6          $ratio \leftarrow size(\{x \in d_{candidate}, D(x) = 1\})/cover$
7   If no rule in $pareto$ has bigger cover and smaller ratio than candidate
              then append candidate to $pareto$
8   If any rule in $pareto$ has smaller cover and bigger ratio than candidate
              then remove it from $pareto$
9   **end**
       `/* If used to find an evidence to support the challenge, ratio`
          `should be bigger as a condition to append and smaller as a`
          `condition to remove.`   `*/`
10   **return** $pareto$

Algorithm 2: Function definition: ParetoOptimalRules

References

1. Abdul, A., Vermeulen, J., Wang, D., Lim, B.Y., Kankanhalli, M.: Trends and trajectories for explainable, accountable and intelligible systems: an HCI research agenda. In: Proceedings of the 2018 CHI Conference on Human Factors in Computing Systems - CHI '18, pp. 1–18. ACM Press (2018). https://doi.org/10.1145/3173574.3174156. http://dl.acm.org/citation.cfm?doid=3173574.3174156
2. Alvarez-Melis, D., Jaakkola, T.S.: A causal framework for explaining the predictions of black-box sequence-to-sequence models (2017)
3. Atkinson, K., et al.: Towards artificial argumentation. AI Mag. **38**(3), 25–36 (2017). https://doi.org/10.1609/aimag.v38i3.2704. https://www.aaai.org/ojs/index.php/aimagazine/article/view/2704
4. Bex, F., Walton, D.: Combining explanation and argumentation in dialogue. Argum. Comput. **7**(1), 55–68 (2011)
5. Biran, O., Cotton, C.: Explanation and justification in machine learning: A survey. In: IJCAI-17 Workshop on Explainable AI (XAI), p. 8 (2017)
6. Biran, O., McKeown, K.R.: Justification narratives for individual classifications. In: ICML (2014)
7. Biran, O., McKeown, K.R.: Human-centric justification of machine learning predictions. In: IJCAI, pp. 1461–1467 (2017)
8. Corfield, D.: Varieties of justification in machine learning. Mind. Mach. **20**(2), 291–301 (2010). https://doi.org/10.1007/s11023-010-9191-1
9. Irving, G., Christiano, P., Amodei, D.: AI safety via debate. arXiv:1805.00899 [cs, stat] (2018)
10. Kim, B.: Interactive and interpretable machine learning models for human machine collaboration, p. 143 (2015)
11. Langley, P.: Explainable, normative, and justified agency. In: Proceedings of the AAAI Conference on Artificial Intelligence, vol. 33, pp. 9775–9779 (2019). https://doi.org/10.1609/aaai.v33i01.33019775
12. Laugel, T., Lesot, M.J., Marsala, C., Renard, X., Detyniecki, M.: The dangers of post-hoc interpretability: Unjustified counterfactual explanations. arXiv:1907.09294 [cs, stat] (2019)
13. Lei, T., Barzilay, R., Jaakkola, T.: Rationalizing neural predictions. In: Proceedings of the 2016 Conference on Empirical Methods in Natural Language Processing, pp. 107–117. Association for Computational Linguistics (2016). https://doi.org/10.18653/v1/D16-1011. http://aclweb.org/anthology/D16-1011
14. Madumal, P., Miller, T., Sonenberg, L., Vetere, F.: A grounded interaction protocol for explainable artificial intelligence. In: Proceedings of the 18th International Conference on Autonomous Agents and MultiAgent Systems, AAMAS '19, pp. 1033–1041. International Foundation for Autonomous Agents and Multiagent Systems, Richland (2019)
15. Miller, T.: Explanation in artificial intelligence: insights from the social sciences. Artif. Intell. **267**, 1–38 (2017). https://doi.org/10.1016/j.artint.2018.07.007
16. Miller, T., Howe, P., Sonenberg, L.: Explainable AI: beware of inmates running the asylum. In: IJCAI-17 Workshop on Explainable AI (XAI), vol. 36 (2017)
17. Mittelstadt, B., Russell, C., Wachter, S.: Explaining explanations in AI. arXiv:1811.01439 [cs] (2018). https://doi.org/10.1145/3287560.3287574

18. Mueller, S.T., Hoffman, R.R., Clancey, W., Emrey, A.: Explanation in human-AI systems: a literature meta-review synopsis of key ideas and publications and bibliography for explainable AI, p. 204 (2019)
19. Swartout, W.R., Swartout, W.R.: Producing explanations and justifications of expert consulting programs (1981)

Impostor GAN: Toward Modeling Social Media User Impersonation with Generative Adversarial Networks

Masnoon Nafees, Shimei Pan, Zhiyuan Chen, and James R. Foulds[(⊠)]

University of Maryland Baltimore County, Baltimore, MD, USA
{masnoon1,shimei,zhchen,jfoulds}@umbc.edu

Abstract. The problem of "fake accounts" on social media has gained a lot of attention recently because of the role they play in generating/propagating misinformation, manipulating opinions and interfering with elections. Among them, "impersonators" or "impostors" are those fake social media accounts that mimic the posts and behavior of a targeted person (e.g., a politician or celebrity) or brand. In this preliminary investigation, we study a GAN-based framework in which an impostor aims to produce realistic social media posts which pass for being created by the target person while the detector aims to identify the posts by the impostors/impersonators. The impostor and the detector are co-trained until an equilibrium is reached, where the impostor is good at mimicking the posts of the target person and the detector is good at identifying the posts of an impostor. Our model allows us to achieve both impersonation and its detection, and also to study how this adversarial scenario might unfold. We applied our method to a Twitter dataset to study its performance. The results demonstrate that our proposed model is promising in generating and detecting impostors' posts.

Keywords: Social media · Impersonation · Adversarial networks

1 Introduction

Fake social media accounts are pervasive. According to Facebook's 2020 Community Standards Enforcement Report, the company estimates that around 5% of its accounts were fake in Q4 of 2020.[1] *Impersonator* or *impostor* accounts, which aim to assume the identity of another social media user, are a particularly problematic type of fake account. Social media impersonation is a widespread problem, motivated by fraud (e.g. "brandjacking"), misinformation, propaganda, brand abuse, and the manipulation of popularity and engagement metrics [10].

In this paper, we propose to study social media impersonation from a machine learning perspective. We propose a method called Impostor GAN, which simulates an impersonator, an impersonation detector, and the adversarial game in

---

[1] https://transparency.facebook.com/community-standards-enforcement.

S. Sarkadi et al. (Eds.): DeceptECAI 2020/DeceptAI 2021, CCIS 1296, pp. 157–165, 2021.
https://doi.org/10.1007/978-3-030-91779-1_11

which these two entities compete with each other, using a Generative Adversarial Network (GAN). This allows us to achieve impersonation and its detection, and to study how this adversarial scenario might play out in an idealized setting, which could provide insights into the real-world impersonation problem. Our experimental results, although preliminary, were quite encouraging.

2   Background and Related Work

There is a large body of work on social bot detection [7,8]. The first-generation social bots were quite simple, with few social connections and limited ability to automatically generate posts. These bots are relatively easy to detect. For example, [7] employs supervised machine learning to accurately detect these bots. Recently, to avoid detection, social bots have become increasingly sophisticated. They are carefully engineered to be like humans. These bots are very difficult to detect for both algorithms and humans [9]. Recently, [10] focused on detecting impostors, who try to mimic a specific person. Our work differs in that we study the impostor, the impostor detector, and their interaction, using a GAN.

Generative Adversarial Networks (GANs) [1] have become quite popular recently. As deception detection is intrinsically adversarial, we apply GANs to generate and detect posts from impostors. The idea of the GAN is to play a min-max game between a generator network and a discriminator network. The discriminator tries to distinguish between real and fake data. The generator tries to beat the discriminator. The game continues until the generator can eventually generate realistic samples that fool the discriminator. More specifically, we base our approach on the WGAN [2]. The WGAN tries to address several issues such as vanishing gradients in the original GAN. WGANs clip the weights in the discriminator to enforce the Lipschitz constraint. They use different techniques like linear activation functions, and most importantly, the Wasserstein loss function which is based on the earth mover distance. WGAN-GP [3] tries to further improve the WGAN. The authors proposed a method that penalizes the gradient norm with respect to its input of the discriminator or critic instead of weight clipping. This method generally works better than WGANs and GANs. Due to these advantages, in this paper we have used a Wasserstein GAN-based formulation to develop our Impostor GAN model.

3   Methodology

Our proposed Impostor GAN model consists of three networks: two generators and one discriminator. The two generators aim to produce ambiguous tweets for impersonation, and the discriminator aims to detect impersonation. The first generator generates data points in an embedding space that are semantically similar to a specific user's tweets (*user 1*, a.k.a. *user*, e.g. the target user to be impersonated), but which are difficult to distinguish from a second user's tweets (*user 2*, a.k.a. *otheruser*, e.g. an impersonating user). The second generator does the reverse: it produces data points that are semantically similar to the second user's tweets, but which are difficult to distinguish from the first user's tweets. The generators thereby try to impersonate users by selecting points in the overlap region common to both users, i.e. ambiguous tweets which could have come from either user.

To circumvent the challenging task of generating realistic content from either user, we simplify the problem to the task of selecting from a set of existing social media posts from an impersonating user. The impersonating user could be chosen to be a specific other user who we want to make look like the target user, or to the content from multiple (or all) other users. In our future work, we plan to generate realistic posts via transformer models such as GPT-3 [11].

The objective of the discriminator is to detect this deception by distinguishing between the user 1 and user 2 tweets created by the two generators. It maximizes the score of the target user's tweets while minimizing the score of the other users' tweets. The discriminator and two generators are iteratively updated in turn. Eventually, the Impostor GAN aims to achieve a Nash equilibrium where the two generators will generate points in the overlapping region of the target user's tweets and the other users' tweets. Such selected tweets will be difficult to distinguish, and hence can be used for impersonation.

More formally, our proposed Impostor GAN model consists of two generators, G_1 and G_2, and a discriminator D. As shown in the architecture diagram in Fig. 1, and algorithm pseudocode in Algorithm 1, G_1 and G_2 take inputs from a common latent space z. Let D_1 be the data set for a specific user and D_2 be the data set for other user/users. D_1 and D_2 both generate data points in the embedding space, but G_1 generates points similar to the specific user's data but G_2 generates points similar to the other user(s)' data. Since these data points may not exactly match an existing data point (e.g., a tweet), we use nearest neighbor search to find a data point from D_1 that is closest to the data point generated by G_1. Similarly the point from D_2 that is closest to the data point generated by G_2 is also returned. We use the Ball-Tree algorithm to speed up nearest neighbor search and cosine as the distance metric [4].

Let N_1 be the set of closest data points from D_1 and N_2 be the closest points from D_2. N_1 and N_2 are passed to the discriminator D. We use a WGAN-style formulation [2]. We formulate the model as a min-max game:

$$min_{G_{user,otheruser}} max_D \left[\mathbb{E}[D(G_1(x_i^{N_{user}}))] - \mathbb{E}[D(G_2(x_i^{N_{otheruser}}))] \right] . \qquad (1)$$

The objective of the discriminator is to maximize the score of the data point in D_1 (i.e., the specific user's data) and minimize the score of a data point from D_2 (i.e., other users' data):

$$max_D \left[\mathbb{E}[D(G_1(x_i^{N_{user}}))] - \mathbb{E}[D(G_2(x_i^{N_{otheruser}}))] \right] . \qquad (2)$$

Following the WGAN, we used a linear activation function in the last layer of the discriminator. While in typical image applications of WGANs it is common to bound the generator's output between $[-1,1]$ using tanh in the final layer, in our case we also used a linear final layer for the generators. G_1's objective is to

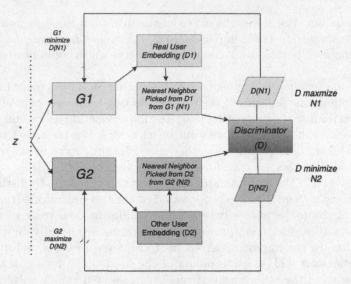

Fig. 1. Impostor GAN model architecture

Algorithm 1: Training of Impostor GAN

Input: Initial Generator $G1$, Generator $G2$, Discriminator D, Real User
        Embedding Data $D1$, Other User Embedding Data $D2$, batch size = x,
        d as number of updates for the discriminator

Parameter: Optimizer = **Adam**, D's learning rate $\alpha_d = 0.00002$,
G_1 and G_2's learning rate $\alpha_g = 0.00001$,
batch size = 32, distance metric = *cosine*

Result: N_1 and N_2 contain most overlapped data

Input of N_1, N_2 in D;

while *Until Converge* **do**

    for $i = 0$; $i < d$; $i++$ **do**

    | Update D to maximize Equation 2 via Adam

    end

    Update G_1 to minimize Equation 3 via Adam

    Update G_2 to maximize Equation 4 via Adam

end

---

minimize the score given by the discriminator for data points from the *user*, and
G_2's objective is to maximize the discriminator score for the *other user*'s data:

$$min_{G_1}[\mathbb{E}[D(N(x_i^{user}))]] \,, \tag{3}$$

$$max_{G_2}[\mathbb{E}[D(N(x_i^{otheruser}))]] \,. \tag{4}$$

The two generators and the discriminator are updated based on the gradients of
the above objective functions, e.g. via the Adam optimizer.

In practice, following [2] we update the discriminator more times than the generators. We found that training the discriminator 3 times more than the generators gave us better results while using a batch size of 32 for both generators. As we have multiple neural networks we also focused on how we can achieve a local Nash equilibrium. We noticed that applying different learning rates for the discriminator and generators provides more meaningful results. We applied the *Two Time-Scale Update Rule* [5] by using a lower learning rate for the generators than the discriminator with the Adam optimizer. Slower learning rates on the generators help the networks to adjust based on the discriminator's feedback.

4   Dataset Description

For the experiment we selected a publicly available tweets data set from Donald Trump and Hillary Clinton [6]. We chose this dataset because these individuals' relatively well-known personalities make the results easier to interpret, and because there is a lot of public interest in any insights into their behavior and the 2016 election which might arise from the study. We made Trump tweets as the target *user* to be impersonated and Clinton tweets as the *other user* whose tweets will be used for impersonation, although note that the model is symmetric and performs impersonations for both users. Both data sets contains around 3000 tweets each. We followed standard text cleaning procedures to clean the text, remove any stop words, numeric values, etc. Then, the cleaned text data was converted into 50-dimensional embeddings. We used a Glove model to get word embeddings and doc2vec to convert the tweets into embeddings. We also generated a synthetic dataset to help understand and visualize the model's behavior and its ability to find the overlap region. The dataset contains 1000 2-dimensional *user* data points uniformly distributed in the range of 3 to 0.5 and 1000 instances for *other user* uniformly distributed in the range of -0.5 to 3.0.

5   Experiments

Results for Synthetic Data: Figure 2 *(a)* and Fig. 2 *(b)* show data points in D_1, D_2, N_1, and N_2 for the synthetic data set at iteration 1 and 7400, respectively. From Fig. 2 *(a)*, we can see that the two rectangle uniform distribution values are overlapped in -0.5 to 0.5 region. Green and Blue values are the nearest neighbor values picked by the two generators. Only 18.75% for both user and non user points picked by the generators lies in overlap region as the other points in N_1 and N_2 are scattered in the whole plot. In iteration 7400, we see that most of the data points selected by Impostor GAN are in the overlap region. This behavior is indicative of success, as points in the overlap region cannot easily be distinguished by the discriminator. This means that the three networks have converged in such a way that the selected data points will be ambiguous.

Results for Twitter Data: We then move to the real Twitter dataset. Unlike for image data, where we can see the quality of the generated images, in our

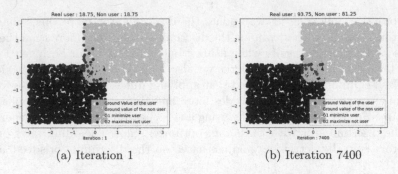

(a) Iteration 1   (b) Iteration 7400

Fig. 2. Results on synthetic data

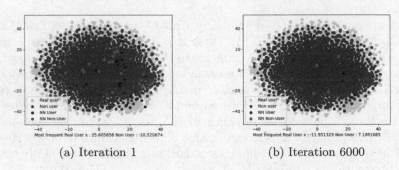

(a) Iteration 1   (b) Iteration 6000

Fig. 3. Results on Twitter dataset (*t*-SNE projection)

case it is difficult to visually observe whether the method is working correctly. To gain some understanding of this numeric data experiment, we used *t*-SNE to convert the 50-dimensional embedding data into 2D for visualization purposes. The plot contains the embedding data for both D_1 and D_2 and the nearest neighbor data points. From Fig. 3 *(a)*, we can see that in iteration 1, the chosen nearest neighbor values are scattered. The most frequent values for both user and non user are also far apart from each other. After the model ran for 6000 iterations, Fig. 3 *(b)* shows that the most frequently selected user and non users points are closer than in the first iteration. Below are some sample tweets from Trump and Clinton. First, as a baseline approach, instead of using the Impostor GAN we report tweets selected based on the shortest distance between them and an embedding from the other user:

Shortest Distance Baseline, *Trump*:

- *"@markgruber1960: @megynkelly @realDonaldTrump That's why he is so successful. He is driven to succeed" True!*
- *Congratulation to Adam Scott and all of the folks at Trump National Doral on producing a really great WGC Tournament. Amazing finish!*

Shortest Distance Baseline, *Clinton*:

- *We have to build an economy that works for everyone, not just those at the top. #DebateNight https://t.co/XPTvh4Dovf*
- *Donald Trump says he "cherishes women". Just not if they're working and pregnant. https://t.co/sd9KHSvQlO https://t.co/MQeMLNtuNG*

We now report tweets selected by Impostor GAN after 6000 iterations.

Impostor GAN, *Trump*:

- *In Hillary Clinton's America - things get worse.*
  #TrumpPence16 https://t.co/WdHbnhhCbW
- *Hillary could lose to Trump in Democratic New York #MakeAmericaGreatAgain #Trump2016 https://t.co/fQR48CVIbt"*

Impostor GAN, *Clinton*:

- *No wonder Donald Trump is hiding his tax returns.*
  #debatenight https://t.co/gcvsadMwHJ
- *"Candidate Trump opposes equal pay, paid leave, and Planned Parenthood. President Trump? Same. https://t.co/H85Ud5jyOe"*

From the model's chosen tweets, we can see that our model has picked Trump's tweets that refer to Clinton, and Clinton's tweets that refer to Trump. It makes sense that these tweets are chosen since the other user's name is likely an effective obfuscation of the tweet author's identity in embedding space. On the other hand, given their understanding of the context of the 2016 election, a human adversary could likely still distinguish the author of these tweets based on the sentiment expressed toward the other person. Note however that this is a relatively challenging scenario. Based on the tweets in this data set that the authors have inspected, the authorship of the majority of the tweets is generally easy inferred, making it quite difficult to choose tweets which comprise effective impersonation against a human adversary in this context. The behavior of the method, in which the chosen tweets refer to the other user, does appear to show promise in a more typical scenario in which the human adversary does not have substantial contextual domain knowledge about the users, or where the adversary uses a machine learning model to distinguish the tweets' authorship.

6   Evaluation

The Impostor GAN's generator, which aims to achieve impersonation, can be said to succeed if it selects social media posts in the overlapping region of its two input users' posts' embeddings. To evaluate this, we have adapted the idea of calculating Frechet Inception Distance (FID) [5], which is commonly used to evaluate GANs for generating images. The FID calculates the distance between embeddings for real and generated images based on the overlap of their distributions, which are modeled as multivariate normal. The images are embedded using the encoding layer of Inception, a large model for image classification. We instead evaluate using the Frechet distance for doc2vec embeddings of the tweets chosen by the Impostor GAN. If the model works as intended, the Frechet distance between the tweets selected by the two generators should decrease. We compared our approach to a baseline which simply calculates the shortest distance between the tweets. From Fig. 4, we can see that as the number of iterations increases, the Frechet distance typically goes down. Finally, the Frechet distance for the trained Impostor GAN was substantially better than the baseline (Table 1).

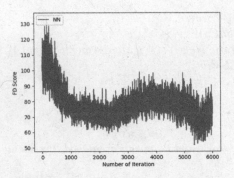

Fig. 4. Frechet Distance vs training iterations for Impostor GAN

Table 1. Frechet Distance (FD) for Shortest Distance Baseline and Impostor GAN (Lower is Better)

Method	FD
Shortest Distance Baseline	168.3
Impostor GAN	70.5

7   Conclusion

We have proposed Impostor GAN, a method for performing impersonation and also impersonation detection based on social media data such as tweets, and potentially, Facebook, Instagram, email, etc. The method used a novel GAN-based formulation involving a combination of three neural networks and a nearest neighbor procedure. Our preliminary experiments with our proposed model showed promising results. Both quantitative and qualitative results on synthetic 2D data and real Twitter data, including a Frechet distance evaluation, show that our model can converge into the overlap region of the data distributions for two users. In future work we plan to extend the model to generate new impersonating social media posts using transformer models such as GPT-3, instead of simply selecting from existing tweets. We will further study the implications of our model regarding the real-world adversarial competition between social media impostors and those who would detect them.

References

1. Goodfellow, I.J., et al.: Generative adversarial networks. arXiv preprint arXiv:1406.2661 (2014)
2. Arjovsky, M., Chintala, S., Bottou, L.: Wasserstein GAN. arXiv preprint arXiv:1701.07875 (2017)

3. Gulrajani, I., Ahmed, F., Arjovsky, M., Dumoulin, V., Courville, A.: Improved training of Wasserstein GANs. arXiv preprint arXiv:1704.00028 (2017)
4. Muflikhah, L., Baharudin, B.: Document clustering using concept space and cosine similarity measurement. In: 2009 International Conference on Computer Technology and Development, vol. 1, pp. 58–62. IEEE (2009)
5. Heusel, M., Ramsauer, H., Unterthiner, T., Nessler, B., Hochreiter, S.: GANs trained by a two time-scale update rule converge to a local Nash equilibrium. arXiv preprint arXiv:1706.08500 (2017)
6. Data World. Tweets dataset for Trump and Hillary (2021)
7. Yang, C., Harkreader, R., Gu, G.: Empirical evaluation and new design for fighting evolving Twitter spammers. IEEE Trans. Inf. Forensics Secur. **8**(8), 1280–1293 (2013)
8. Ferrara, E., Varol, O., Davis, C., Menczer, F., Flammini, A.: The rise of social bots. Commun. ACM **59**(7), 96–104 (2016)
9. Cresci, S., Di Pietro, R., Petrocchi, M., Spognardi, A., Tesconi, M.: The paradigm-shift of social spambots: evidence, theories, and tools for the arms race. In: Proceedings of the 26th International Conference on World Wide Web Companion, pp. 963–972, April 2017
10. Zarei, K., Farahbakhsh, R., Crespi, N., Tyson, G.: Impersonation on Social Media: A Deep Neural Approach to Identify Ingenuine Content. arXiv preprint arXiv:2010.08438 (2020)
11. Floridi, L., Chiriatti, M.: GPT-3: its nature, scope, limits, and consequences. Mind. Mach. **30**(4), 681–694 (2020). https://doi.org/10.1007/s11023-020-09548-1

Studying Dishonest Intentions
in Brazilian Portuguese Texts

Francielle Alves Vargas$^{(\boxtimes)}$ (iD) and Thiago Alexandre Salgueiro Pardo$^{(\boxtimes)}$ (iD)

Interinstitutional Center for Computational Linguistics (NILC), Institute of
Mathematical and Computer Sciences, University of São Paulo, São Carlos, Brazil
`francielleavargas@usp.br`, `taspardo@icmc.usp.br`

Abstract. Previous work in the social sciences, psychology and linguistics has show that liars have some control over the content of their stories, however their underlying state of mind may "leak out" through the way that they tell them. To the best of our knowledge, no previous systematic effort exists in order to describe and model deception language for Brazilian Portuguese. To fill this important gap, we carry out an initial empirical linguistic study on false statements in Brazilian news. We methodically analyze linguistic features using the Fake.Br corpus, which includes both fake and true news. The results show that they present substantial lexical, syntactic and semantic variations, as well as punctuation and emotion distinctions.

Keywords: Deception detection · Linguistic features · Natural language processing

1 Introduction

According to the standard philosophical definition, lying is saying something that you believe to be false with the intent to deceive [11]. For deception detection, the FBI trains its agents in a technique named statement analysis, which attempts to detect deception based on parts of speech (i.e., linguistics style) rather than the facts of the case or the story as a whole [1]. This method is employed in interrogations, where the suspects are first asked to make a written statement. In [25], the authors report an example proposed by [1] of a man accused of killing his wife. In this statement, the accused consistently refers to "my wife and I" rather than "we", suggesting distance between the couple. Thus, for [25], linguistic style checking may be useful in the hands of a trained expert who knows what to look for and how to use language to reveal inconsistencies.

In this context, the deception spread through fake news and reviews is a relevant current problem. Due to their appealing nature, they spread rapidly [37]. Nevertheless, what makes fake content a hard problem to solve is the difficulty in identifying unreliable content. Fake news detection is defined as the prediction of the chances of a particular news article being intentionally deceptive [32], and fake reviews or opinion spam are inappropriate or fraudulent reviews [27].

© Springer Nature Switzerland AG 2021
S. Sarkadi et al. (Eds.): DeceptECAI 2020/DeceptAI 2021, CCIS 1296, pp. 166–178, 2021.
https://doi.org/10.1007/978-3-030-91779-1_12

The psychologists and other social scientists are working hard to understand what drive people to believe in fake news. Unfortunately, there is not yet a consensus on this issue. As claimed by [30], much of the debate among researchers falls into two opposing camps. One group claims that our ability to reason is hijacked by our partisan convictions. The other group claims that the problem is that we often fail to exercise our critical faculties: that is, we are mentally lazy.

The rationalization camp, which has gained considerable prominence in recent years, is built around a set of theories contending that, when it comes to politically charged issues, people use their intellectual abilities to persuade themselves to believe in what they want to be true, rather than attempting to actually discover the truth. In the context of social media, some evidences suggest that the main factor explaining the acceptance of fake news could be cognitive laziness, especially, where news items are often skimmed or merely glanced at.

[13] calls attention to a lack of non-laboratory studies. In [19], the authors comment that their study, examining the deceptive and truthful statements of a convicted murderer, was, at the time, the only known study of its type in a "high-stakes realistic setting". Moreover, as believed by [21], we do not know much about the embedded lies in texts or discourses. With the notable exception of a paper published by [15] and several studies proposed by [22] dealing with fictional discourse in the American television show, there is a lack of empirical research.

Therefore, in this paper, we present a pioneering empirical linguistic study for Brazilian Portuguese language on false statements in texts. We methodically analyze linguistic features from the Fake.Br corpus, which includes both fake and true news. The goal in the linguist approach is to investigate predictive deception clues found in texts. In particular, in this paper, we aim to provide linguistically motivated resources and computationally useful strategies for the development of automatic deception detection classifiers for the Portuguese language.

The remainder of this paper is organized as follows. In Sect. 2, we present the main related work. Section 3 describes an overview of our data. In Sect. 4, we show the entire empirical linguistic-based study. In Sect. 5, final remarks and future works are presented.

2   Related Work

[9] defines deception as a deliberate attempt to mislead others. There are relatively few studies that have focused, specifically, on deceptive language recognition with speech or writing style, specially for Portuguese. Most of the available works have been used to aid in authorship attribution and plagiarism identification [7]. Recent studies have been valuable for detecting deception, especially in the Fake News classification.

[25] examined lying in written communication, finding that deceptive utterances used more total words but fewer personal pronouns. The linguistic-based

features have been employed for fake news detection. In [25], the authors listed a set of linguistic behaviors that predict deception, as tones of words, kinds of preposition, conjunctions and pronouns. In addition, the deception linguistic style includes weak employment of singular and third person pronouns, negative polarity and frequent use of movement verbs. [9] also presents a long study on clues to deception. For [24], the basic assumption is that liars differ from truth tellers in their verbal behaviour, making it possible to classify the news by inspecting their verbal accounts. Accordingly, they present insights, decisions, and conclusions resulting from deception research conference at legal and criminologist psychology society. In [5], the authors proposed a set of features using several linguistic analysis levels. They employed lexical, syntax, semantic and discourse linguistic features. In the lexical level, the authors explored bag-of-words approach using bi-grams. In the syntax level, a probability context free grammar was implemented. For semantic analysis, the context information (such as profile content) has been incorporated. To model discourse features, the authors used the Rhetorical Structure Theory (RST) [20] analytical framework.

Specifically for Brazilian Portuguese, [23] and [34] created the Fake.Br corpus and proposed classifiers for fake news detection. They have also performed a basic linguistic analysis of the corpus. However, to the best of our knowledge, no previous systematic empirical linguistic study exists on dishonest intentions and language-based deception detection for the Brazilian Portuguese.

3   Data Overview

To provide a linguistic analysis on false statements in texts, the first challenges concentrate on the data. The identification of reliable corpora for each language is a relevant task. Most of the research has developed computational linguistic resources for English. In general, few resources are available for Portuguese. As we commented before, for Brazilian Portuguese, we have Fake.Br [23], which includes fake and true news in Brazilian Portuguese. An overview of this corpus is shown in Tables 1, 2 and 3.

Table 1. Corpus overview: Fake.Br [23]

Subjects	Number of texts	%
Politics	4,180	58.0
TV & celebrities	1,544	21.4
Society & daily news	1,276	17.7
Science & technology	112	1.5
Economy	44	0.7
Religion	44	0.7

Table 2. Number of tokens

News	Tokens	%
Fake	796.364	50.80
True	771.510	49.20

Table 3. Number of news texts

News	Number of texts	%
Fake	3,600	50.0
True	3,600	50.0

The Fake.Br corpus was composed in a semi-automatic way. The fake news were collected from sites that gather such content and the true ones were extracted from major news agencies in Brazil, as G1, Folha de São Paulo and Estadão portals. A crawler searched in the corresponding web pages of these agencies for keywords of the fake news, which were nouns and verbs that occurred in the fake news titles and the most frequent words in the texts (ignoring stopwords). The authors have performed a final manual verification to guarantee that the fake and true news were in fact subject-related.

4   Linguistic Features

Most of the false statements present linguistic features that are different in relation to the true statements. According to [6], most liars use their language strategically to avoid being caught. In spite of the attempt to control what they area saying, language "leakage" occurs with certain verbal aspects that are hard to monitor, such as frequencies and patterns of pronouns, conjunctions, and negative emotion word usage [12].

In this section, we aim at understanding relevant linguistic properties of fake and true statements in Brazilian news. We used Python 3.6.9 and the spaCy[1] library to automatically annotate[2] the corpus. We divided our analysis in two main groups: word-level and sentence-level analyses. In the first group, we analyzed the occurrence patterns of (i) sentiment and emotion words, (ii) part-of-speech tags, (iii) pronoun classification, (iv) named-entity recognition and (v) punctuation behavior. In the second group, we evaluated the number of sentences in fake and true news and the average of words for each sentence. We also analyzed the occurrence of clausal relations in syntactical dependency trees on fake and true statements. We present the results in what follows.

4.1   Word-Level Analysis

In the word-level analysis, our goal is to identify differences among word usage behavior and variations in fake and true news.

Sentiment and Emotion Words. According to [41], deception language involves negative emotions, which are expressed in language in terms of psychological distance from the deception object. The psychological distance and

---

[1] https://spacy.io/.
[2] https://spacy.io/api/annotation.

emotional experience reflect an attempt to control the negative mental representation. Therefore, we have identified the incidence of sentiment and emotion words in fake and true statements. We used the sentiment lexicon for Portuguese Sentilex-PT [33] and WordNetAffect.BR [29] to account for the sentiment words. Table 4 shows the results. Note that the incidence of sentiment and emotion words in fake news overcame the ones in true news, except for surprise emotion.

Table 4. Word-level sentiment and emotion occurrence

Sentences	True news	Fake news
Positive	103,376	115,260
Negative	102,54	115,431
Joy	4,941	5,657
Sadness	2,596	3,347
Fear	1,757	1,895
Disgust	1,561	1,667
Angry	2,865	3,232
Surprise	423	419
Total	642,636	665,489

In the fake news, we have observed a difference of 11,49% and 12,57% in positive and negative sentiment when compared to the true news; for joy, sadness, fear, disgust, angry and surprise emotions, the difference amounts to 14,49%, 28,92%, 7,85%, 6,79% 12,80% and 0,95% when compared to the true news. Therefore, we evidence that in our corpus the fake statements presented more negative and positive sentiments and emotions than true statements, confirming what some relevant literature [5,9,25,32] have found, i.e., that dishonest texts have more negative than positive sentiments and emotions.

Part-of-Speech. The growing body of research suggests that we may learn a great deal about people's underlying thoughts, emotions, and reasons by counting and categorizing the words they use to communicate. For [25], several aspects of linguistic style, such as pronoun usage, preposition and conjunctions that signal cognitive work, have been linked to a number of behavioral and emotional outcomes. To exemplify, in [39], the authors identified that poets who use a high frequency of self-reference but a lower frequency of other-reference in their poetry were more likely to commit suicide than those who showed the opposite pattern.

In this present study, we extracted the frequency of part-of-speech in our corpus in order to examining the grammatical manifestations of false behavior in text. The obtained results for part-of-speech occurrence is shown in Table 5. The results show an impressive increase on the number of interjections in fake news compared to the true news. We must also point out that, for many authors, it is clear that interjections do not encode concepts as nouns, verbs or adjectives do. Interjections may and do refer to something related to the speaker or to the external world, but their referential process is not the same as that of lexical items belonging to the grammatical categories mentioned, as the referents of interjections are difficult to pin down [28]. Similarly, the use of space character has shown a relevant occurrence difference. We found 25,864 spaces in fake news and 3,977 spaces in true news. Furthermore, in true statements, the use of the NOUN category is 9,79% larger than in fake statements. The verbal use is also 13,81% more frequent in the true statements.

Table 5. Part-of-speech occurrence

N.	Label	Definition	True news	Fake news
1	NOUN	noun	140,107	127,609
2	VERB	verb	86,256	98,168
3	PROPN	proper noun	109,501	98,757
4	ADP	adposition	109,613	92,166
5	ADJ	adjective	33,433	32,535
6	DET	determiner	77,660	83,169
7	ADV	adverb	25,384	31,534
8	**SPACE**	**space**	**3,977**	**25,864**
9	PRON	pronoun	20,994	24,348
10	AUX	auxiliary	13,529	16,999
11	CCONJ	coordinating conjunction	17,263	16,352
12	NUM	numeral	16,951	12,596
13	SCONJ	subordinating conjunction	8,870	12,392
14	SYM	symbol	10,065	9,458
15	OTHER	other	2,684	3,113
16	**INTJ**	**interjection**	**66**	**220**
17	PART	particle	29	23

Pronouns. Several studies on deception show that the use of the first-person singular is a subtle proclamation of one's ownership of a statement. In other words, liars tend to distance themselves from their stories and avoid taking responsibility for their behavior [14]. Therefore, deceptive communication should be characterized by fewer first-person singular pronouns (e.g., I, me, and my) [25]. In addition, when people are self-aware, they are more "honest" with themselves [4, 10, 36] and self-reference increases [8].

In accordance with deception literature, we investigate the pronoun behavior in our corpus. We identify the occurrence for first, second and third persons of singular and plural pronouns. Table 6 exhibits the results. Surprisingly, the pronoun occurrence in fake news overcame the ones in true news, except in the 3rd person singular (tonic oblique). An unusual behavior, considering the literature on deception, may be noted on the 1st person singular (subject). In fake statements, there has been a jump in the occurrence of the "eu" pronoun (1,097) related to true statements (495). 3rd person singular (subject) and 3rd person singular (unstressed oblique) represent 34,16% and 42,80% respectively on the total occurrence of pronouns in the corpus for the fake news. Differently, for true news, the 3rd person singular (subject) and 3rd person singular (unstressed oblique) represent 36,88% and 47,74% respectively. In other words, the 3rd person occurrence in true news overcame fake news considering the total occurrence of pronouns in the corpus.

Table 6. Pronoun occurrence

N.	Pronoun classification	Example	True news	Fake news
1	**1st person singular (subject)**	**eu**	**495**	**1,097**
2	1st person singular (unstressed oblique)	me	233	447
3	1st person singular (tonic oblique)	mim	39	87
4	2nd person singular (subject)	você, tu	390	683
5	2nd person singular (unstressed oblique)	te	4	24
6	2nd person singular (tonic oblique)	ti, contigo	2	2
7	3rd person singular (subject)	ele, ela	3,344	4,006
8	3rd person singular (Unstressed oblique)	se, o, a, lhe	4,329	5,019
9	3rd person singular (tonic oblique)	si, consigo	44	41
10	1st person plural (subject)	nós	52	71
11	2nd person plural (subject)	vocês	7	26
12	3rd person plural (subject)	eles,elas	128	222

We must also point out that we found that the occurrence differences of 2nd person plural (unstressed oblique) and (tonic oblique) pronouns in fake and true news are statistically irrelevant.

Named-Entity Recognition. According to [21], most scholars in the field of deception research seem to accept standard truth-conditional. In addition, semantic assumptions on deception are rarely made explicit [40]. Moreover, the implicit content extraction is a hard task in natural language processing area, as [35] comments. Nevertheless, we propose a superficial semantic analysis based on named-entity recognition categories. Table 7 shows the results.

Table 7. Named-entity occurrence

Named-Entity	Label	True news	Fake news
Person	(PER)	19,398	22,151
Localization	(LOC)	19,232	15,250
Organization	(ORG)	9,503	8,851
Miscellaneous	(MISC)	8,427	9,119

Based on the obtained results, one may see that the true statements present larger number of localization occurrences (LOC) than fake statements. Otherwise, the fake statements overcome in larger number of person occurrences (PER) when compared to the true statements. Organization (ORG) has occurred more frequently in true statements, while miscellaneous (MISC) in fake statements.

Punctuation. [9] assumes that punctuation pattern could distinguish fake and true texts. Consequently, the punctuation behavior would be a "clue to deception". We evaluate the occurrence of each punctuation mark. The obtained data is shown in Table 8. In agreement with the literature, our results show a noticeable change among the punctuation setting in fake and true news. Note that in fake statements there has been a expressive use of interrogation, exclamation, end point, double quotes, two points, three consecutive points, square brackets, bar and asterisks. For the true news, we observed the larger use of comma, single trace, single quotes and two consecutive points. We also point out that the "Error" label consists on annotation mistakes.

Table 8. Punctuation occurrence

Punctuation		True news	Fake news
Comma	,	43,244	31,610
End point	.	26,311	31,911
Double quotes	" "	5,004	17,200
Parentheses	( )	12,170	11,027
Two points	:	1,674	5,138
Interrogation	?	687	1,808
Exclamation	!	277	2,226
Square brackets	[ ]	237	4,638
Three consecutive points	...	71	2,746
Two consecutive point	..	1,619	127
Error	n/a	1,389	1,320
Single trace	-	910	13
Long trace	—	80	46
Asterisk	*	91	650
Bar	/	123	358
Single quotes	' '	443	3
Four consecutive points	....	0	54
Circle	°	4	4
Double trace	–	12	0
Five consecutive points	.....	0	5

4.2   Sentence-Level Analysis

According to the standard philosophical definition of lying, the intention to deceive is an important aspect of deception [2,3,18,38]. In order to provide an initial understand on dishonest intents in text, we analyze the sentence structure in true and fake statements. In order to achieve that, we evaluate the number of sentences and the average number of words, which is shown in Table 9.

Table 9. Sentence-level analysis

Sentences	True news	Fake news
Total	43,066	50,355
Avg of words	15,45	13,24

Based on data displayed by Table 9, we may note that, in fake statements, there are 14,47% more sentences than in true statements. It is interesting to realize that, despite the greater number of sentences in fake news, the average number of words by sentence is smaller than in true news.

According to [6], analysis of word usage is often not enough for deception prediction. Deeper language structure (syntax) must also be analyzed to predict instances of deception. Therefore, in order to investigate anomalies or divergences in syntactic structure of false and true statements, we also analyzed the dependency relation occurrences in our corpus. We present the results in the Table 10.

A dependency tree, according to [17], is a syntactic structure corresponding to a given natural language sentence. This structure represents hierarchical relationships between words. Figure 1 shows a dependency tree example. Notice that the relations among the words are illustrated above the sentence with directed labeled arcs from heads to dependents. According to [16], we call this a typed dependency structure because the labels are drawn from a fixed inventory of grammatical relations. It also includes a *root* node that explicitly marks the root of the tree, i.e., the head of the entire structure. For the interested reader, the Universal Dependencies project [26] provides an inventory of dependency relations that are cross-linguistically applicable.

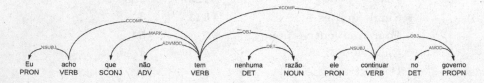

Fig. 1. Dependency tree example

Table 10. Clausal dependency relations occurrence

N.	Label	Definition	True news	Fake news
1	**CASE**	**case marking**	**106,964**	**89,177**
2	DET	determiner	71,070	78,013
3	AMOD	adjectival modifier	29,486	29,580
4	NMOD	nominal modifier	62,406	50,913
5	ROOT	root	43,055	50,035
6	FLAT:NAME	flat multiword expression (name)	45,955	40,025
7	NSUBJ	nominal subject	43,091	49,321
8	OBJ	object	39,787	45,063
9	OBL	oblique nominal	38,901	33,550
10	ADVMOD	adverbial modifier	22,741	28,834
11	CONJ	conjunct	21,316	20,907
12	APPOS	appositional modifier	21.146	20,587
13	CC	coordinating conjunction	18,603	17,586
14	MARK	marker	17,108	19,932
15	ACL	clausal modifier of noun (adjectival clause)	14,239	13,072
16	NUMMOD	numeric modifier	10,034	8,427
17	COP	copula	8,767	11,359
18	ADVCL	adverbial clause modifier	8,210	9,437
19	ACL:RELCL	relative clause modifier	8,177	7,720
20	CCCOMP	clausal complement	7,610	9,380
21	AUX	auxiliary	6,902	9,989
22	XCOMP	open clausal complement	6,208	7,411
23	AUX:PASS	auxiliary	5,931	6,485
24	NSUBJ:PASS	passive nominal subject	5,574	6,014
25	DEP	unspecified dependency	3,017	2,357
26	EXPL	expletive	2,139	2,874
27	NMOD:NPMOD	nominal modifier	2,055	2,093
28	OBL:AGENT	agent modifier	1,329	1,084
29	COMPOUND	compound	1,251	1,119
30	NMOD:TMOD	temporal modifier	1,193	368
31	FIXED	fixed multiword expression	1,135	1,259
32	PARATAXIS	parataxis	934	1,491
33	CSUBJ	clausal subject	769	1,053
34	IOBJ	indirect object	328	466
35	FLAT:FOREIGN	foreign words	13	15

Figure 1 shows the syntactical dependency structure for the following sentence extracted from our corpus: *Eu acho que não tem nenhuma razão ele continuar no governo.* ("I think there is no reason for him to remain in the government"). The NSUBJ relation identifies the subject; CCOMP identifies the complement of the main verb; ADVMOD identifies the adverb modifier; MARK is the word introducing a finite clause subordinate to another clause; OBJ identifies the direct object; DET identifies determinants; AMOD exhibits the adjectival modifier of a noun phrase (NP); and XCOMP consists of an open clausal complement for a verb[3].

Based on the obtained results (see Table 10), in an initial analysis, we found a relevant difference among the syntactic structures in fake and true news. For example, one may notice a significant difference on the occurrence of CASE, OBJ, OBL, NMOD, ROOT, DET, ADVCL, AUX, FLAT:NAME, CSUBJ and PARATAXIS structures. In the future, we intend to perform a deeper syntactical analysis of the dependency trees, looking for argument structure differences, for instance.

5   Final Remarks and Future Work

We know that language may be used to deceive and confuse people. The current context of social media usage is unique, with diversity in format, and relatively new. However, lying and deceiving have been at play in other forms of human communication for ages [31]. In this paper, we presented a study on the statements in true and fake news for Brazilian Portuguese. We performed an empirical linguistic-based analysis over the Fake.Br corpus. We automatically annotated a set of linguistic features in order to investigate actionable inputs and relevant differences among fake and true news. Based on the obtained results, we found that fake and true news present relevant differences in structural, lexical, syntactic and semantic levels.

For future work, we intend to deepen our investigation of syntactical behavior and to explore discourse markers and sophisticate machine learning techniques in order to provide deception detection classifiers for different tasks, such as fake news and reviews detection in several languages.

For the interested reader, more information may be found at the OPINANDO project webpage (at https://sites.google.com/icmc.usp.br/opinando/).

Acknowledgments. The authors are grateful to CAPES and USP Research Office (PRP 668) for supporting this work.

References

1. Adams, S.H.: Statement analysis: what do suspects' words really reveal? FBI Law Enforcement Bull. **1**(1), 12–20 (1996)
2. Augustine, S.: Lying. In: Deferrari, R.J. (ed.) Treatises on Various Subjects (The Fathers of the Church, vol. 16, pp. 47–110. Catholic University of America Press (1952)
3. Bok, S.: Lying: Moral Choice in Public and Private Life (1978)
4. Carver, C.S., Scheier, M.F.: Attention and Self-Regulation: A Control-Theory Approach to Human Behavior. Springer, Heidelberg (1981). https://doi.org/10.1007/978-1-4612-5887-2

---

[3] The typed dependency manual in available at https://nlp.stanford.edu/software/dependencies_manual.pdf.

5. Conroy, N.J., Rubin, V.L., Chen, Y.: Automatic deception detection: methods for finding fake news. In: Proceedings of the 78th ASIS&T Annual Meeting: Information Science with Impact: Research in and for the Community. American Society for Information Science, USA (2015)
6. Conroy, N.J., Rubin, V.L., Chen, Y.: Automatic deception detection: methods for finding fake news. In: Proceedings of the 78th ASIS&T Annual Meeting: Information Science with Impact: Research in and for the Community, ASIST 2015, pp. 82:1–82:4. American Society for Information Science, Silver Springs (2015)
7. Cristani, M., Roffo, G., Segalin, C., Bazzani, L., Vinciarelli, A., Murino, V.: Conversationally-inspired stylometric features for authorship attribution in instant messaging. In: Proceedings of the 20th ACM International Conference on Multimedia, pp. 1121–1124. ACM, New York (2012)
8. Davis, D., Brock, T.: Use of first person pronouns as a function of increased objective self-awareness. J. Exp. Soc. Psychol. **11**, 381–388 (1975)
9. DePaulo, B., Lindsay, J.J., Malone, B., Muhlenbruck, L., Charlton, K., Cooper, H.: Cues to deception. Psychol. Bull. **129**, 74–118 (2003)
10. Duval, S., Wicklund, R.A.: A Theory of Objective Self Awareness, 1st edn. Academic Press, Oxford (1972)
11. Fallis, D.: What is lying? J. Philos. **106**(1), 29–56 (2009)
12. Feng, V.W., Hirst, G.: Detecting deceptive opinions with profile compatibility. In: Proceedings of the Sixth International Joint Conference on Natural Language Processing, pp. 338–346. Asian Federation of Natural Language Processing, Nagoya (2013)
13. Finney, K.L.: Detecting deception through RST: a case study of the Casey Anthony trial. In: Proceedings of the 31st Annual North West Linguistics Conference, vol. 1, no. 1, pp. 12–23 (2015)
14. Friedman, H.S., Tucker, J.S.: Language and deception. In: Robinson, G.W.P. (ed.) Handbook of Language and Social Psychology, 1 edn, pp. 257–270. Wiley (1990)
15. Galasiński, D.: The Language of Deception: A Discourse Analytical Study. SAGE Knowledge, SAGE Publications, Thousand Oaks (2000)
16. Jurafsky, D., Martin, J.H.: Speech and Language Processing: An Introduction to Natural Language Processing, Computational Linguistics, and Speech Recognition. Prentice Hall Series in Artificial Intelligence, 2nd edn. Prentice Hall/Pearson Education International, Hoboken (2009)
17. Jurafsky, D., Ranganath, R., McFarland, D.: Extracting social meaning: identifying interactional style in spoken conversation. In: Proceedings of Human Language Technologies: The 2009 Annual Conference of the North American Chapter of the Association for Computational Linguistics, NAACL '09, pp. 638–646. Association for Computational Linguistics, Stroudsburg (2009)
18. Kupfer, J.: The moral presumption against lying. Rev. Metaphys. **36**(1), 103–126 (1982)
19. Mann, S., Vrij, A.: Telling and detecting lies in a high-stake situation: the case of a convicted murderer. Appl. Cogn. Psychol. **15**(2), 187–203 (2001)
20. Mann, W.C., Thompson, S.A.: Rhetorical Structure Theory: A Theory Of Text Organization (1987)
21. Meibauer, J.: The linguistics of lying. Ann. Rev. Linguist. **4**(1), 357–375 (2018)
22. Meibauer, J., Dynel, M.: Empirical approaches to lying and deception. Int. Rev. Pragmatics **8**(3)
23. Monteiro, R.A., Santos, R.L.S., Pardo, T.A.S., de Almeida, T.A., Ruiz, E.E.S., Vale, O.A., et al.: Contributions to the study of fake news in Portuguese: new

corpus and automatic detection results. In: Villavicencio, A. (ed.) PROPOR 2018. LNCS (LNAI), vol. 11122, pp. 324–334. Springer, Cham (2018). https://doi.org/10.1007/978-3-319-99722-3_33

24. Nahari, G., et al.: 'Language of lies': urgent issues and prospects in verbal lie detection research. Legal Criminol. Psychol. **24**, 1–23 (2019)

25. Newman, M.L., Pennebaker, J.W., Berry, D.S., Richards, J.M.: Lying words: Predicting deception from linguistic styles. Pers. Soc. Psychol. Bull. **29**(5), 665–675 (2003)

26. Nivre, J., et al.: Universal dependencies v1: a multilingual treebank collection. In: Proceedings of the Tenth International Conference on Language Resources and Evaluation (LREC'16), pp. 1659–1666. European Language Resources Association (ELRA), Portorož (2016)

27. Ott, M., Choi, Y., Cardie, C., Hancock, J.T.: Finding deceptive opinion spam by any stretch of the imagination. In: Proceedings of the 49th Annual Meeting of the Association for Computational Linguistics: Human Language Technologies, pp. 309–319. Association for Computational Linguistics, Portland (2011)

28. Padilla Cruz, M.: Might interjections encode concepts? More questions than answers. Lodz Papers Pragmatics **5**, 241–270 (2009)

29. Pasqualotti, P.R.: Reconhecimento de expressões de emoções na interação mediada por computador. Master's thesis, Porto Alegre, Brasil (2008)

30. Pennycook, G., Rand, D.: Why do people fall for fake news? New York Times Ed. **1**, 1–12 (2019)

31. Rubin, V.L.: Deception detection and rumor debunking for social media. In: The SAGE Handbook of Social Media Research Methods (2017)

32. Rubin, V.L., Chen, Y., Conroy, N.J.: Deception detection for news: Three types of fakes. In: Proceedings of the 78th ASIS&T Annual Meeting: Information Science with Impact: Research in and for the Community, ASIST '15, pp. 83:1–83:4. American Society for Information Science, Silver Springs (2015)

33. Silva, M.J., Carvalho, P., Sarmento, L.: Building a sentiment lexicon for social judgement mining. In: Caseli, H., Villavicencio, A., Teixeira, A., Perdigão, F. (eds.) PROPOR 2012. LNCS (LNAI), vol. 7243, pp. 218–228. Springer, Heidelberg (2012). https://doi.org/10.1007/978-3-642-28885-2_25

34. Silva, R.M., Santos, R.L., Almeida, T.A., Pardo, T.A.: Towards automatically filtering fake news in Portuguese. Expert Syst. Appl. **146**, 1–14 (2020)

35. Vargas, F.A., Pardo, T.A.S., et al.: Aspect clustering methods for sentiment analysis. In: Villavicencio, A. (ed.) PROPOR 2018. LNCS (LNAI), vol. 11122, pp. 365–374. Springer, Cham (2018). https://doi.org/10.1007/978-3-319-99722-3_37

36. Vorauer, J.D., Ross, M.E.: Self-awareness and feeling transparent: failing to suppress one's self. J. Exp. Soc. Psychol. **35**(5), 415–440 (1999)

37. Vosoughi, S., Roy, D., Aral, S.: The spread of true and false news online. Science **359**, 1146–1151 (2018)

38. Williams, B.: Truth and Truthfulness: An Essay in Genealogy (2002)

39. Ye, S., Chua, T.S.: Learning object models from semistructured web documents, **18**(3), 334–349 (2006)

40. Zimmermann, T.F.: Model-theoretic semantics. In: von Heusinger, K., Portner, P. (ed.) Semantics: An International Handbook of Natural Language Meaning, 1 edn, pp. 762–802. de GruyterTo the best of our knowledge, Berlin (2011)

41. Zipitria, I., Sierra, B., Sopena-Garaikoetxea, I.: Emotion in deceptive language. In: Proceedings of the 39th Annual Meeting of the Cognitive Science Society, CogSci 2017, London, UK, 16–29 July 2017 (2017)

Author Index